GUERRILLA DAUGHTER

Guerrilla Daughter

Virginia Hansen Holmes

The Kent State University Press

Kent, Ohio

© 2009 by The Kent State University Press, Kent, Ohio 44242

All rights reserved

Library of Congress Catalog Card Number 2008039305

ISBN 978-0-87338-949-5

Manufactured in the United States of America

Library of Congress Cataloging-in-Publication Data

Holmes, Virginia Hansen.

Guerrilla daughter / Virginia Hansen Holmes.

p. cm.

Includes bibliographical references and index.

ISBN 978-0-87338-949-5 (pbk. : alk. paper) ∞

1. Homes, Virginia Hansen. 2. Holmes, Virginia Hansen—Family. 3. World War, 1939–1945—Underground movements—Philippines—Mindanao. 4. World War, 1939–1945—Personal narratives, American. 5. Philippines—History—Japanese occupation, 1942–1945. 6. Girls—United States—Biography. 7. Americans—Philippines—Biography. 8. Mindanao Island (Philippines)—History. I. Title.

d802.p5h65 2009

940.53'16109227599—dc22

2008039305

British Library Cataloging-in-Publication data are available.

13 12 11 10 09   5 4 3 2 1

Contents

Preface

One's past emerges in many forms. Often, rather than being written, it is passed through intimate conversations around a dinner table or a festive event that prompts us to recall and discuss what brought us to where we are now. This was our case. At the outbreak of World War II, my family—parents Charles and Trinity Hansen and older siblings Rudy, Hank, and Charlotte (Peach)— and I were living on the island of Mindanao in the Philippines, where my father was the plant superintendent of the East Mindanao Mining Company, whose gold mine was near Surigao, the capital of Surigao province. Four years later we emerged from the war intact and still alive. Most of all we were free! Still, we each carried many scars and memories of a bad period initiated by the invading Imperial Japanese Army.

During the late 1990s, my brother Rudy became ill and was confined at the Fort Miley Veterans' Hospital in San Francisco. He had been the custodian of the family documents that had survived the war, including a few precious photos. During one of my visits I asked to borrow the photos to have copies made. He suggested that I retrieve them from his files, along with whatever other family memorabilia I might find. I soon learned that his "files" consisted of an enormous amount of miscellaneous old personal records and documents packed in a dozen boxes in his garage. My sister-in-law Clarissa kindly granted me full access and welcomed the opportunity to review and cull their own personal records.

Shortly after commencing our examination of the jumble of paperwork, I came across carbon copies of the first two pages of a letter from my father addressed to "General Sharp, Commanding General, V.M.F. (*Visayan-Mindanao*

Force), Del Monte, Misamis Or." I focused on its date—March 17, 1942—just over three months after the outbreak of World War II. (By coincidence, General Douglas MacArthur left the Philippines for Australia from that same location on that precise date.) As I read the letter, my mind drifted back more than fifty-five years to that Monday morning, December 8, 1941, when my father unexpectedly returned from work and informed us that the Japanese had bombed Pearl Harbor and we were at war. I had never seen him so agitated! Less than seven years old, I had no concept of what being at war meant or of the impact it would soon have on our lives.

The subjects of Dad's letter—"Ordnance" and "Offer of Service"—also intrigued me. The first dealt with his design of a firing mechanism for hand grenades that could be manufactured at the mine power plant using materials available locally. And under the second, he offered his services to the Army for the duration of the war. This part brought a lump to my throat—as a parent, I could relate to the gravity of the circumstances in which my parents found themselves when the war broke out. My father was a U.S. Army veteran who received his discharge in the Philippines in 1922. Twenty years later, at age fifty-two with a wife and four children, he was volunteering to serve his country again.

As I continued to search, I found interspersed with Rudy's own personal papers many old Hansen documents, such as my parents' marriage certificate and the birth and baptismal certificates of their children. But more importantly I discovered a treasure trove of material that is of historical value to not only our family but also anyone with an interest in World War II military operations in the Philippines. I was amazed to find dozens of pages of Dad's wartime records, which outlined his duties and special orders relative to supporting the American guerrillas of Mindanao. This organization, under Colonel Wendell Fertig, emerged in the fall of 1942 to fight the Japanese occupation of Mindanao. The guerrillas included U.S. and Philippine military that refused to surrender, other U.S. military that had escaped from Japanese prisoner of war camps, and American businessmen (like my father). In April 1943 my father joined Fertig's growing guerrilla force known as the Tenth Military District, U.S. Forces in the Philippines, with the rank of captain. He was appointed the 110th Division's liaison officer as well as procurement officer and food control administrator for the Province of Surigao. My brothers, Rudy and Hank, seventeen and sixteen, each added five years to their ages and were also inducted at the same time; however, their roles were quite different—they would became frontline infantrymen in the war against the Japanese.

Dad's communications with division headquarters covered a variety of subjects that ranged from intelligence reports on Japanese movements to weighty and thought-provoking memorandums on the ability of the guerrilla force to survive until Allied forces returned. As the Japanese increased their stronghold on the island, supplies and foodstuffs became extremely scarce. A major challenge for my father was the procurement and transportation of sufficient rice rations for the 110th Division's guerrilla force, which included over five thousand Filipino fighters who required a daily rice staple if they were to endure effectively. I had no idea of the existence of these records and immediately contacted my siblings about my discovery. Peach was surprised as well, but Hank was familiar with them and was glad that I'd found them.

In 1963 John Keats, with the help of a Guggenheim Fellowship, wrote a book on Fertig's wartime exploits as a guerrilla leader. Titled *They Fought Alone,* this book was the only published work about the guerrillas' war in Mindanao to which we could relate. It was something of a wartime bible that helped us link our lives with the war. In fact, one of Rudy's encounters with a Japanese army patrol is mentioned in the book. Prompted by his own desire to gain credit for his wartime service with the guerrillas from 1943 to 1945, Rudy had kept in touch with Fertig through the years. He obtained a letter from Fertig attesting to his service.

Upon my return to the East Coast, my husband, Kent, and I pored over each page of my father's records. A retired CIA officer and history buff who spent most of his career in the Far East (including four years in the Philippines and tours of duty in Indonesia and Laos, where he worked with the hill tribe guerrillas), Kent was as fascinated as I was with this record of my father's service with the guerrillas on Mindanao during World War II. Over the years we had made attempts at setting down on paper my recollections of my family's ordeals during the war, but there was little in our verbal history of those years upon which to construct a definitive record of what the Hansen family had experienced collectively. Missing were detailed time lines of the family's experiences with the guerrillas and specific actions of the Japanese in Mindanao—all in juxtaposition with the course of the war in the Pacific. A mosaic of events, woven into a chronicle, was required to tell this story. Such a chronicle would have been helpful in responding to requests from my children and grandchildren for anecdotes about my life as a young girl. Unfortunately there was no diary to consult, so an accurate account was difficult, with only dimmed memories weaving the history of what we had experienced and endured. I was also interested in how various experiences recalled from my perspective fit into those of the collective remembrances of my older siblings. Geography, work, and family obligations complicated our initial efforts to compile a history of our family's wartime experiences—while my brothers were settled in northern California, Peach resided in the Philippines and Australia, and I lived in Virginia and various foreign countries.

Fortunately, Dad's papers covered most of the war years and provided time lines and a bridge upon which we could reconstruct our respective activities during the period of the war. Kent, now retired, encouraged us to take on this project in earnest and volunteered to spearhead the effort. Peach agreed to fly in from Australia, and we spent several days sitting around Hank and his wife Bobbie's kitchen table with a cassette recorder, just reminiscing. Prompted by Kent's probing questions, memories buried for over sixty years rose to the surface, each of us contributing to or corroborating various aspects of wartime incidents.

During the late 1990s and early 2000s, conversations with members of the American Guerrillas of Mindanao (AGOM) veterans' organization bolstered our individual recollections. Several of these former guerrillas had served with my father and brothers. They have answered many of my questions about the guerrilla movement and its leaders, and we augmented their memories by research that included articles, diaries, and other recorded information about the guerrillas and our family's role in the movement. While Keats's book was a starting point, it became apparent over time that some of the book's assertions did not agree with reflections of other veterans that had fought as guerrillas on Mindanao.

Our efforts to bring this history together, particularly as it pertains to our family, have resulted in this record of the war as we experienced it. As time passed, we continued to find new pieces of information germane to this historical account. However, we have now reached the point that prompts a deadline for any new or additional information being included in this work.

When this story was a "work in progress," my dear and patient husband was a strong supporter. As an avid student of history, Kent took a personal interest in ensuring that we moved toward completion of the final manuscript. At the annual AGOM reunions, he got to know many of the charter members, which facilitated their recollection of events and people in the guerrilla movement. These personal accounts were important in getting their own individual historical record of what happened in the war. Their motto is, "We Remained—1941–1945." Kent also did a tremendous amount of research and wrote commentaries to balance and put into perspective the recollections of the surviving members of the Hansen family.

We hope that this final rendition of our family's experiences in the war will be informative and stimulating, especially to historians as they attempt to better understand the daily lives of Americans who stayed behind in the Philippines to resist the Japanese occupation.

Acknowledgments

I am indebted to my husband, Kent, who developed time lines and commentaries to complement what I have written about my personal experiences during World War II. For example, he describes in chapter 1 the Philippines' preparedness for war. This would have a direct bearing on the beginning of my family's odyssey in evading the Japanese Army that lasted almost three and a half years. Similarly, he assisted me in underscoring those events leading to the return of American forces to the Philippines in late 1944 and early 1945 that did have the effect of bringing us out of harm's way in 1945. Finally, he assisted me in writing the "Afterword" (chapter 10) concerning the guerrilla movement on Mindanao and its contribution to the war effort.

ONE

The Gathering Clouds of War

Most Americans born in the 1930s and earlier will never forget the shock and horror of December 7, 1941, that day of infamy. For Charles and Trinity Hansen and their children—Rudyard, Henry, Charlotte, and Virginia—who were living on the island of Mindanao in the southern part of the Philippines, it was already Monday, December 8; in fact, the attack on Pearl Harbor occurred at approximately 2:00 A.M. Manila time. Japanese bombers would not hit Luzon until midday on the 8th. However, at 6:30 A.M., Japanese Navy dive-bombers from the aircraft carrier *Ryujo* off Mindanao did attack the USS *Preston*, a U.S. Navy seaplane tender, and two patrol bomber seaplanes (PBY) in the harbor of Davao.

We were getting ready for our weekly trip back to boarding school after a most enjoyable weekend, the highlight of which was a joint birthday party celebrating my brothers' birthdays—Rudy's sixteenth and Hank's fifteenth. It was shortly after 7:00 A.M. when Dad came bounding up the steps to our house from his office at the machine shop of the East Mindanao Mining Company. He was very agitated and asked if we had been listening to the news on the radio, then announced, loudly: "The Japs have bombed Pearl Harbor. We're at war!"

The implication of Dad's words did not make much of an impression on me. I was not quite seven years old and could not fully comprehend the word "war." However, I could sense from Dad's demeanor that something bad must have happened. For one thing, he seemed to be scolding Mom for not monitoring the news, and I had never heard him speak to Mom in such a sharp tone of voice. True, Dad had a quick temper and I had heard him yell at my brothers when they misbehaved, but to my knowledge he had never, ever raised his voice toward Mom. I also remember that we were running late on that particular Monday morning, probably because of the birthday festivities, which had included a picnic on the beach near Placer on Saturday and a nice dinner followed by multiple servings of birthday cake on Sunday evening.

Because of that fateful morning's events, life would not be the same for us over the next four years. We did not go to school that day and, though we did not know it then, would not do so again until late 1945.

The reality of the situation that we now found ourselves in prompts me to provide the reader with some background on the Hansen family and how fate brought us to be a part of this war experience in the southern part of the Philippines. My father, Charles Hansen, was born in Syracuse, New York, in 1890 and grew up on a nearby farm. He attended local schools and worked his way through college, studying mechanical engineering at Syracuse University. After a series of jobs in different parts of the country he ended up back in New York, where he worked as a toolmaker at the Watertown Arsenal. In the summer of 1919 he enlisted in the U.S. Army. After his basic training, he was sent to Siberia as a member of the American Expeditionary Force (AEF), numbering almost ten thousand, ordered there by President Wilson in fall 1918. Wilson took this action in conjunction with the other Allied powers, with two main purposes. It sought first to save the Czech Legion, which was transiting from western Russia to Vladivostok. This legion was largely composed of prisoners of war who had been captured on the eastern front. They were making their way eastward, along the Trans-Siberian Railroad to Vladivostok, with the objective of repatriation back to Czechoslovakia. The AEF's second purpose was to maintain law and order along the Trans-Siberian Railroad following the 1917 Russian Revolution. During his service in Siberia Dad joined the 27th Infantry Regiment—which was deployed to Vladivostok from Fort William McKinley, near Manila—and returned with the regiment to the Philippines in April 1920. After completing his service obligation in 1922, he joined the army's Manila Arsenal as a foreman and instructor. During this period he received a commission as captain in the U.S. Army Reserve.

Upon arriving in Manila, Dad quickly recognized the many opportunities for Americans in the Philippines. This island nation had come under U.S. control as a result of the Spanish-American War in 1898, when Commodore George Dewey destroyed the Spanish fleet in Manila Bay. Within weeks, U.S. troops were in charge of the archipelago. Initially, Congress was cool toward annexation but narrowly voted to go along with it. Even so, there was a growing number of Filipinos opposing this U.S. action. Eventually the armed actions by the U.S. Army brought the insurrection under control and the United States found itself preparing the country for nationhood.

William Howard Taft was the first civilian governor of the Philippines, arriving in 1900. He launched economic and education programs that would have lasting effects on the country. Congress's liberal import-export laws gave U.S. businesses a free hand with goods imported into the country while Philippine corporations had export trade to the United States free of tariff. As American interests flourished in the islands, the Philippines did indeed become the "Pearl of the Orient." On the political side, the United States was gradually giving the Filipinos greater control over their future.

While U.S. rule in the Philippines was unspecific regarding the future, the U.S. Congress became increasingly interested in granting the Philippines self-rule, as demonstrated by the second Philippine Organic Act, U.S. Congress, 1916. While not fixing a date for independence, it implied that the long-range goal of the U.S. government was to grant Philippine independence when a stable government came into being. It established a framework for representative government, including a House and a Senate. However, an American governor general still wielded executive power over the country.[1] The United States granted the Philippines commonwealth status in 1935, with the passage of the Tydings-McDuffie Act. The act also contained provisions for a president and a definite independence date ten years hence.[2]

With its vast resources in lumber and mining, and U.S. corporate interest in exploiting these for export, the Philippines was a dream come true for an engineer. Dad's experience in working with the two U.S. military arsenals and his university training in engineering immediately qualified him for many positions in the growing and expanding Philippine economy. His specific technical skills would become invaluable to the many American entrepreneurs arriving in the Philippines during the 1920s.

Not long after his arrival in Manila, Dad met my mother, Trinity Harris, through mutual friends. Mom was the only child of William Harris, a U.S. Army Spanish-American War veteran who opted to remain in the Philippines, and Maria Aguilar, a member of one of numerous families of Spanish descent that had declined to be repatriated to Spain at the conclusion of that conflict. For the Aguilar family, the outcome of the war was quite dramatic. The American occupation of the Philippines ended 350 years of Spanish rule and drastically altered the privileged status of countless Spanish families that had prospered in that island nation for many generations. The Aguilar family did not approve of my grandmother's marriage to an American—they still considered America "the enemy"—and this caused a rift in her relationship with her family. Sadly, both of my grandparents died when Mom was quite young, and she became the ward of her mother's sister.

My mother had remarked to us that her independent, headstrong nature strained her relationship with her aunt and that as a consequence, she spent many years as a boarding student at a convent school in Manila run by Belgian nuns. She felt more at home in the convent than at her aunt's house—her fellow boarders were her real family. After Saturday morning class, the girls were allowed to go home for the afternoon or the whole weekend. Parents came to pick up the young ones, but those sixteen and older were allowed to make their way home on their own. Mom preferred to spend her free time with her friends at their homes, and during one of these visits she met Dad, the friend of a friend of the family. He was immediately attracted to her, and she was flattered that this handsome man was interested in her—not yet seventeen, this was her first romance.

After a brief courtship, Mom and Dad became engaged, and on April 12, 1921, they were married in the Iglesia Cristiana Gloriosa, a Protestant church in the Pasay section of Manila. Mom was Catholic but agreed to marry in the Protestant church because the pastor did not know the Aguilar family and had no reason to question her age.

Fortunately, despite her youth, the education and training she had received from the nuns would prepare her well for the future she had chosen. As far as her aunt was concerned, however, Mom's marriage was "history repeating itself," and the damage to their relationship became irreparable.

Dad was also orphaned at an early age and had lost contact with relatives in Syracuse. So when they started married life, Mom and Dad literally had only each other. Their commitment to their marriage, however, helped forge a strong partnership, which held as one of its goals achieving financial stability. Ever mindful of the financial difficulties his family had experienced at the turn of the century, Dad was determined that his own family would be raised in a secure and comfortable environment.

Throughout the 1920s and 1930s Dad's engineering background afforded him employment opportunities in the mining and lumber sectors, both in the field and in Manila. Life then, particularly in Manila, was busy and exciting, though touched with sadness and loss. Mom and Dad's first baby, Alice, survived only hours after birth. Their second child, Charlie, born in 1923, died at age two of complications from diphtheria. Then three more baby boys arrived in quick succession: Edward in November 1924 and Rudyard and Henry in December 1925 and 1926, respectively. Another son, Robert, was born in 1928 but died soon after birth.

Mom matured and adapted well to her role as wife, mother, and active member of the American community. She was president of the Daughters of American Veterans and served on the high commissioner's committee for organizing the observance of American public holidays. And in the midst of this activity, my sister Charlotte joined the family in 1930. When she was a toddler a family friend named "Pop" Henderson, who owned the Independent Shoe Shop—renowned in the Philippines for its custom-fitted leather shoes and boots—commented that Charlotte was "as sweet as peaches and cream." From then on she was "Peach" to family and close friends. I should mention here that since my brothers were so close in age, they were referred to as "the boys." After my arrival in December 1934, Peach and I became "the girls."

As Peach grew older she tried hard to keep up with her brothers, but the differences in age and size made it difficult. They dubbed her "Skinny" and teased her mercilessly. Naturally she reported their behavior to Mom, who invariably gave them a stern talking-to. This resulted in taunts of "Skinny squealed! Skinny squealed!" from the boys, and the cycle would repeat itself. In time, however, Peach learned to gain acceptance without Mom's intervention, and the boys relented and allowed her to participate in some of their activities.

The boys attended Bordner School in Manila, where they forged friendships with the children of friends and neighbors of my parents and enjoyed endless after-school and weekend activities. When Peach reached school age she attended the American Central School, smaller and located closer to our home. Attending a different school gave Peach the opportunity to make new friends and become less dependent on her brothers for companionship.

The growing Hansen family prompted my father to pursue more lucrative job opportunities, thus we moved to the southern part of the Philippines in 1937, when he accepted a managerial position with a sawmill near Iligan, Lanao. This was our introduction to the island of Mindanao, where living conditions were quite different than in metropolitan Manila. The sawmill was located in the interior, along a river. Our home was large and airy, built several feet above the ground for the dual purpose of allowing maximum ventilation and protection from rainy-season floods. Located next to the sawmill was a Moro village. The Moros (also called Mohammedans in those days) were Muslims who migrated to the southern part of the Philippines from Borneo and Malaya. They retained their religion, culture, and customs—resisting the strong wave of Christianization that took place after Spanish colonization of the islands. Peach remembers walking through the Moro village and admiring their colorful attire and shiny brass jewelry and decorative household items. The women were openly friendly, but the children hovered in the background, too shy to come forward.

The sawmill's location made it necessary for my siblings to attend boarding school. The best school for boys in the area was the Ateneo de Cagayan, a major Jesuit school founded by Bishop James Hayes. In the early 1930s the faculty of the college was young—all under forty—and chiefly composed of American Jesuits, with some Filipino priests and seminarians. Though still rather small in 1937, it grew from a hundred boys and one building to a student body of just under a thousand and five concrete buildings by 1941. Father Edward Haggerty (the future unofficial chaplain of the guerrillas on Mindanao) was rector. Attending a Catholic all-boys school was a new experience for my brothers, but they had no trouble making the adjustment.

Also located in Cagayan was Lourdes Academy, an excellent Catholic day/ boarding school for girls. Peach was enrolled there but was not happy about being a boarder—she was not quite eight years old and, unlike her brothers, did not have any siblings to keep her company at school. She was lonely and homesick. She looked forward to brief glimpses of her brothers on Sunday mornings, when the students of both schools, in full uniform, attended High Mass at the huge cathedral. Hank and Peach recall the ritual of the Ateneo boys walking toward the cathedral in a single line and, as they passed the Lourdes campus, the girls formed a similar line and walked with them to the cathedral and settled into their designated pews—Ateneo students on the right side, Lourdes students on the left. Once a month, Mom picked up the kids and took them home to Iligan for a long weekend. On occasion Ed, Rudy, and Hank made the trip home by themselves using the local bus service, but it was a long and bumpy ride, which took the better part of a day. The bus was open on both sides with wooden benchlike seats for the passengers, while extra bundles and other cargo were lashed to the roof. Unfortunately for Peach, Mom and the nuns were in agreement that she should not be permitted to accompany the boys on these trips, so she had to content herself with monthly visits home.

Although Dad was Protestant, the Hansen children had all been baptized Catholic. For some reason, however, the boys had not yet received the Sacraments of Penance and Holy Communion. Most of the schools in Manila were Catholic institutions, with religious instruction as part of the curriculum; Bordner, a private secular school, did not offer any religious education. Now that the boys were attending a Jesuit school, however, immediate attention was given to the matter of their religious education. Peach was also receiving instruction at school, and in 1938 all four of my siblings received their First Holy Communion in St. Augustine Church.

Hank recalled very vividly an incident at Ateneo that brought him to the attention of Father Haggerty. All boarding students had assigned duties; some served at the early morning Mass; others worked in the school's dining hall. Hank was to bring fresh eggs from the chicken house to the kitchen each morning. One of the college brothers had a pet baboon that he kept in a wire cage in the chicken house. Actually, it was a mean-tempered beast that was friendly to its master but had no tolerance for the young students that invaded its territory. Every morning when Hank entered the enclosure, the animal jumped up and down, shaking its cage and making all sorts of grunting noises. This daily performance began to wear on Hank's nerves, so one morning he decided to get back at it. Seeing a stick on the floor, he picked it up and went over to the cage, ran the stick along the bars of the cage and then poked the baboon. Suddenly, it grabbed the stick and retaliated. Hank realized that since the stick was in the cage he would be blamed for disturbing the animal. He thrust some fruit, which he'd found in the enclosure, into the cage to distract the baboon. While it was busy, Hank opened the cage door and reached for the stick. Just then the baboon whirled around and grabbed Hank's arm and pulled him into the cage and gave his arms and body major bites, scratches, and abrasions. Hank's injuries were so serious that he was in the hospital for almost two weeks. When he returned to the college he was summoned to Father Haggerty's office for a tongue-lashing that he never forgot.

My father loved the lumber business, but he and Mom soon realized that the school arrangement was less than ideal. They were particularly concerned about Peach's situation, and they decided that a change was necessary. (Mom's own memories of her lonely years in boarding school may have influenced them.) In late 1938 my father accepted a position as plant superintendent with the East Mindanao Mining Company, a gold-mining enterprise expanding its operations. At this juncture the company employed approximately eight hundred personnel. The mine was located near Tinabingan, south of the port of Surigao on the northeastern tip of Mindanao.[3] By this time, the Hansen boys were almost fourteen, thirteen, and twelve; Peach was eight; and I was almost four. One important advantage of the new job location was its proximity to Surigao and San Nicolas School, a large Catholic institution run by Dutch Missionaries of the Sacred Heart.[4]

Dad went on ahead to Surigao to start his new job and supervise the renovation of a home for us at the mine site, and we stayed in a hotel in Cagayan until the end of the school year. My earliest memories are connected to this hotel, set back from a well-traveled, dusty road. Typical of the roads of that era, it was built up higher than the surrounding terrain, with a ditch on either side. To reach the front entrance to the hotel, one had to cross a footbridge over the ditch, then follow a path through the front garden to a set of five or six steps that led up to a large open porch. This lounge area was furnished with rattan sofas with loose cushions and square tables with woven white rattan chairs. Beyond was the lobby, at the end of which were steps that led down to the rear garden, and the bedroom wing extended from the lobby. Every evening two young men in white uniforms sprayed the whole area with insecticide to keep away mosquitoes and other pests. There was no escaping the strong smell as they pumped away on hand-held repellent guns. Although the bedrooms were also sprayed—the odor still lingered at bedtime—each bed had a white mosquito net attached to the bedposts that had to be tucked in tightly under the mattress to keep any pesky survivors at bay. A mosquito could slip in through the tiniest opening; the following morning it would be found clinging to the net, engorged with blood and too logy to fly. We had to resist the urge to squash the pest because that invariably resulted in an ugly red stain on the net or the bed sheet—best to have the room maid take care of the matter.

I remember an incident that got me into trouble. I was not allowed to go near the busy road, but one day I decided to go to the other end of the footbridge. Unfortunately, I decided to walk a few more steps along the top of the ditch. The ground was loose and I slipped and very quickly found myself on my back in the muddy, dirty water, legs extended and arms outstretched. I did not know how to swim but knew I had to find a way to stay afloat. Something Ed had said flashed through my mind—he claimed that inflated balloons could serve as lifesavers. There were no balloons handy, but I thought that if I puffed my cheeks they would have the same effect. As I puffed, I felt my feet sinking into the mud, then touch bottom. I quickly stood up and discovered that the muddy water was only about knee-deep! I scrambled up the embankment and hurried to the hotel entrance, hoping I could sneak past the lobby to our bedroom without anyone noticing me; however, Mom was sitting there with some ladies and leaped to her feet when she saw me walking by, dripping mud and debris all over the shiny wood floors. I could tell from the expression on her face that she knew exactly where and how I had gotten into such a mess and braced myself for the scolding I knew was coming. Mom angrily grabbed my arm and led me to the bathroom, where she washed my hair and scrubbed me all over, all the while telling me how displeased she was and that it would serve me right if the horrible smell could not be washed away. Although I was crying, no sympathy was forthcoming and the scolding continued for quite a while.

All things considered, our stay at the hotel was pleasant. Hank and Peach have fond memories of its amenities, especially the varied lunch and dinner choices on the dining room menu—what a change from boarding school fare! For me, the best part of the arrangement was that my sister and brothers, as day students, were able to come home at lunchtime and at the end of the school day.

When school ended in late March, we went to Manila for a short vacation, where Dad joined us for part of the time. He and Mom purchased furniture, appliances, and miscellaneous household items for the new home. They also bought a new black 1939 Studebaker Champion sedan that Dad road tested in Manila before returning to Surigao. Prior to shipping the car, Mom drove us to Baguio, a popular mountain resort, for a brief holiday. The upholstery still had that new car smell, and as Mom negotiated the sharp turns of the notorious zigzag road up the mountain, some of us succumbed to carsickness. The discomfort was all forgotten when we reached the city of Baguio, nestled among beautiful pine trees. The temperature was gloriously cool, and our favorite hangout was Burnham Park.

Toward the end of our vacation in Manila, Mom could not resist the soft brown eyes of a little rat terrier, and suddenly we had a new pet. Mom named her Princess, and the dog immediately bonded with her new mistress. She was not as playful as our friends' dogs and often had a haughty attitude, befitting her royal title.

Mom was anxious for us to be reunited with Dad, and we all looked forward to seeing our new home at the mining company's site approximately thirty-five kilometers from Surigao. Dad had told us that living conditions would be different from what we had experienced in Iligan and Cagayan and the school situation would be better. We were actually glad when our holiday ended and we sailed on the SS *Corregidor*, arriving in Surigao late on a Thursday afternoon. As the ship docked, we saw Dad waiting on the pier, standing next to our Studebaker, which had arrived the previous week. He came up the gangplank and, before he had a chance to give us each a hug, was introduced to the newest member of our family. It was not a surprise—Mom had already written to him about Princess—and the little dog acknowledged Dad's importance by wagging her short stub of a tail.

Dad went off to ensure that the outgoing cargo from East Mindanao to its head office in Manila was loaded and consigned to the appropriate SS *Corregidor* officer (later on we learned that part of that cargo was precious indeed). An East Mindanao employee, who welcomed us with a warm smile, took care of loading our luggage and the incoming office pouch from Manila onto the company station wagon. Dad drove the Studebaker and both vehicles were filled to capacity with Hansens and luggage and cargo as we left the pier. We stopped at a store owned by a Mr. Egling—a general store with a market on one side and an assortment of mining supplies and equipment on display across the room. A rear door led to a wide wooden pier that extended out over the water. There was a refreshment bar against the wall and small tables and chairs scattered about. Dad pointed out where he had been sitting as he watched the SS *Corregidor* slowly put into port, adding that he saw us standing at the railing. We sat at "his" table and had some refreshments as more customers arrived. The arrival of the SS *Corregidor* was the highlight of the week in Surigao; people came from the neighboring areas to greet or bid farewell to family and friends or simply to socialize with each other. The ship was tied up a short distance away, and Peach and I watched the activity on the dock while Mom and Dad shopped for groceries and the boys explored the equipment side of the store.

Finally it was time to head to the mine site. It had been a long and exciting day, and everybody was tired but eager to arrive at our new home. By then darkness had set in. Due to the poor condition of the road, the trip, which usually took over an hour, took much longer at night.

The site of the mine was a tropical wonder. Our house was perched on the side of a hill overlooking the mine site, the bay, nearby islands, and the Surigao Strait (site of the epic sea battle which would take place in October 1944 between American and Japanese naval forces) in the distance. The road ended at the bottom of the hill, and we had to walk up thirty or forty zigzag steps to the house level. Dad carried me, sleeping, up all those steps on the night of our arrival.

Settling into our new home was relatively easy. Though not very large, it was quite comfortable. A work crew supervised by a Japanese master carpenter had added a master bedroom suite and a wraparound veranda. Dad also had wire screens installed in the windows, eliminating the need for mosquito nets above each bed. In short order, Mom hired the household staff. Her primary helper was a cheerful young woman named Romana, who occupied a room next to the kitchen. Romana was assisted by two women from a nearby barrio who came in daily to help with the laundry and housecleaning. Additionally, Mom took on two gardeners to clear excess growth on the slope between our house and the road and form terraces for her future garden. The furniture and household items shipped from Iligan and Manila had arrived in good order, and Mom soon had everything arranged to her liking. The dining room was her pride and joy, with its large table, sideboard, and hutch filled with her favorite china and fine crystal. An open doorway led to the living room, with comfortable seating arranged near the RCA radio console. Large glass windows separated both rooms from the veranda.

The floors of the living areas were beautiful. Part of the original structure, they were made of wide, dark wood planks burnished to a high gloss. The secret to the gleaming floors was Johnson's Floor Wax and a coconut husk polisher. A mature coconut was neatly cut in half and the edges of the inner hard shell trimmed away to expose about half an inch of the stiff brushlike outer husk. I can still picture one of Romana's helpers, a circular coconut husk under one foot, buffing each plank to a beautiful shine.

The mine was largely self-contained—in addition to several administration buildings, there was a dispensary and a movie theater. Dotting the hillside were a few private residences for the American and European members of the management team; oddly enough, none of the team members had children living with them. The mine's general manager was Fred Varney, a German American (he spoke with a distinct German accent) whose wife's name was Nelle. For the convenience of East Mindanao personnel, there was a general store run by R. Yang that carried everything from clothing to canned and fresh food. Yang extended credit to the mineworkers, and on paydays they lined up to settle their bills for the month; they'd start another month's tab the following day. A two-hundred-foot pier accommodated the various boats and barges that brought in supplies for the mine operation. East Mindanao had two motor launches—the larger was the *Gold Bug* and the smaller the *Henry Joy*. One of the duties of the latter was to tow the oil barge to Placer to be filled with crude oil from the mine's storage tank. On these occasions we tagged along, but our destination was the sandy beach north of Placer, where we would enjoy a swim and a picnic until the boat picked us up on its return trip. Our frequent excursions led me to believe that it belonged to our family and was named after my brother Hank, with "Joy" added because our outings were really joy rides.

We were surprised to learn that the mine had a mascot—a spirited horse named "Old Timer." He was left over from a herd of twenty-four Australian horses used in the early years to pull the ore carts from the mine to the smelter. However, as the mine modernized and installed narrow gauge rails, the horses were no longer needed and were rounded up for transport back to Australia. Old Timer somehow evaded the roundup crew and later showed up at the mine site after the ship had departed. The management then decided to allow him to remain as the mine's mascot. Old Timer was the curse of many of the *lavanderas* (launderers) in the community—after they had washed the laundry and hung it up to dry, he often came along and snatched the clothing with his mouth and pulled it to the ground. In the early evenings, for amusement, the miners put out pots of *tuba* (fermented sap from young coconut blossoms) for Old Timer to drink; this really got him going with all sorts of bucking and snorting antics.

One day, while Mom was at Yang's store, I joined Fred Varney as he stood outside his office feeding Old Timer some lemon drops. Varney gave me one lemon drop and then Old Timer another. Well, Old Timer apparently did not like the competition. All of a sudden, he whirled around and attacked me. Lowering his head, he pushed me to the ground with his muzzle and held me down with one of his hooves. With teeth bared, his head came straight toward my face. Fortunately I moved my head in time and he took a bite out of my left shoulder instead. Varney immediately intervened and knocked him away. Sweeping me up in his arms, he rushed me to the dispensary, at the same time yelling at staff members to find Mom and also advise Dad. My most vivid memory of that incident is not the pain—although I still have a scar the size of a dollar coin on my left shoulder as a reminder of the attack—but my fear of being in the dispensary. There was a large *balete* tree (relative of the banyan) right next to it, and the locals believed that "little people" dwelled among its limbs and roots. It was rumored that the flashlights of the security force that patrolled the mine site nightly mysteriously failed whenever they passed near the tree and the guards heard light footsteps behind them as they beat a hasty retreat. As soon as Mom and Dad arrived, I pleaded with them to take me home immediately. I was safely in my own bed when the anesthetic wore off and I felt the pain in my shoulder and chest. Strangely, my right instep was swollen and sore as well—Old Timer had managed to stomp on it at some point during the attack.

Since the mine operated seven days a week, Dad's work routine seldom changed. At around 6:00 every morning, he walked down the many steps from the house to his office at the machine shop; at noon he retraced his steps to the house for lunch. After lunch, he relaxed a bit by lying on the floor and listening to news broadcasts from Manila and Singapore on the RCA radio. During that period my parents and their friends and colleagues were becoming increasingly concerned about Japanese intentions in Asia, particularly as Japan became more successful in its military adventures in China. From our tiny hamlet of Tinabingan, on the northeastern coast of Mindanao, that all seemed a world away.

Dad's domain at East Mindanao consisted of the machine shop, where he maintained his office; the power plant, which housed the two generators that supplied electricity for the mine operations; and a large structure about three stories high called "the mill," which was built against the hillside. The mill's most important function was the production of gold bouillon. While all aspects of the mining operation interested my brothers, they were particularly fascinated by the process of converting ore into pure gold. According to Hank (and probably unbeknownst to Mom) they often hitched rides on the railroad cars filled with ore from the mineshafts. The track snaked its way around the back of our house to the top of the hill, where the rocks (some the size of a basketball) were dumped into a hopper in a metal bin, then into a chute that placed them on a conveyor belt, which carried them to the crusher in the mill. The two cylinders of the crusher, one inside the other rotating in opposite directions, reduced the ore to the consistency of sand, which was then carried by another conveyor belt to the first of three big wooden vats of water for the stirring process to eliminate soil particles. The resulting concentrate was crushed into fine dust and transported to the main administration building for evaluation, after which it was placed in a vat with a mixture of cyanide and water. After the cyanide had dissolved most of the extraneous material, the concentrate (still in fine dust form) was removed and mixed with mercury, which picked up minute ore particles. This mixture was placed into molds and subjected to high temperatures in the kiln. The mercury was allowed to evaporate, leaving gold amalgam. My brothers watched this process through a thick glass window—Hank can remember being fascinated by watching the glowing red molds in the furnace. When cooled, the gold ingots easily slid out of the molds and then stored in the company's safe in Varney's office to await transport to Surigao on Thursdays and consignment to an SS *Corregidor* officer for delivery into the eager hands of the East Mindanao treasurer in Manila.

To my regret the summer vacation soon ended; in June my siblings started the new school year at San Nicholas School in Surigao. Unlike their previous schools in Cagayan, San Nicolas was coeducational, with separate classrooms for boys and girls from grades 1 through 7, followed by four years of high school. A combination day and boarding school, it was ideal for the children of the families who lived at mines, lumber mills, and ranches in the northeastern part of Mindanao. Mother Adela, the principal, ran a tight ship—I remember the boys remarking later in the year that they dreaded being called to her office for some infraction of the rules. Rooms on the third floor of the Little Flower Dormitory, the nuns' convent, were made available for the female boarding students. The male boarders were housed in a separate building across the square. For my sister, Peach, this was a welcome change from her experience at Lourdes Academy. Always an excellent student, she thrived in this new atmosphere. Furthermore, her mature attitude and demeanor impressed her teachers. My siblings adjusted well to the new school routine of leaving for Surigao early each Monday morning and returning home either Friday evening or Saturday at midday, depending on school activities. Weekends were short but jam-packed.

In contrast to my siblings, I was a shy little girl. While they were at school during the week, I enjoyed being the center of attention at home. Although my nickname was Ginger (eventually shortened to simply Gin), Dad's pet name for me was "Babe," and I loved his addressing me in this special way. Without the other kids around, Dad was able to relax and cast off his role of disciplinarian. Because he tended to be on the strict side, especially with the boys, Mom often acted as mediator (although she could mete out punishment as well).

During the early years of their marriage, my parents had their hands full trying to keep three active young boys in check. One of the youngsters' escapades almost turned deadly. When they were in the lower grades at Bordner School in Manila, it was the fashion of some of the older boys to wear spent bullets, pierced with holes and strung on a fine leather thong, around their necks. My brothers did not have the money to spend on these necklaces, so they decided to make their own. Although Dad kept his revolver locked up, they could access his supply of ammunition and simply helped themselves. Somehow they had learned the trick of getting a bullet to explode. They anchored the bullet in a few inches of soil, covered it with twigs, set the twigs on fire, and dove behind a large rock or mound of dirt to wait for the explosion. The bullet, now separated from its cartridge, could be pierced and strung on a leather thong. Well, one of their friends also wanted one of these fashion statements and persuaded the boys to make him one. They followed the same procedure, but this time it took longer for the bullet to explode. After a while the friend grew impatient and raised his head to see why nothing was happening. In that instant the bullet exploded, sending a piece of shrapnel in his direction, piercing him in the neck. When he started to bleed, Hank, as the youngest, was sent to summon Mom and face her initial angry reaction. She immediately calmed down, however, and came in the car to take the friend to the nearest hospital. Frightened, the boys sat quietly in the back seat. To everyone's relief the wound was not serious, and the boy was released after treatment. Now came the difficult part, explaining the accident to the mother of the friend. Mom's explanation and sincere apology averted a rift between the two families. The boys could now only steel themselves for Dad's reaction. Mom had the gardener wash the bloodstains off the upholstery but the car seat was still wet when she picked Dad up from work. He was furious by the time he arrived home to confront the boys and immediately removed his belt and gave each of them a thrashing that they never forgot. He did not enjoy punishing his children, but he believed that they would benefit from good discipline in the long run.

When my older siblings returned to school after the hot season break, I was content to play with my toys and our newest pet, a cat named Bootsie. She was almost all white, fairly young but no longer a kitten. Mom brought her to me one day, saying that she had been looking for a family with a little girl and decided to come and live with us. I tried to get more details, but Mom just smiled and would not elaborate. To my delight, Princess became more friendly toward me after Bootsie's arrival. Mom was not sure if this was because of jealousy or the calm atmosphere without the other kids around—in any event, I welcomed her company, and she and Bootsie tolerated each other's presence. My favorite play area was the veranda that extended along the entire front of the house. It had large hinged windows that could be propped open or lowered, depending on the weather, providing protection from both the sun and heavy weather such as typhoons. The large glass picture windows of the main house were thus shielded from the elements. Weather permitting, breakfast and lunch were served at one end of the veranda, and it was here, in the early evenings, Dad enjoyed sipping his favorite drink—Scotch and water, no ice. Romana would prepare it, and I would always beg her to let me serve. She did not always acquiesce because she knew that on the way from the kitchen I would help myself to a sip or two. My parents favored more formal dinners, so the dining room was the venue for the evening meals and Sunday dinners. I must confess that I did not fully participate in these mealtime gatherings—I was a picky eater, and even stories of "the poor children in Russia and China who didn't have enough food" could not persuade me to eat my meals. Mom had no patience with this kind of behavior and would give up in anger and frustration. Romana had better success in getting some sustenance into me—she would coax and cajole, playing my favorite tunes on the record player ("Popeye the Sailor Man" seemed to whet my appetite the best) as she spoon-fed me. My brothers thought this was outrageously childish and called me a ninny.

Every Thursday, my parents accompanied the gold shipment from the mine up to Surigao. The gold bars were packed in heavy wooden crates with rope handles at each end and were loaded aboard the company station wagon for transport to town. The driver assigned to Dad drove the station wagon. (We grew fond of him and considered him our driver because he drove the Studebaker as well; regretfully, none of us can remember his name.) In Surigao the crates were then brought aboard the SS *Corregidor*. Thursdays were always special shopping days for our family. One of Mom's new stops was the general store owned by the Ong family—not only was it well-stocked, but Mr. Ong also took orders for items not normally in his inventory. In addition, this family operated Surigao's only movie theater and the best Chinese restaurant in town.

Meanwhile, down at the waterfront bar behind Egling's store, Dad would spend time socializing with his colleagues as he waited for the loading of the gold shipment and the delivery of the East Mindanao pouch, which also contained our personal mail and newspapers. Later on, the socializing would continue in the bar on board the ship, where Dad and his friends could be found rolling dice (probably playing "liar's dice"). We would be treated to dinner and delicious Magnolia ice cream in the ship's dining room. I can also remember youngsters dancing in the upper deck salon to popular tunes: "San Antonio Rose," "I'll Get By," and "Moon over Burma." However, their favorite by far was "Beer Barrel Polka." Lucy McCarthy, a friend of my siblings (daughter of Frank McCarthy, who ran a sawmill near Surigao), was especially pleased when the band played "Come Away with Me, Lucille, in My Merry Oldsmobile."

Mom oversaw the creation of an extensive garden with many varieties of tropical plants and flowers growing on the terraced hillside. Behind the house was a large tree, which became the site for a tree house my brothers built in its upper reaches, using lumber they had scavenged from the mine. It had a ladder and an escape hatch through which a long rope could be lowered. Also, the boys built a swing that hung from a coconut tree. It was rigged so that you swung around the tree, kicking the trunk for propulsion, until the length of rope got shorter and shorter, and eventually you collided with the tree. Another project for my brothers was replicating a small mine in the hillside behind the house—they dug in the tunnel in search of quartz crystals, which they pretended were diamonds.

Peach, though only four and a half years older than I, was mature for her age. The lonely, miserable year she spent boarding at Lourdes Academy taught her how to be independent and self-sufficient. She had always tried to keep up with her older brothers in their antics, and could hold her own in most situations. But she did not turn into a tomboy, and as she grew older she was able to straddle both the arena of boys' rough activities and the more gentle girls' world of dolls and tea sets. She made friends easily at San Nicolas School and was soon enjoying a busy social life on the weekends, with frequent sleepovers at the homes of school friends. I tagged along when Mom drove Peach and, seeing the group of girls assembled, wondered if I, too, could have a similar circle of friends when I reached her age.

Too timid to attempt to participate in activities up in the tree house or in the backyard mine or swing around the coconut tree, I frequently retreated to my own private playground, the area underneath the house. Many houses in the tropics are built several feet above the ground, with wooden posts set in large cement footings. Each cement support was surrounded by a reservoir of oil that kept termites, ants, and other creatures from entering the house. Often the accumulation of dead insects actually formed a pontoon bridge for a fresh brigade of advancing ants. Mom assigned to me the responsibility of advising one of the gardeners when this happened, lest the house be overrun by ants.

We spent part of the school breaks of 1940 and 1941 vacationing in Manila, with mini-holidays at the cool mountain resort of Baguio. My siblings would visit with friends and indulge in shopping sprees. Peach particularly enjoyed staying with the Holmes family, old neighbors from when our family lived in the San Juan suburb before I was born—the boys and the Holmes kids played together and attended Bordner. Peach and Lynn Holmes (now Parsons) were best friends for many years and remain close today. Most of the time, we would stay with Pop Henderson, whose adopted daughter Flora ("Boots") and her sisters Helene ("Belle") and Grace were close friends of Mom.

The whole family enjoyed Manila's big-city amenities—department stores and other specialty shops along the Escolta filled with goods imported from around the world and local markets with a wide variety of Philippine merchandise. I especially liked our visits to the Botica Boie, a huge pharmacy with a soda fountain that served the best ice cream sodas and sundaes in town. One of our favorite eateries was a Chinese restaurant called "Panciteria Nueva" at Plaza

Santa Cruz, which had three floors filled with tables large and small draped with white linen tablecloths, plus several private dining rooms. Our group, consisting of family and friends, was usually large enough to warrant a private room. We passed around a seemingly endless array of beef, pork, duck, chicken, and seafood dishes, and everyone feasted on their own favorites—Hank's was bola-bola (spicy beef/pork meatballs) in a sweet-and-sour sauce. The teenage boys had enormous appetites, so there was not much food left at the end of the meal—but the lovely white tablecloth sported many spots and stains, which let the restaurant management know that we had really enjoyed the food.

Although we enjoyed our vacations in Manila, no one protested when it was time to return to our home at the mine site. My brothers were always eager to learn more about the different aspects of the mine operation and proudly donned the miners' helmets they had bought at Egling's shop with their own money. Pleased at their interest, the workers let them watch but also kept a close eye on them to make sure they stayed out of dangerous situations. When Ed turned sixteen, Dad let him learn how to operate some of the equipment in the machine shop. He soon became an apprentice lathe operator and was actually paid eighty centavos a day.

Dad and Mom were planning to send Ed to the States after his graduation from high school to study engineering and join Dad in the mining business. Hank recalls how they studied the classified ads in the American newspapers that arrived every week to get ideas on the availability of private rooms or boarding house accommodations suitable for Ed in various cities on the West Coast.

I will never forget an accident that occurred at the mine when some of the shoring in a tunnel collapsed. Unfortunately, one of the miners suffered serious head injuries. He was taken to the dispensary down the hill from our house where the local doctor decided he was too badly injured to be moved to the hospital in Surigao. I remember wondering if the miner knew the story of the balete tree that was close to the dispensary. I also felt sorry because he could not go home immediately, like I did. All night long we could hear him, and when there were no more moaning sounds the next day, Mom told me that he had died from his injuries. A pall settled on the community of miners as they mourned the passing of one of their fellow-workers. I was about six years old and had only a vague idea of the meaning of this sad phenomenon. Little did I realize that in a few months the full concept of death and its impact on our family would come home to me distinctly and unequivocally.

In June 1941 I joined my brothers and sister at San Nicolas School. This caused a drastic, difficult change in my life—for starters, I did not like having to wear the school uniform. We kids normally left for school early on Monday morning, in the Studebaker, accompanied by Romana. To accommodate us all in the crowded sedan, Romana set me on her lap, and I always asked that she position herself next to a window. My siblings, however, insisted that window seating be rotated, and for good reason. On particularly hot days, the smell of the mohair upholstery, combined with the heat and humidity, made us feel queasy. Tense and upset, I was the first one competing for a window seat as nausea set in. This would cause a chain reaction, and soon we all needed a turn at an open window. Romana helped us rid ourselves of the early morning meal by squeezing our stomachs as we held our heads out of the car window. To the utter embarrassment of our driver, the black Studebaker often reached San Nicolas School with its sides streaked with vomit from our mad dash down the mountain road from the mine. On Thursdays Mom visited us at school, bringing fresh clothes and special food, and took us to the SS *Corregidor* for the weekly dinner and ice cream treat.

I did not adjust well to life at school. I shared a room with Peach and another young girl at the Little Flower Dormitory. The morning schedule included daily Mass, followed by breakfast in the dining room—usually hot chocolate, bread, and fruit. Breakfast over, we would go to our respective classrooms. After lunch we would return to class. After-school activities included piano lessons, choir practice, and dance rehearsals (we seemed to be constantly preparing for a recital or musical program). Dinner was varied but always included rice. After dinner we would have some free time before doing homework. Some evenings, during recreation time, the older male boarders (including my brothers, no doubt) gathered in the courtyard to surreptitiously smoke cigarettes. Then someone started strumming a guitar, and soon they were serenading the girls in the convent. Surprisingly, the nuns did not object. Nevertheless, I hated the routine and was always looking for ways to return home with Mom on Thursday evenings, often by coming up with some contrived malady before her arrival. I found that I could actually make myself sick by not eating. Whether real or imagined, my ailments often succeeded in convincing the nuns to allow me to leave with Mom before the end of the school week. It also came to Mom's attention that Peach was not overly fond of the food served in the dining room; in fact, she often cajoled the nun in charge of kitchen operations to prepare something different for her. Peach recalled that one of those concoctions was a dish of rice and vegetables topped with an egg. The cook would mix cooked vegetables into steamed rice as it was being fried in a pan, and plop a fresh egg on top. The heat generated by the rice and vegetables cooked the egg in almost no time, and Peach would have a reasonably healthy one-dish meal. Mom decided to negotiate a special arrangement for our meals. Mother Adela agreed to have a couple of tables set up in a separate room where a modified version of the day's menu would be served. Soon several other boarding students joined us. There were some additional costs involved, and Mom made sure there was always a supply of bread, butter, and jam for us, thus ensuring that no one starved.

In 1940 and 1941 our family was sheltered from many of the world's problems. We had no concept of the extent of the economic depression in the States and Europe. As an engineer, my father had always been well compensated by the firms with which he had been affiliated. At night, in front of our shortwave radio, we tuned to Manila or overseas stations for broadcasts of our favorite programs, notably *The Shadow*, *The Edgar Bergen and Charlie McCarthy Show*, and *Amos and Andy*, as well as the latest news from the United States and Europe. Important events in Europe—Germany's seizure of Austria in 1938 and invasion of Poland in 1939—were like developments on another planet. However, when France fell in 1940 and Great Britain faced Germany alone, my parents began to sense that events in the rest of the world might somehow catch up with us on Mindanao. Still, they felt safe in knowing that General MacArthur was now in command of U.S. and Philippine forces.

After our annual vacation to Manila during the school break of 1941 my parents became increasingly concerned about the escalation in Japanese war activities in Southeast Asia, particularly in July when the Japanese invaded French Indochina. This was during the same period when the United States froze Japanese assets in the United States and halted trade. Also, during the summer of 1941 the U.S. high commissioner recommended that dependents and nonessential personnel return to the States. Great Britain issued similar precautions to its personnel in Singapore. However, for our family leaving was not a viable option. After leaving New York for his Army enlistment, Dad lost contact with his family, and Mom never had a chance to get to know the Harris family in the States. Without relatives or friends there, going to the States without Dad, five young children in tow, was too daunting an undertaking for Mom to contemplate.

On Friday, September 26, 1941, an incident occurred at San Nicolas School that would devastate our family. It all happened in the main dining room. My brother Ed happened to be walking by when he saw one of the boarding students (the son of the mayor of a town in the northwestern part of Mindanao) badgering a "working student" who was clearing the breakfast tables. Ed told the student to stop pestering the working student. There were words between him and the other student, but since they were friends and classmates, the argument ended after a few minutes. By then it was time to go to their first class and, considering the matter closed, Ed suggested they proceed to their classroom. The student left to go to the boys' dormitory, ostensibly to get his books, while Ed waited for him in the hallway. A few minutes later the student returned, apparently still angry, and resumed the argument. A scuffle ensued and the other student ended up on the floor. Suddenly he reached for a brass stiletto that he had hidden in his high-top shoes and thrust it into Ed's abdomen. Initially, because the stab wound was small and did not bleed profusely, Ed thought it was just a minor cut. By the time the nuns arrived to investigate, however, blood was seeping through Ed's pants below the belt. As a safeguard, he was taken to the local hospital in Surigao for treatment of what seemed a superficial wound. Someone was dispatched to the mine to summon my parents. Unfortunately, the stiletto had penetrated more deeply than anyone realized, causing internal bleeding and infection. Throughout the day and night the infection continued to spread despite the best efforts of the local doctors. Ed developed a high temperature that could not be brought down. Peach recalled being in Ed's room when Mom, overcome with shock and fear and sadness at the realization that Ed's life was slowly ebbing away, fainted beside his bed. A doctor revived her and gently suggested she get some rest, but she refused to leave Ed's bedside. Sadly, late in the afternoon of the second day, with all of us standing around his bed, our beloved Ed died. I remember the event vividly. The priest who had administered the Last Rites had just departed. It was a great shock to all of us, especially my mom—I had never seen her so sad. Dad, who seldom showed his emotions, stood rigidly by Ed's bed, his eyes red-rimmed. Rudy, Hank, and Peach were weeping softly. I moved toward the window and started to cry also, although I still did not fully grasp the implication of Ed's death. It was not until Ed's funeral several days later that I truly understood that he would never come home and be part of our family again. It was the first time in my life I had ever experienced such a feeling of deep sadness.

After Ed's funeral in Surigao, we all gathered at Mr. Ong's restaurant. School friends and their families were in attendance, and everyone seemed to be in a state of shock over the tragedy that had so senselessly ended the life of such a promising young man (Ed was two months short of his seventeenth birthday). Adding poignancy to the occasion was the revelation that, unbeknown to Mom and Dad, a budding romance had been blossoming between Ed and sixteen-year-old Adela O'Dell, a boarding student whose father was in the lumber business.

It was ironic that this tragedy occurred just as my parents were in the process of arranging separate housing for us in Surigao. The idea came about when they learned that Boots Henderson's sister Grace and her husband and young son, Bucky, were moving to the Surigao area. Grace's husband had recently secured a job in a nearby mine, but there was no family housing available at the site. Grace was willing to live in Surigao and be our housemother during the week. According to Hank, Mom and Grace had already found a suitable house but it needed some renovation. Of course, at the time I was not aware of the change that was being planned, but I cannot help wondering: if our move had somehow been accelerated and we were living in a separate house, perhaps Ed would not have been near the school dining room that fateful morning. I imagine this thought occurred to Mom and Dad, but it was never mentioned.

Surprisingly, despite his family's political standing, the young man who had inflicted the fatal stab wound was quickly charged, convicted, and sentenced to a juvenile detention facility. On those occasions when the driver took my mother in our Studebaker and they passed the inmates of the jail doing work along the road, the driver, outraged at Ed's murder, would ask Mom's permission to finish off his assailant. Of course, she would say no. But after about a month Mom felt she was sinking into depression. Despite her deep faith, she found it difficult to accept the loss of her eldest son, who had matured into a responsible young adult and a role model for his younger brothers, even keeping a watchful eye on them while they were at school.

Mom's dear friend Boots came from Manila to visit us and help her cope with her grief. Shortly after Boots's arrival, however, my parents decided that, as a diversion, Mom should take a trip to Manila, visit old friends, and do Christmas shopping for the family. Boots would remain to oversee the running of the household until Mom's return and spend time visiting Grace and her family.

Mom made the trip on the next voyage of the SS *Corregidor*. She planned to return to Surigao in early December, but first she ordered Christmas gifts and special goodies to bring home. She also bought a Hotpoint refrigerator that was to replace the kerosene model in our kitchen. However, not long after her arrival in Manila Mom had a dream about Ed, in which he urged her to return immediately to Surigao. According to Mom, he said to her, "Go home, Mom, your family needs you." The next day she changed her reservation and took the next sailing of the SS *Corregidor* back to Surigao. She was able to bring the new refrigerator, but due to the Christmas rush the gifts and special foods were not quite ready for shipment and had to wait for a later sailing.

Relations between the United States and Japan were going downhill fast. Every day as usual, after his noon meal, Dad would lie on the floor in the lounge in front of the radio console and listen to the latest news, usually on KZRH from Manila. In the evening, if the atmosphere was favorable, he might tune in to KGEI in San Francisco or the BBC broadcasts from Singapore. In the weeks prior to the attack on Pearl Harbor, Dad waited with bated breath for the news reports concerning talks in Washington between Secretary Cordell Hull and Admiral Nomura. The talks, of course, went nowhere but did allow time for some miniscule war materiel to flow to General MacArthur's forces in the Philippines.

While Mom was on her trip, Boots listened along with Dad to the ever-worsening news of impending war in the Pacific. She became anxious to return home to Manila, and Dad agreed that she should leave as soon as possible. She hurriedly made preparations to sail on the very next voyage of the SS *Corregidor,* feeling a bit guilty because she had promised to stay at least until Mom's return. Imagine her astonishment when Mom arrived via the very ship on which she was planning to depart! Although Boots did not know it at the time, her decision to return to Manila earlier than planned was fortuitous— had she delayed her departure, she could very well have been trapped with us on Mindanao, and the course of her life would have taken a drastically different direction.

For our family, it was truly a blessing that Mom had decided to return home early. A footnote to this event is that the SS *Corregidor* hit a mine as it exited Manila harbor on December 17. As a defensive measure, the U.S. Navy had mined the harbor. Bruce Elliot, a petty officer who was assigned at Sangley Point at the time and who later served with the guerrillas on Mindanao, later remembered participating in the mining operation. Ironically, the ship was carrying much needed supplies for U.S. Army Forces in the Far East (USAFFE) forces on Mindanao. With the sinking of the SS *Corregidor* went our Christmas gifts Mom had ordered during her trip, but she was home safe—and we had a new Hotpoint refrigerator as well.

COMMENTARY ON PHILIPPINE PREPAREDNESS FOR WAR

During the summer of 1941 events began to spin out of control in the Far East. Particularly disturbing was the military campaign Japan was waging in nearby China. In July 1941 General Marshall had activated the U.S. command that MacArthur was to head. It was designated as USAFFE. It included not only U.S. Army units in the Philippines but also those military units of the Philippine Commonwealth. Prior to the establishment of USAFFE, the Philippine Department was responsible for all U.S. Army units in the islands. This department also had responsibility for the Philippine Division that was made up of mostly Philippine Scout units. These were Filipino enlisted men serving under American officers. Prior to July 1941, MacArthur had no command responsibility to the Philippine Department. He reported to President Quezon as a military adviser regarding the defense of the Philippines and the development of a Philippine army commanded by a Filipino general.[5]

On Mindanao the American/Filipino force, under General Sharp, numbered some thirty-five thousand troops. Moreover, the island did have a B-17 bomber base at the California Packing Corporation's airfield, located near its pineapple plantation at Del Monte, near Cagayan in Misamis Oriental. This was activated in late 1941. During late 1941 and early 1942, General MacArthur had ordered the Commander FEAF (Far East Air Force) at Clark Field, Major General Lewis Brereton, to move a number of B-17 aircraft to the Del Monte airfield to keep them out of harm's way should the Japanese attack. However, before Del Monte could be used, Colonel Hugh Casey, Corps of Engineers, had to marshal fifteen hundred construction workers to upgrade the small airstrip that had been used only by light aircraft of the California Packing Corporation. The airstrip was extended to five thousand feet and became capable of handling the heavy B-17 bombers. However, it was not a hard surface runway and it was without any modern airfield infrastructure.

Just prior to the attack on Pearl Harbor, sixteen B-17 bombers were finally deployed to Del Monte. The remaining B-17s at Clark were all destroyed during the Japanese attack on December 8, 1941. In late 1941, the personnel of the 19th Bomb Group were shipped from Clark to Del Monte to support the remaining B-17 presence in the islands. Some of these personnel later became a part of the resistance movement on Mindanao.[6]

The U.S. Navy elements in the Philippines were not a part of the USAFFE command structure. They reported to the commander of the U.S. Asiatic Fleet. Though the command was located in the Marsman Building in central Manila, its elements were dispersed throughout Asia and included the 4th Marines in China. In the Philippines the Navy had installations at Cavite, Sangley Point, Mariveles, and Subic Bay. These facilities supported air patrol squadrons, submarines, minesweepers, and patrol craft.[7]

The newly increased Army Air Corps strength at Del Monte made Americans residing on Mindanao feel somewhat more secure. However, they knew very little about the real state of readiness of USAFFE ground units, particularly on the island of Mindanao. Most of their equipment consisted of hand-me-downs from the U.S. Army. Few supplies were available for issue to the troops. The basic weapon was the vintage Enfield rifle or the Springfield '03 rifle; other supporting weapons such as grenades were nonexistent. This is why in the early months of 1942 General Sharp's staff had approached East Mindanao and other mining facilities about using their mine machine shops to repair weapons and manufacture firing mechanisms for grenades. Thus, in many respects, the USAFFE force on Mindanao was no more than a paper force. The U.S. Congress was, in a sense, derelict in the paltry funds it authorized for the defense of the Philippine Archipelago against a modern Japanese army that soon breached its meager capabilities. Had Americans known this, they would have had no hope for USAFFE units repulsing the Japanese invaders.

Another factor in the defense of Mindanao was the large number of Japanese civilians already working and living throughout the islands. While their presence in Surigao was limited to Japanese shopkeepers selling Japanese-manufactured goods, little did the average person realize the extent of their numbers and the influence exerted on the Philippine economy. In the 1930s, the Japanese had a strong presence on the island of Mindanao, especially in the Davao area in the south. The Japanese commenced to arrive in the Philippines after the turn of the century. Their focus was on the abaca fields—related to the banana plant, abaca produced tough fibers used for making rope, matting, et cetera. By 1941 the Japanese controlled almost all of the hemp produced in Davao province. Almost all sixteen thousand Japanese were located in the province. Davao City was called "Little Tokyo" by some. Moreover, the Japanese had strong economic influence in shipping, fishing, lumber, and mining. The Philippine Commonwealth government recognized this control and passed legislation mandating that 60 percent of the equity in any firm or corporation must be owned by Filipinos.[8]

The large presence of Japanese in Davao province was recognized in Japanese war-planning efforts. Within days after the war started, Japanese military elements were dispatched to Davao and Jolo, where their presence was designed to support the Japanese invasion of Borneo. A significant Japanese presence in the rest of Mindanao did not materialize until after April 1942. With this breathing space, the U.S. forces had the opportunity to develop a base in the interior of Mindanao from which to launch guerrilla operations after the invasion of the Japanese main force. Unfortunately USAFFE wasted this chance, and surrender became the fate of the U.S./Philippine military presence. From this debacle would come the leadership and determination to build a guerrilla resistance movement.

TWO

Moving to War and Awaiting
the Invasion of Mindanao

On December 8, 1941, after Dad rushed home from his office at the mine and announced that Japan had attacked Pearl Harbor, we gathered in the living room to listen to the news on our shortwave radio. My siblings and I sat on the floor, still wearing our school uniforms. I had recently learned that Manila was known as the Pearl of the Orient, so I asked if Pearl Harbor was near Manila. One of my brothers explained that Pearl Harbor was across the ocean in the Hawaiian Islands, closer to the States. I was relieved and wondered why everyone was worried about something that was happening in that far-off place.

I decided to take advantage of the unexpected day off from school. After changing into play clothes, I went to the veranda in search of Princess and Bootsie. Activities over the weekend—picnic at Placer on Saturday, birthday party for my brothers on Sunday—had left little time for me to spend with them. And, of course, being in school during the week limited my playtime with my four-legged friends.

Dad continued to monitor the news broadcasts throughout the day. I was in the living room in the afternoon when the Manila radio stations and the BBC broadcast the initial bulletin of a Japanese aerial attack on Clark Field, north of Manila. I was startled to see Dad leap to his feet in anger. He paced around the room, muttering expletives. Suddenly the war was no longer an ocean away, but just 750 or so kilometers to the north of us. How soon would the Japanese attack Mindanao? The bombing on Luzon prompted Fred Varney to call a meeting of the management team that evening. They decided to halt operations, put the mine in caretaker status with a skeleton force, and furlough the rest of the workers. Varney and Dad would remain to see what was going to be done by U.S. and Allied forces to stop the Japanese and end the war. Hundreds of Filipino workers were asked to return to their barrios until further notice while the other American employees considered their options regarding how or where they would wait out the war. Dad and Varney agreed that if it became necessary to abandon the mine, the last one to leave would oversee the disabling of the mining equipment to render it useless to the enemy forces. East Mindanao's large crude oil tank located in nearby Placer would also have to be destroyed so the Japanese couldn't use that precious commodity.

As news of more attacks followed, Dad seemed to calm down, but his demeanor was intense and serious as he listened to the reports. The names of the bombed places were not familiar to me at the time, but my parents' reaction to these reports made me feel uneasy and I often retreated to my play area on the veranda. In the evenings I stayed close to the radio in the vain hope that our regular serial programs—especially my favorite, *The Edgar Bergen and Charlie McCarthy Show*—would return to the air.

The battle losses the Japanese planes had inflicted on the U.S. Pacific Fleet at Pearl Harbor were severe, but we did not yet know the extent of the damage sustained by U.S. military installations closer to home on Luzon—Clark Field, the U.S. Navy facilities at Sangley Point, Cavite, Mariveles, and Subic Bay, and Nichols Field right in Manila. If we had known the extent of these losses from the raids of December 8 and later, we would have lost all hope of the Japanese being neutralized in their military thrust against the Philippine Islands. As it was, we did have hope, and believed that somehow this ugly Japanese action would soon come to an end.

In the early days of the war, Philippine president Manuel Quezon had ordered the schools closed. Assuming a Japanese invasion, he did not want the schools to be used by the Japanese occupation as a platform for spreading propaganda and ideology. Thus, my siblings and I didn't return to school after the December 8 bombings.

Unlike the joint celebration of my brothers' birthdays on the previous weekend, my seventh birthday on Wednesday, December 17, came and went with little fanfare. This did not bother me because my birthday celebrations were usually simple family affairs anyway. Since I had no friends or playmates at the mine site, there were no potential little guests for a party. However, I received a very special gift—a pair of brand new brown-and-white saddle shoes custom-made for me at Pop Henderson's shop. On her recent trip, Mom had ordered a pair of brown-and-white spectator pumps for herself, and she chose the same color combination for my shoes. She knew how much I enjoyed it when we wore matching mother/daughter dresses with color-coordinated shoes.

On the day after my birthday we received news of the sinking of the SS *Corregidor* as it exited Manila Bay the night before. The ship's normal schedule had been disrupted by the Japanese attacks on Luzon, and this voyage was supposed to depart at midnight. However, the shipping company decided to let it depart several hours ahead of schedule, leaving behind a number of passengers. These were the lucky ones, for as the ship proceeded unescorted through the mine fields laid by the U.S. Navy in Manila Bay, it struck a mine near Corregidor Island. Filled to capacity with cargo and several hundred passengers anxious to return to their homes in the various islands to the south, it sank within minutes. The patrol torpedo (PT) boat squadron stationed on Corregidor Island acted quickly and rescued hundreds of survivors, but many perished as well. The ship was carrying much needed supplies for USAFFE forces on Mindanao. And somewhere in its cargo hold were the Christmas gifts and special holiday treats that Mom had ordered when she was in Manila.

In contrast, my birthday the year before had marked the start of the buildup to the Christmas holiday. Most of the presents ordered from Manila had arrived and were stored in various places, out of sight of curious eyes. There were visits to the stores in Surigao for last-minute gifts. The Christmas tree, which had traveled all the way from Baguio, came with its branches tied with twine and its roots, encased in a big ball of soil, wrapped in burlap. The gardeners put the tree in a round wooden tub on the veranda, adding more soil to make a snug fit. It seemed to come alive right before my eyes as they watered it and released its branches. The tree-decorating ritual took place on the weekend, when my siblings were home. (My favorite part was hanging the tiny strands of shiny tinsel on the branches.) But at Christmastime in 1941, there was no tree to trim; in the chaos following the initial Japanese bombing raids on Luzon in early December, filling Christmas tree orders was not a priority. The mood at home was somber. The phonograph and records of Christmas songs lay untouched. The radio was always on, but I don't remember any Christmas carols coming over the airwaves. No one in our family had made a trip to Surigao since the outbreak of the war—Dad wanted to avoid our being seen by potential informants—so we didn't buy any last-minute Christmas gifts from the local stores. As was the case for millions of families all over the world, for us Christmas 1941 was not a happy occasion.

A big blow to our morale came on the day after Christmas when we heard the news that Manila had been declared an "open city."[1] The term piqued my interest so I asked what it meant. My parents told me that the Japanese Army was marching toward Manila, and no one was going to stop it from coming into the city. One of my siblings wondered aloud what Pop Henderson (and Boots and her sisters) and the Holmes family and all our other friends would do when the Japanese arrived. Should they try to run away and hide? Where could they hide, when the Japanese now controlled virtually all of Luzon? No one wanted to continue discussing the matter, as though the reality of an enemy force occupying Manila was almost too awful to contemplate. I was relieved that we did not live in Manila. I concluded that even if the Japanese came marching into Surigao itself, our home at the mine site was so far away from the city that it would not be possible for them to find us.

I was unaware that, as the Japanese offensive continued unabated, my parents were already thinking seriously about their options on Mindanao, a large island with mountains and abundant jungle areas, when the Japanese fully occupied the island. The consensus was that its extensive coastline would exhaust Japanese efforts to control all but the major towns and ports of the island. The initial Japanese landings on Mindanao were in Davao (in the south) and Jolo (to the west). With those areas under their control, it was only a matter of time before they started to establish their presence in the northeastern part of the island, where we lived. It was impossible to predict their plan of action, but so far their strategies in conducting this war had been successful.

As the days passed, it became abundantly clear that surrender to a Japanese occupation force was not an option. Moreover, if we were to go that route, my father's personality would immediately clash with the authoritarian nature of the Japanese and he would be dead within a few days' confinement in a Japanese internment camp. Already my parents had heard stories of the atrocities the Japanese had committed in China. They had reasoned that if the Japanese treated other Asians with such cruelty, their actions against Americans in the Philippines would certainly be worse. Furthermore, Mom and Dad had the safety and future of their four children to consider. Evading the Japanese by living in the mountains and out-of-the-way enclaves appeared the best option for sitting out the war until American forces returned. Of course, they knew that such a life would not be easy. In addition to the possibility of capture, the family would face many other threats in the jungle—malaria, tropical ulcers, worm infestations, dysentery, fungus, and infections, to name just a few.

As the reality sank in that we were now in the midst of a war, Mom and Dad began in earnest to prepare for the day when the Japanese occupation of the northern part of Mindanao would force us to leave the mine and our comfortable surroundings. We still had time; the Japanese advance toward Manila was steady but not rapid, and the American forces had consolidated at Bataan and Corregidor. As long as the mine generator had fuel, we could continue to have electricity for the radio, lights, and kitchen appliances. The mine movie theater continued to operate and was reshowing *The Shadow* (my favorite) and a couple of other recent movies. Before the start of the show, the few of us assembled there rose and sang "The Star-Spangled Banner" and "God Bless America," which bolstered our morale and inspired hope in our ever-dwindling mining community.

Shortly after Christmas, Varney decided that it was time for him and his wife, Nelle, to leave the mine site and go into hiding. They planned to join some friends at a lumber mill site in Misamis Oriental, in the midwestern part of Mindanao. That left Dad solely in charge of the mine. However, before Varney's departure, he and Dad still had the major task of hiding the last two gold bars that came from the mine's smelter, so they would not fall into the hands of the Japanese Army. They had the gold bars packed in a sturdy wooden crate and carried to the mine site to one of the horizontal shafts running off the main vertical shaft. Workers then placed explosives in both shafts. The subsequent detonations closed the mine entrance, preventing the Japanese (or anyone else) from looting the gold.

On Sunday, December 28, a Manila radio station broadcast that the city had been heavily bombed. Widespread destruction included the historic Santo Domingo Church in the Intramuros (walled city) area. This aerial attack seemed unnecessary because Manila had been declared an open city and the Japanese could have entered and occupied it unopposed. By Thursday, January 1, 1942, Manila radio was reporting that Japanese forces were very close—less than twenty kilometers from the city. The station indicated that this broadcast might be its last. Fortunately, we were still able to receive broadcasts from the BBC and KGEI in San Francisco on our short-wave radio. They were reporting that Manila was still under friendly forces. However, the next day a radio report from the BBC indicated that Manila had fallen. Our spirits were crushed, but we hoped that the USAFFE on Bataan and Corregidor could turn the tide.

Radio news reports over the next few weeks were not encouraging. One sad note was the fall of Singapore. "So soon," was my Dad's only comment. It should have held much longer—after all, it had been touted as an invincible stronghold for the British in Asia. Even so, we were riveted by Winston Churchill's radio announcement over the BBC:

And now, I have heavy news. Singapore has fallen. That mighty bastion of the Empire, which held out so long against insuperable odds, has honorably surrendered to spare its civilian population from further useless slaughter. And so let us go on, into the storm and through the storm.

Yes, for us in Mindanao the storm, like a typhoon, was about to strike. We, too, prayed that we would have the mettle to negotiate the many challenges that we would surely meet.

While Corregidor and Bataan might hold until the promised U.S. reinforcements could arrive, what defense did we have on Mindanao? When would the Japanese move an invasion force southward to Mindanao? When would they strike, and how much time did we have to prepare for evacuation? Some apprehension was eased when in January 1942 General MacArthur decided to move elements of the 61st Division southward to Mindanao. Though the Japanese presence on Mindanao was limited to two battalions in the Davao area and some troops on the island of Jolo, the rest of Mindanao was under U.S. military control. With the exception of forays up the Agusan River to threaten Japanese garrisons north of Davao, the U.S. forces were static, preparing for an anticipated Japanese invasion that would probably occur in Lanao, Zamboaga, Cotabato, Cagayan, and the Agusan areas. In the meantime, East Mindanao and other mines were using their machine shops to assist the USAFFE units with sorely needed equipment repair. Having a U.S. Army Air Corps contingent at Del Monte airfield did give us a degree of confidence. But we did not know that its capabilities were limited and most of its aircraft had been destroyed, or that it was now relegated to launching sporadic and limited raids in the defense of Luzon. Increasingly, particularly during February and March, it was supporting the evacuation of personnel and aircraft to Australia; its useful days were numbered. Nonetheless, there was elation throughout Mindanao in early January when elements of the 81st and 93rd Divisions arrived in Surigao from the islands to the north. Later deployed to the Butuan area, their presence gave us some sense of security, knowing that USAFFE troops were being deployed to protect us. The Philippine Constabulary maritime detachment in Surigao was making a name for itself in sweeping some thirty Japanese mines from the strategic Surigao Strait. The recovered mines were salvaged for use in defensive weapons; for example, the explosive material was used to fabricate grenades and land mines.

Sometime in January a runner arrived with a note from Fred Varney, wherein he indicated that the *Gold Bug* would be very useful for an operation to move U.S. forces up the Agusan River to Camp Kalao. He asked Dad to bring the launch to the embarkation point, and Dad immediately complied, in what was his first contribution to the military effort. He was gone for about two weeks and returned by land. Roy Welbon, a lumber mill manager, also assisted, particularly in maintaining communications.

In February Dad received a letter delivered by an emissary of Henry Gasser, representing the mine owners, advising him that the East Mindanao Mining Company would officially cease operations effective February 13 and, with regrets, that his services "were no longer required." We were now on our own!

Shortly thereafter a Captain Brundrett from General Sharp's headquarters at Del Monte, near Cagayan in Misamis Oriental, came to the mine inquiring about facilities to manufacture spare parts for weapons used by the U.S. Army. Of particular interest was the possibility of devising firing mechanisms for hand grenades. He also mentioned that 15 percent of the Enfield rifles in service had broken extractors that needed replacement. Dad told the captain that all the parts could be manufactured in the mine machine shop. Moreover, he had done similar design work for the Watertown Arsenal in New York. Not receiving a return visit from the captain, Dad wrote a personal letter to General Sharp offering his services to the U.S. Army for the duration of the war. The letter further reviewed the discussions Captain Brundrett had with my father on February 7, 1942, as explained below.

According to Captain Brundrett the army wants to manufacture several thousand grenades and having that many 22 cal. shells on hand which could be used as primary ignition devices the undersigned has designed a positive firing device which could be used with either a 22 cal. shell or even a primer for magnesium flares used in night photography; and as the whole mechanism consists of only four small parts very easily adaptable for mass production with machinery and materials available here, the undersigned firmly believes that a simple but effective hand grenade could be manufactured in quantity as long as there are 22 cal. shells available.

Dad also included a resume of his education, military service, and work history at the Watertown and Manila arsenals. Subsequent pages are missing but they would have outlined his service with the 27th Infantry Regiment in Siberia.

We have no record of a response to Dad's letter. However, very soon thereafter Dad learned that Sharp's forces had established a district headquarters in Surigao. He immediately made contact with military forces there to volunteer his services and expand on his ideas contained in the letter to the general. In short order, he was involved in the procurement and repair of weapons and other materiel from the local populace. Invariably, many of the old rifles would need replacement cartridge extractors or sights. Dad's experience and a fully equipped machine shop afforded him the capability to manufacture spare parts, and he had the expertise to repair and restore malfunctioning firearms. "Chief," his chief mechanic and right-hand man in the operation of the machine shop and member of the skeleton crew that remained at the mine, assisted him in these efforts.

Dad wrote his letter to General Sharp on March 17, 1942, the very day that General MacArthur departed the airfield at Del Monte on a B-17 bomber destined for Australia. He and his family, plus several staff officers, had been spirited out of Corregidor and transported to Cagayan, Misamis Oriental, by three PT boats under the command of Lieutenant John D. Bulkeley. It should be noted that after MacArthur's departure from the Philippines the War Department designated the remaining military presence as U.S. Forces in the Philippines (USFIP).

Tom Mitsos, a member of the 30th Squadron, 19th Bomb Group, assigned to the Del Monte airfield, vividly described MacArthur's arrival in Cagayan:

At 7:00 A.M. we heard the drone of engines. The sound was coming from the sea but we couldn't see any planes. After about five or ten minutes of this tense situation we saw three P.T. boats heading for the docks. They were numbers 34, 35 and 41. For a while we thought they were reinforcements, but they docked and we saw General MacArthur standing there; we knew they had come from Bataan. We watched General MacArthur shake Lt. Bulkeley's hand, thank him, and tell him he was awarding the Silver Star to him and every man in his squadron for bravery. The General, his family and staff got into cars waiting for them and were transported to Del Monte airfield.[2]

This historic escape by MacArthur was happening just 170 kilometers from us. Later in the month Lieutenant Bulkeley and his PT boats made another trip to Mindanao bringing Philippine Commonwealth president Manuel Quezon and his party for their evacuation to Australia via a U.S. Army Air Forces B-17 bomber from the Del Monte airfield.

A number of the crew on these three PT boats bringing MacArthur and Quezon to Mindanao remained and later joined the guerrilla movement. Among them was John Tuggle, a chief petty officer on Bulkeley's boat, who joined the guerrilla movement in December 1942. Initially responsible for logistical support for the guerrillas, he was later assigned to the airfield-building project in Domingog.

Although I did not fully understand what was going on, I did not complain. The Japanese bombings on Luzon and the fall of Manila had happened far away from us. Even though some Japanese were in Davao and Jolo, those areas were clear across the island from us. Besides, the American military forces that were in many parts of Mindanao, including Surigao, would surely protect us. The atmosphere at home was not as tense as it had been during those first few weeks following the start of the war, so it was easy for me to return to the routine I enjoyed before I started school. With my siblings at home, it felt like vacation time, though eerily different. There was no activity at the mine, and it was virtually deserted. Rudy and Hank spent more time observing Dad and Chief's activities at the machine shop than they did at their usual backyard haunts. During Dad's frequent absences, the boys kept themselves busy restoring an old abandoned *baroto* (dugout canoe) they had found on a nearby shore. It had a big hole in the bottom that they patched up, using scraps of wood and tar. After successfully rendering it seaworthy, they proudly made several trips along the coast almost as far as Placer, keeping close to shore. Our favorite launch, the *Henry Joy*, was still moored at the pier, but we did not take any more joy rides around the bay or trips to the beach at Placer.

In the midst of our new wartime life, on April 9, 1942, General Edward P. King, commander of the force holding Bataan, surrendered unconditionally the 78,000 American and Filipino members of the force holding Bataan. For three months, they had kept the Japanese advance in check. However, disease and starvation had also contributed to their defeat. They now confronted the infamous Bataan Death March to the concentration camp at Camp O'Donnell, more than a hundred kilometers north of Manila. Corregidor, with its eleven thousand defenders, continued to fight on until May 6, when USAFFE announced its acquiescence to surrender.

Dad turned over East Mindanao's station wagon to the military forces in Surigao, but the *Henry Joy*, unlike the *Gold Bug*, was deemed too small for current military operations. Dad also contributed our Studebaker, although he continued to use the car for his procurement efforts.

In addition to the various items Dad was able to procure for the U.S. forces from the local populace, the crude oil in East Mindanao's tank in nearby Placer was also made available to the military. Unfortunately, there was a shortage of empty oil drums for storage and transport.

As the weeks went by, the general mood at home became more somber. Dad had ceased his procurement activities, but he still made trips to the USFIP headquarters in Surigao City to discuss the latest developments. We were all disappointed that there was nothing coming through military channels to contradict the news we were receiving via short-wave radio. It was only a matter of time before the last stronghold on Corregidor fell. How much longer could those brave Americans and Filipinos resist the unrelenting onslaught of superior Japanese forces?

Mom accompanied Dad to Surigao a couple of times to search the shops and marketplace for items useful to take into hiding, such as canned food and material for clothes. Unfortunately, these were highly valued items, and the stocks that were in *bodegas* (warehouses) when interisland shipping ceased had since been depleted, snapped up by eager buyers or held back by the owners for their personal use. After her last trip, Mom remarked that only a few stores remained open, and their shelves were almost bare. She was all the more thankful that when Mr. Yang closed his store at East Mindanao a couple of months earlier, she'd purchased as much of his supply of canned goods as he was willing to sell. He also sold her several khaki shirts and pairs of trousers that would fit the boys.

Our day-to-day routine was different—in fact, there was no routine at all. The warm rolls we all enjoyed had not appeared at the breakfast table for many weeks. Both Mom and Romana were busy with household matters, so meals were snacks throughout the day. This did not bother me, but my siblings were accustomed to regular meals at designated times. However, they adjusted quickly.

Mom's demeanor had certainly changed—her lips were usually pursed tightly, and she seemed preoccupied as she went around the house sorting and separating our household items. Romana was usually at her side, following instructions but also making suggestions or offering her opinion on the potential usefulness of certain items. Piles of clothing and bed and table linens often remained on the floor for days; I remember thinking that such clutter would normally not be tolerated. Even Peach, usually cheerful and fun to be around, was pensive and spent a lot of time in our room going through her books and personal belongings and was not interested in playing games with me. I could sense that she missed school, her friends, and their fun social activities. The weeks of uncertainty as to the future were worrisome for anyone, of any age, and I am certain Peach had many questions on her mind but realized they were unanswerable.

I was most disappointed at the change in Romana's behavior toward me—she was less solicitous of my needs and went about her work without her usual smile, often dabbing her eyes with a corner of her apron. While there was not much I could do about my family's inattention, I could certainly let Romana know of my displeasure at her behavior and did not hesitate to do so. She didn't respond, but there was a strange look in her eyes as she leaned down and gave me a hug. (Sometime later I received a sound scolding from Mom for my petulant behavior. As a rule, we were not allowed to berate the servants—we were to bring problems to Mom's attention, and she would deal with them as appropriate. After disciplining me, Mom explained that Romana was sad because she wanted to accompany us into hiding, but her parents had forbidden her to do so and told her they would pick her up when we evacuated.)

One day we were surprised when Dad came home from a trip to Surigao by *banca* (outrigger canoe). His tone was serious as he announced that Corregidor had fallen and General Jonathan Wainwright had ordered the surrender of all troops. USFIP forces on Mindanao had received the dreaded order to surrender, and all U.S. and Philippine units were to report to designated surrender points. All available vehicles, including our Studebaker and the mine's station wagon, were needed to transport the troops on their journey to Japanese captivity. I could tell from the grim look on Dad's face that he was very worried. It saddened me that our Studebaker was gone, but I could not really comprehend the significance of its last trip.

The surrender of the American and Filipino military units on Mindanao on May 10 had a major impact on those of us still remaining at East Mindanao. Most of the Filipino employees had already returned to their hometowns and barrios. Americans and other Allied nationals in the Surigao provincial area had a disheartening choice: surrender to the Japanese forces, or go into hiding in the remote areas of Mindanao. We felt deserted and left to deal with a situation not of our making. MacArthur and his staff had fled to Australia, the American and Philippine troops on Luzon and Mindanao had surrendered to the Japanese, and now we were faced with the coming Japanese invasion and occupation of an island that we had called home.

As we listened to these broadcasts, my family began to realize the enormity of the war and the fact that Japan had designs on Hawaii and Australia. Of particular note were reports concerning the battles of the Coral Sea and Midway. The former transpired on May 7 and 8 as we were preparing to go into hiding, with Japan endeavoring to secure the approaches to Australia via the Solomon Islands and the Louisiade Archipelago. American carrier-based aircraft inflicted heavy losses on Japanese naval forces and checked any Japanese plans to invade Australia. To this day, the Australians have not forgotten this major engagement that saved their nation from a Japanese invasion. The Japanese military was so confident that they could invade and occupy Australia that Japanese government–issued currency in pounds, shillings, and pence were printed for use in Australia; I saw samples on display at the MacArthur Museum in Brisbane.

My parents were lucky. Realizing our predicament, as a hiding place Chief offered us a small house he owned in his hometown of Tagana-an. Dad, Rudy, and Hank immediately went to investigate it. The house was a modest *nipa* hut (so called because its roof and walls were made up of dried fronds of the nipa palm) right in the middle of town, but everyone concluded that its location made it unsuitable. However, another resident of Tagana-an, Peping Lisondra, upon learning of the purpose of Dad's trip, offered a somewhat larger and newer nipa hut on the outskirts of town. It was the best option available, so Dad gratefully accepted. When he and the boys returned to the mine and described our future home, Mom's face contorted as she struggled to control her emotions. The inevitability of imminent departure from the mine site was setting in. Despite everyone's hopes and prayers, there was no escaping the grim reality of the war and the impending arrival of the Japanese.

Before leaving the mine, however, Dad had to perform some important tasks. He made several trips to Placer to determine how and where to plant explosives around the crude oil tank in preparation for its destruction before it fell into the hands of the Japanese. But there was a problem: when the storage tank was built, Placer was a small seaside barrio; however, mining operations in the area brought population growth, and many homes were built in close proximity to the tank. Dad had considerable expertise in ordnance matters, and blowing up the tank would have been an easy task, but the resulting fiery explosion would also wreak havoc on the town. The risk of engulfing the area with flaming oil was too great, and he was forced to abandon the idea.

The time was fast approaching when we would have to abandon the mine. The uncertainty of what lay ahead for our family must have weighed heavily on my parents' minds. Capture by the Japanese was their greatest fear. Like most parents, their concern was less for themselves than for their children. During the early weeks of the war, the subject of life as Japanese prisoners of war was an important one in conversations with friends and colleagues. Where family groups were concerned, it was the consensus that young girls faced greater danger than boys. With this in mind, Mom and Dad came up with the notion that if captured by the Japanese, Peach and I might fare better if we were disguised as boys. So, our parents summoned the barber from a nearby barrio to our house to give us haircuts. To finish our disguise they called a seamstress, who often came to sew the maids' uniforms and do mending jobs, to fashion appropriate boys' attire in a hurry. They, like most of the people in the area who derived their livelihood from the mining operation, were not happy that East Mindanao had shut down. Expressing their regret over our plight, they promised to keep our secret. Luckily, Rudy and Hank had growth spurts during the previous year and had outgrown their clothes. These were cut and altered to fit Peach and me. In short order, our outfits were completed—khaki shirts and short pants. I was thrilled at my transformation into a little boy! Too young to participate in my brothers' activities, I nevertheless felt that everything the boys did was exciting and daring. Now, as a boy, I looked forward to becoming brave and adventurous like my big brothers.

With Dad's work finished at the mine, preparations were made for our departure. Rudy and Hank were extremely helpful to my parents in this process. Essential household items—clothing, bed and table linens, a few dishes, cutlery, canned food, and basic medical supplies—were packed into boxes. Mom also decided to bring the treadle sewing machine and miscellaneous sewing supplies, anticipating their usefulness in making clothes for us from the bed sheets and tablecloths she had packed. High on Dad's list were his shotgun, hunting rifle, and .38 caliber revolver. Other very important items included a small short-wave radio; several miners' helmets (with carbide lamps attached); and a portable typewriter, along with extra ribbons and paper. The only large item of furniture Mom decided to take was a carved wooden Chinese chest with an elaborate mother-of-pearl inlay. Into this chest went important documents—Mom and Dad's marriage certificate, children's birth and baptismal certificates, family photographs, stock certificates. After some thought, Mom agreed with Dad that her jewelry, with the exception of her wedding ring set, should also be kept in the chest.

My first disappointing experience as a boy was learning that it would not be possible for me to take even one of my favorite dolls with me. Since my brothers were in their teens, there were no little boy toys in the house that I could pack up for myself. Furthermore, all the pretty dresses hanging neatly in the closet of our the bedroom had to be left behind, although that was a bigger disappointment for my almost twelve-year-old sister than for me.

Not wanting to leave Old Timer at the soon-to-be abandoned mine site, Dad decided that he should go to Tagana-an with us—he might be useful for transportation purposes. However, mindful of Old Timer's violent reaction to being loaded onto a floating craft, Chief agreed to take him by way of the narrow road that ran inland, then back to the coast near Tagana-an. Before our actual evacuation, Dad and the boys made a couple of trips to Tagana-an on the *Henry Joy* to leave the Chinese chest and other items in the care of Peping Lisondra. Then they turned the *Henry Joy* over to the mayor of Tagana-an, who planned to hide it in the mangroves for the duration of the war.

All mining supplies and equipment that might be of use to the Japanese were destroyed. The gleaming machinery in Dad's beloved machine shop, so well maintained by his staff of engineers and mechanics, was disabled in such a manner as to be repairable when mining operations resumed. The loss of the generators at the power plant that supplied the mine and our house with electrical power was the final blow to our spirits. We did not dream that it would be four years until we again would enjoy the convenience of electricity. Yes, our modern conveniences were being stripped from our everyday lives. Father Edward Haggerty, in his book *Guerrilla Padre in Mindanao,* summed up our situation and our uncertain future:

> Most of us have lost our material possessions. Our homes have been burned, our furniture, our clothing is lost. Our cities lie in ruins, our bridges blasted, our fields unplanted, our harbors ruined. But we have lost nothing that cannot be rebuilt. Material things can be restored but the things of the spirit, if once lost, crush down a man and a nation so that they can never rise, even to rebuild burned homes, ruined cities and peaceful countries. If you ever lose your faith and hope in God, and your love for one another; if you ever abandon your ideals of Christianity, and sink back into the pagan way of life your country abandoned centuries ago—then all things are really lost. But with faith strong, hope unshaken, and unity among ourselves, nothing really is lost. With these some day we will build anew a more beautiful land.[3]

We left the mine site about a week after the surrender of U.S. forces on Mindanao. Early in the morning the day maids and the gardeners gathered to say good-bye before leaving for their respective homes. They had already made their selections from the array of household goods and clothing we were leaving behind. I sat numbly as my precious collection of dolls and tea sets were bundled up. One of the day maids, who had four young daughters, was the happy recipient of my dresses and Peach's. She also took our cat, Bootsie, and promised Mom that she would take care of her "until you come back, Ma'am." My heart jumped to my throat when I heard this, for I had assumed Bootsie, like Princess and Old Timer, was coming with us. I burst into tears and asked Mom why our cat could not come with us and she explained that Bootsie may not adjust well to our move to a strange place and might run away. This way we could be sure that Bootsie had a nice home with a woman she knew and young girls who would play with her. Although I wanted to argue, I could tell from the look on Mom's face that she was in an emotional state herself and was not receptive to a prolonged dialogue on this matter—certainly not in the presence of our household helpers who were waiting to say their final goodbyes.

It was fortunate that Romana's parents came to fetch her, because she had the lion's share of our belongings. They thanked Mom and Dad and wished us good luck. Romana was crying as she hugged the boys and Peach, and I was weeping loudly when she turned to me and gave me the tightest and longest hug of all. Everyone had tears in their eyes as she and her parents departed, promising to pray for our safety.

I remember very well the day we left our home on the hill. There was a lot of last-minute packing. The boys and Peach (or perhaps I should say "the three boys," because Peach now looked like a smaller version of Hank) were able to help my parents, but I didn't know what I could do, so I just stood by in my new khaki shirt and short pants and tried to keep out of the way. In the preceding weeks, no one had thought to explain to me the plan of action on this final day and what I should be doing to help. Like most parents, Mom and Dad always tried to shield their children from anything unpleasant, so I guess keeping me out of the loop was their way of sparing me possible fear and worry.

It was midafternoon when we finally left the house and made our way down the hill, past the dispensary and the various mine buildings, to the pier area. The two boatmen Dad had previously hired, with their large banca, were waiting to transport us to Tagana-an. I was charged with carrying Princess and making sure she didn't try to run back home. We couldn't carry our boxes and bundles from the house to the pier area in one trip, so we left some items at home for pickup on a second run. Apparently the Filipinos from the surrounding areas, knowing that Dad represented the last vestige of mine authority, were just waiting for us to depart so they could start helping themselves to every-thing left behind. After loading our belongings onto the banca Dad, the boys, and Peach returned to the house for the remainder of our things while Mom and I stayed on the *banca.* As they were going up to the house, they saw several people, who had already been there, coming down the path with many of our belongings. Peach encountered a woman carrying a bundle of books she had packed and asked the woman to give it to her, but she clutched it more tightly and shook her head. Peach was devastated, as they were some of her favorites.

Dad and the others were gone for a long time, and it was starting to get dark. Although I felt secure with Mom, I also started to feel a twinge of fear that something awful might happen to the others. There were bancas and barotos of various sizes at the same location, and people were loading them with all kinds of household goods, furniture, and metal items that had been taken from residences, offices, and the power plant. One of the barotos was already fully loaded and ready to depart. On board was a family with a young boy leaning over the side, pulling two objects resembling small boats attached to strings that he held in each hand. Curious to see his floating toys, I took a closer look and was dismayed to see my almost brand-new brown-and-white saddle shoes being pulled along by their laces, like garbage barges I had seen being towed on the Pasig River in Manila. I had completely forgotten about those shoes, having only worn them around the house and on the veranda to break them in. In fact, I used to keep them in a corner near my play area so I could quickly slip them on and walk back and forth along the length of the veranda, enjoying the sounds of the soles on the wood floors. Sadly, from my birthday to evacuation day, there had not been any social events where Mom and I could show off our coordinated mother/daughter dresses and matching shoes. As we were preparing to pack up the boys' outfits that the tailor had delivered, Mom decided that tennis-style canvas shoes were more practical for the type of terrain we would be traversing, so I'm not sure I could have worn those saddle shoes even if I had remembered to take them with me. Still, I was sad to see them being so unceremoniously towed to—where? I wondered—as that family's baroto left for their barrio.

By this time, it was fairly dark, and people started using bamboo torches to light their way. Finally, Dad and the others returned, saying that the looters at our house did not interfere when they gathered the last few useful items that could be accommodated on the banca. They also related how, as they went down the path that last time, they all looked back and said a final goodbye to the home where our family had experienced both happiness and sorrow. As we slowly pulled away from shore, we all sat watching a parade of torches moving up, down, and sideways around the entire mine site. I could make out the outline of various pieces of furniture on men's backs, colorful bundles of clothing on women's heads, and children running along with whatever they could carry. No one spoke. I glanced up at my mother's face and saw tears streaming down her cheeks, but the only sound I could hear was the noise made by the paddles as they cut into the water and then hit the side of the boat. As I sat clutching Princess, that little twinge I had felt earlier was gone, but in its place was a hollow, sinking feeling I had never felt before.

It was late by the time we reached Tagana-an, physically exhausted and emotionally spent. Chief was waiting for us and helped unload the banca and transport our belongings to his house. He invited us to join him and his family for dinner and to spend the night before proceeding to our new home. Mom and Dad accepted both invitations without hesitation.

COMMENTARY ON THE AMERICAN DEFEAT

Following the attacks on U.S. military installations in the Philippines there was much talk that General MacArthur's forces would be reinforced with several divisions from the States. It was believed that relief would come in short order. In fact, prior to the attack on Pearl Harbor, a convoy led by the heavy cruiser USS *Pensacola* had departed the Hawaiian Islands heading for the Philippines. The convoy carried 4,600 troops and 70 planes. Whether the convoy should continue on to the Philippines was even discussed at the White House level. Finally, on December 12 the Joint Board decided that the convoy should proceed to Brisbane, Australia, instead.[4]

As the Hansen family continued listening to the news broadcasts, rumors flew in all directions about future Japanese intentions in Southeast Asia. On December 10, the first reports about the Japanese sinking of the British battleships HMS *Prince of Wales* and HMS *Repulse* off the coast of Malaya were broadcast. Apparently Japanese bombers from Indochina had hit them. Later, historians asked why these warships were deployed without proper air cover; the simple answer was that Great Britain was stretched too thin. She did not have an aircraft carrier for deployment or fighters to operate from the many airstrips in Malaya. These fighters were being used for the defense of Britain, the island nation. Within the week, Japanese troops moved toward Hong Kong, landed in Malaya, and seized American facilities on Guam. These fast-moving actions made people's heads swim.

While the American civilians on Mindanao did not have a great deal of information on U.S.-Filipino defensive capabilities, they did know from military parades on the Luneta in Manila and ROTC activities in the universities that some sort of military capability existed. U.S. Navy ships had visited the various ports in Mindanao, and occasionally B-17 and P-40 operational flights over Mindanao had been seen. But how well were U.S./Filipino forces prepared? It would be somewhat unfair to say that plans, facilities, and equipment were not available to meet the initial raids and follow-up invasion. In some regards, Japan's thrust into the Philippines hung on a thin reed. The attack on Pearl Harbor had taken the major portion of its military assets to ensure the success of the operation. By contrast, sufficient aircraft and ships were not available for the Philippine operation to guarantee a high level of success. Despite this weakness, Japanese forces were able to take advantage of frail U.S. ground, air, and naval defensive capabilities. Luck and U.S. mismanagement of air capabilities allowed the Japanese to secure air superiority over Luzon in the second week of the war. This resulted in U.S. naval shore facilities being made vulnerable to air attacks. Japanese raids on Cavite in the early days of the war rendered the U.S. Navy ineffective. With U.S. air and naval capabilities all but destroyed, the Japanese were able to launch amphibious operations against U.S. and Filipino ground forces on Luzon. This in no small measure contributed to the early crumbling of the U.S-Filipino defense on Luzon. By late December, U.S.-Filipino forces were relegated to a defensive posture on Corregidor and the Bataan peninsula.

While Bataan had fallen on April 9, 1942, there was a small bright spot in this new war. On April 23 a group of B-25 bombers, under the command of General James Doolittle, hit Japan in a daring raid. They had been launched from the aircraft carrier USS *Hornet*. Most of the bombers that survived the raid crash-landed in China.

In history books this raid would overshadow another attack on the Japanese which was almost as brazen and audacious as the one on the mainland of Japan. Just prior to the fall of Bataan, General Wainwright, the commander of USFIP, made a strong plea to General MacArthur in Australia that bombers be sent to the Philippines to break up the Japanese stranglehold on shipping of supplies to Corregidor from Cebu. General Ralph Royce, with the U.S. Army Air Forces elements in Australia, was charged with developing a bombing mission that might break part of the Japanese blockade. The "Royce Mission" was deployed to Mindanao from Darwin, Australia, on April 11, 1942, two days after the fall of Bataan. The mission consisted of ten B-25s and three B-17 bombers. Because of the approximately 2,400-kilometer route to Mindanao from Darwin, the B-25s were equipped with auxiliary fuel tanks. After arriving at the Del Monte airfield they were deployed to other airfields on Mindanao. During the following days, this mission attacked ships and docks in Cebu and Davao, as well as Nichols Field in Manila. The aircraft participated in over twenty sorties, sinking one ship and damaging others. Japanese aircraft were also shot down. Despite this heroic effort, the large Japanese military presence already in the Philippines prevailed and Corregidor fell.[5]

The only military obstacles now standing in the way of the Japanese Army were the coastal guns on Corregidor, controlling the entrance to Manila Bay. Eleven thousand U.S. and Philippine troops would now endure an unrelenting land and air bombardment by the Japanese, which continued until May 7, when General Wainwright ordered the surrender of all U.S and Philippine armed forces in the Philippines. A debate exists over whether the surrender of U.S. forces by General Wainwright should have included forces in Mindanao. Obviously, it was to the advantage of the Japanese to have them included, avoiding continued combat and difficult occupation problems. MacArthur believed that the Mindanao and Visayan Forces were separate from the Luzon and Harbor Defense Forces that were in the surrender terms. The Japanese did put pressure on Wainwright to include all U.S. forces. Implied by the Japanese was that a failure to do so would risk the humane treatment, under the Geneva Conventions, of the eleven thousand defenders of Corregidor. Wainwright finally did agree to the Japanese demand despite MacArthur's opposition. One wonders if the Mindanao and Visayan forces could have transitioned into a viable guerrilla fighting unit. If the performance of the U.S.-Philippine forces in the early stages of the war was any indicator, it would have been difficult for a regular U.S. Army unit that depended on an elaborate supply and support structure to become guerrilla fighters. As it was, the forces surrendered and ceased to exist except for personnel and equipment remnants. In this phoenix-like situation, the ashes of the former army became the basis for the emergence of a lean and efficient force that could rally the people of Mindanao until U.S. forces returned to liberate the Philippines.

THREE

Evacuating the Mine and
Evading the Japanese

Our first hiding place was a typical, modest nipa hut. The hut was built on stilts about four feet above the ground, with a bamboo ladder leading to the entrance. The floor was composed of bamboo slats tied together with slender strips of the rattan vine, with enough space between the slats for air circulation. There was one main room with a few pieces of basic furniture made of wood and bamboo and an open doorway that led to a smaller room, which became Mom and Dad's bedroom. A makeshift partition separated the bathroom, which was simply a small private area with a large clay jug of water for washing. To the rear of the main room was the kitchen area. The stove was an oblong sand-filled box (similar to a child's sandbox) set on a wood counter made of long, two-inch-wide pieces of wood set about an inch apart. Its burners were two sets of uniform sized rocks arranged in a circle, on which clay cooking pots with rounded bottoms (the local name for this type of pot was *culon*) would be balanced. There needed to be sufficient space between the sand base and the bottom of the pots to accommodate small pieces of firewood. We brought in water from a nearby stream in bamboo stems and stored it in tall clay vessels. Bamboo stems are hollow but have joints at regular intervals that close off separate sections. To make a water carrier, one punched through the joints of a long pole, leaving the last one intact to maintain a seal. The larger the diameter of the bamboo, the greater its capacity. We prepared food and washed dishes on the counter, kept clean by frequent scrubbing with a piece of coconut husk and rinsing with water. There was no sink, so the water simply drained through the slatted bamboo floor to the ground. A short distance from the rear of the house was the outhouse, built so that it extended over a slope to provide maximum elevation.

In the evenings, clam shells filled with coconut oil, with wicks held in place by pieces of wire, provided dim light. If brighter illumination were needed, Rudy or Hank activated the carbide headlamp on one of the miner's helmets we'd brought with us. Its light was bright enough to read by, but we had no reading material besides Peach's magazines. Peach and the boys lamented how much they missed the week-old newspapers from Manila that would arrive on the SS *Corregidor* every Thursday, including the popular Sunday comics section that featured *The Katzenjammer Kids, Maggie & Jiggs, Prince Valiant,* and other strips. I used to grab the comics section right away because it was the only part of the newspaper that I could relate to; because of my stubbornness and recalcitrant attitude during the few months that I technically attended first grade, I had not yet learned to read when the war broke out.

At bedtime all the furniture had to be pushed against the walls so that we could set up sleeping arrangements. Mom and Dad slept in the small room on folding cots with mosquito nets, and the rest of us slept on woven straw mats on the floor, using the bed linens we had brought from home. Several mosquito nets were strung from the walls in the main room, but they proved ineffective—we could not keep them tucked tightly under the mats. Mosquitoes were a real problem—not only were they maddeningly annoying pests, they were also dangerous carriers of malaria. While they were still available, we placed mosquito-repelling coils, which smoldered when lit, at strategic locations around the house. When supplies ran out, we used the local method, we burned the husks of mature coconuts; the smoke was an effective insect repellent. At bedtime, my brothers placed these smoking husks under the house so the smoke could waft upward through the gaps in the floor. Coconut husks tended to smolder rather than flare up, so they lasted for a reasonable period of time. However, we fell asleep amidst a cacophony of coughing. We found it cooler to sleep directly on the mats and not bother with bed sheets. This was fortunate, because as the war progressed those sheets were put to more useful purposes.

Naturally there was a big change in our cuisine. Meals were simple, usually a canned food we had brought from home, supplemented with whatever local produce, rice, chicken, seafood, and other food items might be available at the market. Papaya trees abounded in the area, and we simply helped ourselves to this delicious fruit. Several varieties of bananas grew nearby—regular-sized as well as small fingerlings, long plantains (excellent for cooking), and a short, stubby variety that was also tasty when boiled or fried. Even if Mom had wanted to prepare more elaborate fare, the limitations of our so-called kitchen would have made it impossible. Mom and Dad often collaborated on menu decisions, with an eye to conserving as much of our canned goods as possible.

To the surprise of everyone in the family, I found this new diet appetizing and ate heartily. This was a relief for Mom, who I'm sure did not need the added worry of whether I had enough sustenance. She insisted that I drink a daily glass of milk ("Klim," powdered milk mixed with water), but it was not very palatable at room temperature so I'd grimace with every sip.

Poor Princess—she really had a difficult time adjusting to our new living conditions. Try as she might, her short legs just could not negotiate the bamboo ladder that led up to the front entrance of the house. With my siblings helping Mom and Dad with daily chores, it became my responsibility to take her up and down the ladder several times a day. Old Timer was safely corralled at a local farm, and the boys took care of his needs. For a change of scenery, they often rode him to areas outside his enclosure, usually in wooded areas out of sight of the townspeople.

One of Dad's top priorities was to devise a way to power our battery-operated short-wave radio—during those early months of the war an indispensable item in keeping our family informed of the outside world. With Chief's assistance and materials he had scavenged from Tagana-an, Dad and my brothers rigged a contraption that generated enough power to operate the radio. Taking the battery and generator from an inoperative vehicle, they mounted these on a long board; behind this was a stationary bicycle with the tire taken off the rear wheel. They attached a long belt between the pulley on the generator and the rim of the bicycle wheel. With Rudy or Hank pedaling on the bike, the generator maintained the charge on the battery to which the radio was attached. Dad always had an anxious look on his face as he fiddled with the dials and then was greatly relieved when he heard the BBC announcer.

While we were listening to the broadcast, Dad took notes. Peach typed his notes, and we then circulated the news among our neighbors. I remember watching, fascinated, as Peach formed words by hitting letters on the typewriter with her fingers. I recognized the letters on the keyboard but couldn't read the words they formed.

All our new friends and neighbors, especially Chief and the Lisondra brothers, were extremely helpful in those early days in hiding. Peping Lisondra's older brother Juan took a special interest in us kids—we addressed him as Mano Juan (*Mano* was a term of respect for an older person, probably from the Spanish *hermano*), and he delighted in teaching us how to help our parents adjust to the day-to-day challenges of life in the boondocks.

When we moved in, Mano Juan provided the coconut oil for our lamps, and when that was exhausted he showed us how to make more oil for cooking and lamps. First the husk of mature coconuts had to be removed and the shell split in half, exposing the pulp, or meat, which had become thick and hard as it matured. The pulp had to be grated with a *kudkuran,* a crude metal implement with sharp, sawlike teeth shaped to fit the interior contour of the coconut half. It took practice to learn the knack of placing the kudkuran on a low stool and using one's foot and body weight to anchor it and then, holding the outer shell with both hands, scraping the meat from the inside of the shell. After a few mishaps where the grater slipped and hit their hands instead of the coconut, the boys learned how to keep the kudkuran firmly in its place while applying enough pressure to strip away the meat. The moist flakes, when combined with a little water and squeezed, produced *gata,* a thick milky substance that was an excellent base for sauces for seafood and vegetables. To make oil, one boiled the coconut milk until it thickened and clarified. The residue that settled on the bottom of the pan turned into a slightly burnt, sticky sweet substance that was delicious as a snack or dessert.

After about a month, my parents decided to move to a different area, as they realized that our family was becoming too well known by the locals. Also, Dad learned that there was a mountain trail running near the house that connected the town of Tagana-an with the Mindanao Mother Lode mine. When the Japanese landed, this would be their route from the coast to the mine. Once again, Peping Lisondra offered us a hiding place. Shortly after the outbreak of the war, he had built a small hut up in the hills a couple of kilometers out of town to serve as a *bakwitan* (evacuation place) for his family, should the Japanese make an incursion into Tagana-an. It was not unusual for people of means to make bakwitan arrangements. (The word *bakwit* was a corruption of "evacuate," and dropping the "e" and adding the suffix "an"—(e)vacuate-an— turned it into a term meaning hiding place.) Although small and primitive, Lisondra's bakwitan was located halfway up a hill and well concealed from the neighboring areas, and therefore safer. It was a crude hut, meant to be used only as temporary shelter until the Japanese departed the area. In the meantime, we heard that some American and European families were turning themselves in to the Japanese military authorities in Surigao. However, my parents had decided that evading the Japanese was preferable to internment.

Our new hideout was on a hill called Binaguiohan (stormy or windy place). We immediately named the place "Little Baguio" to remind us of the popular mountain resort area in northern Luzon where we had spent part of our summer holidays. The first day of moving into this new refuge was not without incident. Peach and I were carrying bundles of linens and other articles up the trail to the hut, which was perched on a hill. Prior to our arrival, several villagers had been cutting down a large tree near the trail that was host to a huge beehive. To avoid dislodging the hive and scattering the bees when the tree came down, they had tied two or three lengths of rope to the upper part of the trunk. They planned to anchor the ropes to neighboring trees and loosen them slowly to control the tree's descent to the ground. However, needing materials to wrap around the hive and thus contain the bees before setting fire to the hive, they had halted the process and returned to their barrio. As we made our way to the bakwitan, Peach and I decided to rest before fording a stream and sat down on a rock beside the trail. All of a sudden, a strong gust of wind materialized and the tree came crashing down. Unfortunately for us the hive came with the fallen tree and broke apart on impact. In an instant the air was filled with the loud roar of thousands of swarming bees. Peach, who was carrying her precious bundle of magazines atop her head (essential items for her in the days ahead), quickly put me in the water and covered me with the bed sheets that I was carrying. For some reason she decided to make a run for the hut, a good distance up the hill. Of course the annoyed bees attacked her. She received numerous stings and spent almost a week in utter misery, swollen from head to toe. Her only diversion was reading and rereading the magazines she had carried. How she wished she had successfully retrieved her bundle of books from the woman who had taken them from our house at the mine!

This new hut was very small, with one main room that was living room, dining room, and bedroom combined, containing a few items of basic furniture fashioned from bamboo bound with rattan strips. The floor was composed of medium-sized bamboo poles split in half. The rounded bamboo halves did not provide a comfortable sleeping surface, and we soon learned to lie lengthwise on the bamboo, rather than across the curves.

Like most nipa huts, it was elevated about three or four feet, but the cooking area was on ground level and very rudimentary—three rocks arranged in a triangular shape on the ground. Water had to be brought in from the stream at the bottom of the hill in long, hollow bamboo tubes and stored in large clay vessels. We also bathed and washed in the stream, and while the houses in Tagana-an itself had separate outhouses, there were no toilet facilities of any kind for this hut.

My siblings and I didn't mind bathing in the stream—after all, it was no different than our beach outings at Placer, and this had the added advantage of being fresh water. The lack of a toilet, on the other hand, was a major inconvenience, especially for my parents. Children have an easier time of adjusting to unpleasant situations; after some trial-and-error learning experiences, we took it in stride. In retrospect, however, I can only imagine how degrading it must have been for Mom and Dad to perform necessary toilet functions while perched on a fallen log behind a bush or a tree. Mano Juan had pointed out the bushes to avoid when collecting leaves or twigs to use as toilet paper—some could cause severe rash. Actually, we learned that coconut husk served the purpose quite well.

Since Mom did not dare shop in person at the market in Tagana-an, Peping Lisondra or his brother Mano Juan took orders and brought us whatever they could get. I always put in a request for *camay,* solid brown sugar molded in coconut shells, from which one could break off small chunks to suck on like hard candy. We all yearned for bread, which was completely unavailable—how we missed the basket of freshly baked *pan de sal* from R. Yang's store at East Mindanao that one of our day maids used to bring up to our house each morning.

There was a coconut grove nearby, and we all enjoyed drinking the refreshing juice of the young coconut. The boys quickly learned how to climb the coconut trees and dislodge several of the young fruit. Climbing the branchless trunk of a coconut tree, with only shallow notches as footholds, required some effort, so they chose the younger, shorter trees. Once the fruit had fallen, the boys lopped off a thin slice of the husk with one swing of a sharp *bolo* (machete). If made at the proper angle, this first cut produced a slice of husk resembling a flattened spoon. A few more swings and the shell was exposed. After they used the tip of the bolo to poke a hole through one or two of the three "eyes" at the stem end of the coconut and then through the inner flesh, we could drink the juice straight from the coconut. Afterward, they split the coconuts open so we could scoop out the sweet soft pulp using the spoon they had fashioned from the coconut husk.

Sometime during this period we acquired a new pet—a colorful pesky parrot with a large curved beak—courtesy of one of the townspeople. His vocabulary consisted of four words, *"Periko pikoy, periko tao,"* which he repeated over and over. While the boys could explore the surrounding area, Peach and I were somewhat housebound because of security concerns, and this lively and noisy creature provided welcome moments of diversion. Strangely, Dad became really fond of the parrot, which readily climbed onto his finger, crawled up his arm, and perched on his shoulder.

Three weeks or so after we moved in, Dad became sick, running a high fever. Surmising that this might have been caused by polluted drinking water from the nearby creek, Rudy and Hank decided to check out the source of the stream—it was a wallow for *carabaos* (water buffalo). Our friends in Tagana-an persuaded Mom to move us all back to our former house nearer town. Dad was in a comalike state for about three weeks, not speaking and experiencing violent attacks of hiccups that could be heard all over town. Someone suggested putting a bag over his head so he could inhale carbon dioxide from his own breath, but that did nothing to change his condition. Finally, Mom located the only person in the area with some medical knowledge, a dentist named Dr. Saquilayan. He gave Dad some shots, and eventually he came out of his stupor.

As soon as Dad had recovered, my parents, still concerned about our exposure, jumped at the opportunity to move to another hiding place deeper in the interior. The area was known as Pulang Lupa (red earth), but we referred to it as "Red Mountain" because our nipa hut was located behind a small hill of red soil with an elevation of about thirty feet. There were two structures making up the compound, both owned by a woman named Lisa Ga. She had been living in one hut with her young son while her brother and his wife occupied the other. When she learned of our need for another hideout, she asked her brother and sister-in-law to move in with her and offered us the second hut, which was actually a bit larger. My siblings and I cannot recall any prior relationship with this family, but believe that they might have been relatives or friends of the Lisondra family. A short distance from Pulang Lupa was a tiny trail that led to a small nipa structure in an area close to the mangroves, where Peping Lisondra had hidden the chest containing the family valuables.

Our new hut was almost luxurious compared with the one at Binaguiohan. It was also built aboveground and had several steps leading to a front porch that ran the width of the hut. The bamboo slats that comprised the floor were so narrow they were almost flat. To the left of the main room was a separate kitchen area. It had the same simple stove made of rocks arranged in a circular pattern embedded in sand on a small platform. And the hut's back door provided access to a bamboo footbridge (with handrails, no less) that led to the outhouse. The ground behind sloped down under the outhouse to a small creek bed, which filled with water when the tide came in; a few hours later the outgoing tide "flushed the toilet."

Following our neighbors' example, we started raising chickens for eggs and meat. Peach was very much involved in this endeavor. Forewarned that chickens were always prey for the iguanas that roamed the area, she kept track of the little chicks and each day made sure they were all present and accounted for. One of the chicks was a little smaller and slower than its contemporaries and often lost out on the choicest morsels of leftover rice that Peach threw out at feeding time, so she adopted this one and made sure it received its fair share of the food. It soon learned to expect her special attention and scampered toward her as soon as she approached. To our dismay, we discovered that there was, indeed, a local iguana hunting our chickens. The boys found that it was living in a decayed log not too far away. By inserting burning coconut husks into one end, they smoked it out and Rudy shot it as it exited the other end. The beast was about five or six feet long. Our neighbors shared in this bounty, and it provided meat for several meals for us all. Not surprisingly, it tasted like chicken.

On July 25, 1942, we observed Peach's twelfth birthday with a special dinner and some local treats. This celebration wasn't nearly as festive as her usual parties, which included a fancy cake and presents from her friends, often followed by a boisterous slumber party.

As we settled into life at Red Mountain, our patience with the parrot wore thin—he had the run of the house and had developed the nasty habit of nipping at our toes while we were eating or sleeping. We had tolerated this annoying behavior because he was a source of amusement for us and was always friendly to Dad, the only one who could touch and control him. Unfortunately, he once bit Mom so hard the wound drew blood. That was the last straw. Dad summarily eased him out of the household, but did not disclose his fate to us.

A rooster we named "Big Red" soon replaced the parrot as a pet. He was a beautiful, tame Rhode Island Red. He spent his days with the hens and chicks and retired with them at sundown; but later in the evening, for some strange reason, he flew through the window and settled down on the floor with us; at dawn he flew out and greeted the day with the rest of the chickens. Many families in the area also had roosters sharing their homes—these were their prized fighting cocks that were tethered indoors (usually in the kitchen area) to keep them safe from predators. One family told of a large python entering their hut one night and, quite satisfied after making a meal out of the hapless cock, curled up for a nap with the family, right next to their baby.

I can remember learning to climb a very young coconut tree near the house at Red Mountain. Someone had already cut notches into its trunk, and I used them to reach the clump of fronds at the top. The tree was just starting to produce blossoms. Using the strongest stalks of the young fronds, I pulled myself to the very top, where I was surprised to find enough space to squeeze into a sitting position. After a few minutes I realized that getting down was not going to be as easy as coming up. Suddenly, I heard a loud roar and saw a Japanese Zero fighter, with the red ball on its wings, flying low over the area. It seemed so close as it flew above me that I ducked my head and sat perfectly still, my heart racing. I felt certain that I had been seen. Fortunately, the pilot was undoubtedly focused on other matters. Yes, the Japanese were nearby, but for the time being we were able to keep our distance from them.

It was during this period that Hank learned to make tuba from coconut blossoms. One of his new friends gave him a special knife for this purpose. He used the knife to cut through the pods to the young blossoms clustered inside, and the sap from the blossoms flowed into a bamboo tube attached to the pod. From the tube it dripped into a container suspended beneath the pods. Depending on the size of the container, he would harvest a fair amount in a twenty-four-hour period. Afterward, Hank put the fluid in a glass container and let it ferment for about three days. The alcohol content at this point was about 3 percent, but with access to proper distilling equipment, the alcohol content could be raised to 100 percent. Alcohol produced in this manner was a convenient source of fuel for gasoline engines, with only a slight adjustment to the carburetor.

During our stay at Red Mountain my siblings and I sometimes went digging for clams with our neighbors. Following their lead, we gamely proceeded through mud almost to our knees, feeling for the clams with our toes and squealing triumphantly with each find. Peach and the boys soon learned to recognize the feel of the burrowed mollusk, but I didn't enjoy the sensation of the thick mud between my toes and did not match their finds.

My brothers often went shrimping at night with local fishermen. One night, they returned from their expedition late, about midnight. Rudy was wearing a miner's helmet with its carbide lamp lit, and he and Hank were talking as they moved up the trail toward the house. Their voices awakened Dad, but he could not make out what was being said, and all he could see was a light beam bobbing up and down, moving in the direction of our hut. Thinking they might be approaching Japanese soldiers, he pushed the window open a little wider as he reached for his .38. Mom had also awakened and was peering out the window next to him. Dad cocked his revolver and sighted on the first figure with the lamp, Rudy. He couldn't see Rudy's face, but luckily, Hank overtook Rudy on the trail, and the beam from the lamp illuminated Hank's face. Mom clutched Dad's arm and screamed, "Hon, don't shoot! It's the boys! It's the boys!" By then Peach and I were also awake. When Mom realized what had almost occurred, she became hysterical. Aside from her silent tears as we left the mine, this was the first time I had seen any change in the brave demeanor Mom had adopted ever since our evacuation. When the boys arrived at our hut, we could see that Dad was shaking with emotion.

This incident forced my parents to face the unthinkable—but real—possibility that a Japanese patrol could, at any time, march up that same trail right into our compound behind Red Mountain. We knew they already occupied and controlled Surigao, but we did not know how long it would take them to establish a permanent presence in the coastal areas south of that city. On several occasions their patrols had moved through the area but did not remain. Certainly they were developing agents that could report on any hiding Americans. As a precautionary measure, Mom and Dad decided to move our family to another hideaway. Once again, the Lisondras offered a solution—this time Mano Juan's own bakwitan, in the mangrove swamp nearby.

The new sanctuary, designed for short-term use only, was smaller than Peping Lisondra's little hut at Binaguiohan and could accommodate only a very limited amount of our household goods. We packed the remaining items and left them in the care of Lisa Ga and her family. For their protection, Dad took special precautions to conceal the now-useless radio. (I remember when the old battery gave out and no amount of frantic pedaling by the boys could give it a charge. Try as he might, Dad could not get anything more than faint static. "Not enough juice," was his terse comment.)

We arrived at Mano Juan's bakwitan by baroto through a small entrance from the river hidden by an old fish trap. While this one could also be called a nipa hut, it was dissimilar from our previous abodes in that it was simply perched on the curved roots of large mangrove trees. Peach and I learned to rate nipa huts by their flooring—the higher standard of construction used narrower pieces of bamboo, resulting in a flatter, more even surface. Using this criterion, the rough pieces of split bamboo that made up the floor of this hut were at the lowest end of bamboo floor quality. The simple, square structure, with no amenities whatsoever, was the crudest we had ever come across. The kitchen area was simply one corner near the entrance equipped with a shallow square box of sand with three rocks upon which a culon could be perched. A makeshift wall screened off an area in one of the corners to the rear where a hole in the floor served as the toilet.

We bathed and washed toward the rear of the room, using a good-sized basin made from galvanized iron. We tried to perform these activities during high tide, when it was easier to haul water up using a bucket tied to a rope. Because we were close to the coast, the water was brackish, so we used fresh water brought in with our food supplies for the final rinse.

About three times a week, a man named Palabuano (Palab, for short) came in his baroto, bringing food, water, and other necessities. He was our trusty shopper and bearer of the latest rumors. In addition to fresh water, he brought coconut oil, dried fish, rice, *camotes* (local yams), and fruit. Depending on availability at the local market, he would also buy fresh seafood or chicken and produce. Palab was a kind man who spoke some English, so our verbal exchanges were conducted in a combination of English and Visayan. Never in a hurry to conclude his visits, he gave us lessons in Surigaonon (the local dialect of the Cebuano language) while we, in turn, expanded his English vocabulary. Like most Filipinos, Palab started learning English in elementary school, he but lacked opportunities to practice what he had been taught. Most of the people in that part of the country did not speak Spanish, so Mom's fluency in that language was not an advantage.

Cooking for a family of six under such difficult conditions was a huge challenge, but Mom, with Peach's able assistance, somehow managed. She usually prepared a pot of rice before the rest of the meal. And the full menu choices depended on whatever food Palab brought us. Perishables like chicken or seafood were cooked without delay. When prepared in a spicy sauce, these dishes remained edible for a day or two before spoiling. With two teenaged boys around, however, leftovers never reached that stage. In fact, the remainder of our supply of canned goods was quickly depleted. There was no distinction between "breakfast" food or "lunch" food or "dinner" food. Dad had a harder time adjusting to rice at every meal than the rest of us did—after all, rice was always served at lunch and dinner in the dining rooms at school. Until our supply of canned pork and beans ran out, his preference was a bed of boiled rice topped with pork and beans.

Living conditions in this hideaway were really primitive. We lounged, ate, and slept in one room. There was nothing to do and nowhere to go. For entertainment I often sat at the front entrance dangling my feet when the tide was coming in. As the water rose, it reached my feet, then slowly moved up my legs almost to my knees—it was a long process, but helped pass the time. At high tide, the brackish water rose to within inches of the bamboo floor of our hut then gradually receded. When I voiced concern that the water might rise higher and come up through the bamboo floor, Mom and Dad assured me that such a phenomenon happened only if there was a big storm or typhoon. Not completely convinced, I worried that one night we could be rudely awakened from a sound sleep by a higher than normal tide.

There were two ways to reach our hut—by baroto from the river through the small entrance hidden by the old fish trap or by a crude footbridge made of long bamboo poles lashed together with rattan strips and anchored to mangrove trees. The rickety bridge required surefootedness and a good sense of balance. Dad was a big man and not very agile, and the one time he attempted to negotiate it he had to sit on the bamboo poles and pull himself along. It was a humiliating experience for him.

Mom and Dad were constantly worried about fire, as a single spark could easily ignite the old nipa fronds that made up the walls and roof of the hut. The whole structure would be engulfed in flames immediately. They especially wanted me to be aware of the danger of fire, so, to his embarrassment, they told me about Hank's early brush with fire. A couple of years before I was born, Hank went down by himself to the cellar of the house where they were living in Manila and decided to play with matches. Just as he struck the first one, he was summoned to dinner. Before going up the steps he hastily threw it against the wall, thinking it had burnt out. Instead, the smoldering match landed on wood shavings and ignited. While the family was at the dinner table, Dad smelled the smoke coming from the cellar. After dousing it, he saw that the fire had already burned a large hole in the wall. Of course Hank eventually confessed to his mischievous act and suffered the consequences.

Three weeks after moving into the rustic hut, our group was joined by a small animal resembling a civet cat that the boys had found on the footbridge. It was frightened and starving and soon adjusted to its new environment. Even Princess didn't seem to mind the newcomer. Crowded as we were, this pitiful creature was a welcome diversion. However, it doubled the daily pet waste clean-up operation. Since the boys were real animal lovers, they took on this unpleasant task. They lowered a bucket and brought up as much water as they needed to wash the bamboo floor.

My parents had always tolerantly allowed us to take in abandoned or orphaned little animals, which eventually became pets. During our stay in Iligan, Hank became friendly with the workmen at Dad's sawmill. One day, they showed up with a small black monkey they had found wandering alone in the jungle, and Hank agreed to take care of it. It was small and cuddly and soon became the family pet; it was particularly partial to my dad's shoulder. On one occasion, we could find the monkey nowhere, though we looked high and low. Later, we heard sounds coming from the privy—it had fallen into the pit. The boys and Dad immediately went to work and shifted the privy structure away from the pit. They then removed the poor creature from its horrible surroundings and immediately raced with it to the nearby river for a thorough cleansing. As the monkey grew bigger, it became a bit of a problem, so Hank began looking for a new owner. Father Haggerty suggested Bishop Hayes as a possibility, since he liked animals. Later, Father Haggerty arranged for the monkey to be given to the bishop, and Hank was more than happy to deliver it to the Bishop's beautiful residence. Perhaps this harmless initial experience with a monkey led Hank to attempt his ill-fated contact with the ill-tempered baboon at the Ateneo de Cagayan.

As the days passed in monotonous succession, we started to suffer from cabin fever. We occasionally distracted ourselves with a short trip by way of the footbridge to the outer edge of the mangrove, where we could indulge in walking, even running, on solid ground and possibly climb trees to pick some fruit. We were not the only ones who enjoyed these outings—Princess went berserk with excitement. However, Mom and Dad were uncomfortable about letting us go, fearing possible exposure to unfriendly eyes.

We were not the only Americans hiding in or near the mangrove swamp. About two kilometers away Bob and Lily Owens, also from East Mindanao, had their hideaway. The chief electrician at the mine had found it for them, adjacent to the mangrove swamp. Bob handled the lumber supply for the mine, and for some reason he and Dad did not get along, but Mom and Lily were friends. Mom, Peach, and I visited the Owenses via the footbridge a couple of times. Lily was pregnant and welcomed Mom's counsel and advice. These rare excursions afforded my mother precious breaks from her monotonous daily routine. A friendly and gregarious woman, Mom had always enjoyed balancing family responsibilities with a busy social life—the veranda of our home at the mine had been the venue for frequent card parties and other social gatherings.

There was a navigable channel adjacent to the swamp that led from the ocean and continued on to Surigao. Once the Japanese Army occupied Surigao, they routinely cruised this channel by motor launch—we could actually hear them talking as they passed close by. We were especially careful to keep Princess from barking. Because she had a peculiar yap that could be heard from a distance, concerned locals had cautioned us that they could identify our location by her yaps. As a precaution, we took turns holding her snout when we heard Japanese launches patrolling the waterways in our area.

This hideout was a low point for my father. The coming of the war and the invasion of the Japanese Army on Mindanao had changed his world. The pleasant and easygoing days of the Commonwealth period were now gone. For him, it was a turning point in his life. No longer was he in control; all that he had worked for was gone. Now, he had nothing but a miserable shack in a mangrove swamp in which to house and protect his family. Soon after we moved in, he went into a violent rage, uttering invectives that our young ears had never heard. In retrospect, it's clear he was experiencing a syndrome many other Americans did after the Japanese invasion of the Philippines. No longer were they in charge of their lives; an aggressive Asian country now controlled their environment and their future. In this new situation they were required to accommodate a hostile world dictated by a foreign force. The challenge for my parents and many other Americans was dealing with this situation until an American military force could return, restoring order and a world that existed prior to December 1941. Now, it seemed that for the foreseeable future, Dad would have to suffer a situation not of his making.

Looking back at that period in the war, I can understand Dad's anger and frustration. However, I cannot remember Mom ever losing control and exposing her own feelings about our predicament, which is odd, because she was more outwardly emotional than my father. Instinctively following her example, we kids stifled our own impulses to whine or complain about our situation.

After enduring the hardships of life in the mangrove swamp for over a month, Mom and Dad decided we should move back to our hut at Red Mountain, even though the Japanese had control of Surigao and were constantly patrolling by launch and on foot. They were encouraged by the fact that Japanese offers of a reward (10,000 pesos, equal to $5,000 at that time) for information leading to the capture of Americans in hiding went unclaimed. Judging by the advice and admonitions passed on to us from the Filipinos in the area, our presence was obviously known to the local population—yet no one betrayed us. My parents concluded that our physical location was not necessarily the sole determinant in our survival; the loyalty of the people in the area was a much more important factor. Though unpleasant and perhaps unnecessary, the experience of living in the swamp was a positive exercise, giving us confidence that we could effectively go underground should the Japanese develop an active presence in the area.

We were a happy bunch as we marched up the trail to Red Mountain, with Princess delightedly skipping along on her short legs. The ungrateful civet cat had scampered away as soon as we hit dry land. Our hut and everything in it were as we had left them, including Big Red and the chickens. Some of the older chicks had grown large enough to become the main course of a celebratory dinner. Killing, plucking, and preparing these chickens was a joint effort involving Mom, Peach, and the boys, with Dad supervising. I was secretly thankful my services were not needed.

As Mom sorted through some of our things left hidden on Lisa Ga's property she discovered a mouse's nest in one of the bundles. The mother mouse had scampered away, leaving a litter of four newborn mice. Mom was angry at the amount of damage they had done to several bed sheets and other items. She scooped up the tiny creatures with a piece of cloth, handed them to me, and instructed me to run to the river and throw them in. Upon reaching the river, however, I found that the tide was low and there was a wide expanse of mud with occasional puddles of water between the shore and the deeper part of the river. Not wishing to walk in ankle-deep mud all the way to the flowing river, I stopped by one of the larger puddles and deposited the mice into the shallow water. Curious to know what might happen next, I lingered and watched, transfixed, as they wriggled for what seemed like a long time before they simply lay still. I felt a knot in my stomach as I realized that they were dead, and that I was responsible. I wondered what I could have done differently but found no answer—not doing what my mother had asked was out of the question. I was reminded of the ants that used to drown in the oil wells under our house at the mine, but this was different, and I wished I hadn't stayed to watch them drown.

Shortly after our return to Red Mountain, Dad was informed of a number of people willing to organize some form of resistance against the Japanese, and Macario Diaz, former mayor of Surigao, asked Dad to participate in a meeting being held in Tagana-an. The group was called the Filipino-American-Chinese Guerrilla Association (FACGA). While he was at the meeting, a contingent of Japanese soldiers from Surigao came by launch to hold a meeting in the town plaza to distribute propaganda and announce rewards for information leading to the capture of Americans. Fortunately, they took their time getting to the square, cleaning their boots at the town well/pump. This delay gave Dad the time to jump out the back window of the meeting place and head for our hideout. He hurt his knee in the process but did escape from the Japanese soldiers. Unfortunately, this knee injury would trouble him for the rest of his life.

Soon, we learned that Lily Owens was nearing her delivery date, so Mom went to their bakwitan to help with the arrival of the new baby. While she was gone, Peach took over the household responsibilities. Several weeks earlier, Mom had taken advantage of a rare opportunity to purchase one of the piglets from a litter on a neighboring farm, to be butchered and delivered to our house when it reached maturity. As luck would have it, the butchered pig arrived while Mom was away. Peach nonchalantly went about putting to work the lessons she had learned from Mom and our neighbors. I was pleased and proud when she asked me to help as she made preparations to use as much of the pig as possible; without refrigeration, the pork would spoil quickly in the tropical heat. Unfortunately, despite my eagerness to prove that I could help, I was not a good assistant—the spirit was willing but the stomach was weak. The sight of the butchered pig (its bristles shaved, revealing pale skin), complete with ears, snout, hooves and curly tail, made me ill. At home at the mine, I had often watched Romana preparing raw meat for meals, but it was usually in the form of a roast neatly tied with string, or individual pieces of steak. I was filled with admiration as Peach, without a word of protest, set about cutting up the carcass. The choice pieces went to make adobo and *tapa* (dried meat similar to jerky). First, Peach boiled all the meat and skimmed off the fat to make lard. She placed several chunks of meat in an empty square cooking oil can and covered them with the rendered fat; when the fat solidified, the lard formed a good seal, and thus the meat could be preserved for a period of time. She sliced other pieces thinly, soaked them in vinegar or brine, then hung them up on a line to dry for future meals. If we had to move in a hurry, this was very durable as a trail ration. The only downside to the hanging tapa was the many flies it attracted during the drying process. It was my job to examine each piece several times a day and flick off the eggs deposited by the flies. I was glad I could be of some help to Peach, who was doing Mom's job—to my mind, she was just a kid like me. Later, when Dad learned Peach had taken care of cutting, cooking, and preserving the meat, he complimented her on a job well done.

Several neighbors served as Peach's mentors in the selection and collection of vegetables and greens, such as young camote tops, bamboo shoots (carefully avoiding the prickly outer hairs) and the succulent young leaves of the *gabi* (taro) plant. Even the red heart of the banana plant, which usually shriveled up after the banana hands took form, was edible when properly prepared and cooked with coconut milk. Peach also learned the difference between the edible and poisonous species of mushrooms that grew on decayed logs. A short distance away was a pond that hosted the *kangkong* water plant, whose young leaves were a source of iron, like spinach. Unfortunately, we had to wade through marsh grass and chest-deep water to reach the plant. While it was always a treat to take a cooling dip in the pond, we learned not to tarry too long in the water and risk picking up leeches. They were easy to flick off before they attached themselves to the skin, but once the heads and/ or tails became embedded, one had to find someone to "persuade" them to let go. (We usually tried to find Lisa Ga's brother first, because he habitually chewed tobacco and a squirt or two from his mouth did the trick. Alternatively, a burning cigarette or match held close to the leech would make it fall off. Either remedy was not pleasant, but simply pulling off the stubborn creatures was not a good idea because the suckers would break off and stay embedded in the flesh where they would fester and cause painful, ugly sores.)

Shortly after Mom's return from the Owens bakwitan, my parents decided that Peach and I should resume our identities as girls. By then, our hair had grown longer and we looked like our old selves again. Several years later, I learned that Peach had started menstruating during this time, which was another reason to shed her disguise. Besides, she had become Mom's principal helper, and it would have appeared odd to the locals for a young boy to be doing so much woman's work. Lisa Ga could operate Mom's treadle sewing machine, so she made several simple chemise-style dresses for Peach out of the sheets that the rats had chewed, with the holes disguised by patches that resembled pockets or cleverly placed seams. Her boy's clothes were then passed on to me, which was timely because I had started to outgrow my own outfits; besides, there was nothing else to wear and it did not matter whether or not I looked feminine. We had long since worn out the canvas tennis shoes we had brought with us and went around barefoot all the time.

December 17, 1942, was my eighth birthday. After dinner Mom surprised me by bringing out a birthday cake that she had improvised using *bibingka,* a steamed rice cake, and frosting she had made with a combination of raw sugar and cocoa powder (from local cacao beans). She must have made a special request to someone for this cake because it was larger than the customary bibingka, which usually nestled on a piece of banana leaf. There were four stubby white candles stuck into it, not eight. Mom apologized and explained that since little birthday candles were unavailable, each of the white candles counted as double. Everyone sang "Happy Birthday" before I blew out the candles and cut the cake. The party was a total surprise—I did not realize that day was my birthday. Although we had celebrated the boys' birthdays (Rudy's seventeenth and Hank's sixteenth) earlier, I couldn't keep track of the days. It was a happy occasion, and I thoroughly enjoyed being the honoree that evening. Over a year had passed since our world in the Philippines had been shattered by the Japanese onslaught. We now had adjusted to the reality of Japanese troops being nearby. The possibility of moving on a moment's notice was now a fact of life. With the help of our Filipino friends, we were making do with what was available in our immediate environment; we had basic food items, and we were not in danger of starving, but we missed the luxuries that life in the mine had afforded—electricity, running water, a real kitchen, bathrooms, and toilets.

A few days later, Lisa Ga brought over some local Christmas star-shaped decorations that we could hang outside our hut. The stars were rattan reeds, fashioned to make five-pointed frames and then covered with colored paper. Colorful streamers hung from each point. Some of the larger stars had a nail pointing upward from a crosspiece in the center, to hold a lighted candle; on Christmas Eve, we used my birthday cake candles for this. Our hut looked so festive with those stars hanging from several strategic places—after a quiet Christmas Day dinner, we relit the candles to showcase those beautiful stars again.

Throughout this period while our family was settling into life in hiding, other Americans on Mindanao were making similar adjustments. A focus for American servicemen evading the Japanese was an evacuation area called Deisher's Camp. Located on the Lanao-Bukidnon border some two hundred kilometers southwest of our hideaway in Surigao, it had been conceived by Jacob Deisher, a former Spanish-American War veteran who had settled in the region in 1902 and owned a coconut plantation, sawmills, and mines. In February 1941, sensing that that Japanese expansion would spread to the Philippines, he had applied for U.S. passports for himself, his wife, and two sons. The passports had not arrived when the Japanese invaded in 1941, and the Deishers were stranded. Deisher did not want his family to be taken prisoner. Accordingly, he made plans to build his evacuation camp in Bukidnon province, some nine hours' walk from his plantation. Deisher's Camp became a reality on May 4, 1942, when he and his family, plus eight U.S. servicemen, arrived at the site. Several days later, the group heard over their radio that Wainwright had surrendered all U.S.-Philippine forces to the Japanese.

The first task for these evaders was to build huts for shelter. The camp was near a stream so water was not a problem. Deisher had made arrangements for rice to be delivered to the camp every few weeks by Filipino *cargadores* (bearers). Camote, dried fish, and carabao meat were also available through this system. Although their diet was not too dissimilar to ours in Surigao province, they faced a big problem in transporting the food. The Filipino cargadores became frightened because they were traveling through Moro country, where the population was predominantly Muslim. To keep food available to the camp, the American servicemen themselves also took turns serving as cargadores; each person carried over ten kilos on his back over muddy and hilly terrain for the long trek from Momungan. Many of these personnel filled vital leadership roles in the guerrilla movement that was later organized by Colonel Wendell Fertig and supported by MacArthur's command in Australia.

The American servicemen at Deisher's camp included Paul Owen, U.S. Navy, MTB-3 (torpedo boat squadron); Marvin DeVries, U.S. Navy, MTB-3; Dewit Glover, U.S. Navy, MTB-3; Henry Rook, U.S. Navy, MTB-3; John Tuggle, U.S. Navy, MTB-3; Francis Napolillo, U.S. Navy, MTB; Harold Martin, Army Air Corps, 30th Bomb Squad; Thomas Mitsos, Army Air Corps, 30th Bomb Squad. The U.S. Navy personnel had been with the torpedo boat squadron that brought MacArthur to Mindanao. The Army Air Corps personnel had been assigned to the Del Monte airfield to support the B-17s that had been flown there from Clark Field on Luzon.

The population of Deisher's Camp occasionally swelled to as many as twenty-six personnel. Visitors to the camp included Weyman McGuire, USA, Medical Corps; Wendell Fertig, USA, Corps of Engineers; Charles Hedges, USA, Corps of Engineers; Elwood Offret, USN; Charles Smith, Mining Engineer; Jordan Hamner, Mining Engineer; Bill Johnson, USN; Don LeCouvre, Army Air Corps, 14th Bomb Squad.[1]

The experiences of the Deisher Camp are representative of the transition American military personnel went through in becoming guerrillas and continuing to fight the Japanese. They had different but critical roles in paving the way for the U.S. liberation of the Philippines. Had fate been less kind, they might have become POWs and possibly perished under the cruel internment of the Japanese Army. Instead, they became part of the Tenth Military District, an effective fighting and intelligence-gathering force. My father and two teen-age brothers also served in this organization.

In Agusan province, other American civilians also evaded the Japanese. Several families from Mindanao Mother Lode, another gold mine not too far from the East Mindanao mine, evacuated to the Gomoco Goldfields, located far up the Agusan Valley near Rosario. Though in caretaker status, it was well equipped to handle a small community of refugee Americans. The group was headed by Douglass McKay, manager of Mindanao Mother Lode, and included his wife, Harriet, and young daughter, Mary. Mary chronicles their story in *My Faraway Home.*

FOUR

A Guerrilla Movement Is Formed,
and Family Fighters Join

By late 1942, there was a growing guerrilla movement developing throughout Mindanao. Though not organized, there was a synergy to become so. After the surrender of U.S forces in May 1942, those who did not obey the orders of Generals Wainwright and Sharp went into sort of a mental hibernation as they evaded the Japanese and came to terms with their new environment. Also, they must have weighed an important ethical aspect of their action—not obeying a lawful military order to surrender to the Japanese authorities. Surely they thought about whether they would be considered deserters after American forces returned. Moreover, shock over the suddenness of the Japanese onslaught and the growing realization that help was not coming fostered more negativity in their mental outlook. Once my parents had accepted the situation, they became determined to survive in this changed world. As this was the case with my family, we have to assume that it was similar among those American and Filipino military that decided not to surrender to the Japanese.

The growing movement came from many sources. A group of military officers, both American and Filipino, had refused to surrender in May 1942. These were augmented by a number of Army Air Corps personnel from the 19th Bomb Group (B-17s), which had been assigned to the Del Monte airfield after its expansion in December 1941. U.S. Navy personnel from the motor torpedo squadron that brought General MacArthur to Mindanao from Corregidor were also a part of the group. Many of them had come together at Deisher's Camp in central Mindanao; in the months after the surrender additional U.S military personnel, evading the Japanese in the islands to the north, made their way south to Mindanao. Some had escaped from Japanese prison camps and hoped to get to Australia. Those who refused to surrender had serious questions about Wainwright's capacity to give such an order—they believed he was under Japanese control and was thus not in a position to order Sharp and his forces to surrender. While the total number of Americans on Mindanao refusing to surrender to the Japanese is unclear, estimates range from one hundred to two hundred, including both military personnel and civilians like my father.

Several Americans and Filipinos were responsible for bringing my father and brothers into the guerrilla movement. Wendell Fertig was by far the predominant personality in the movement. An engineer like my father, he had come to the Philippines in search of gold and silver. Before the war, again like my father, he had a commission in the U.S. Army Reserve. In 1941, during a trip to Manila from his mining job on Samar, he volunteered his services to the U.S. Army. That summer, when the American High Commissioner had recommended the return of dependents to the United States, Fertig had sent his family home to Colorado. With no immediate family responsibilities, he went on active duty on June 1941 with the rank of major. Working under Colonel Hugh Casey, Corps of Engineers, USAFFE, his assignment during this period was the construction of military airfields throughout the Philippines. Prior to the fall of Corregidor, he was sent to Mindanao in April 1942 to supervise the construction of airfields there. Because the war situation was deteriorating so quickly, he was instead ordered to supervise the destruction of roads and bridges that might be useful to the Japanese. When Wainwright and Sharp gave the order to surrender, Fertig refused and went into hiding in Lanao province, 220 kilometers away from our hideaway in Surigao. Like many of the military who refused to surrender, he went through a contemplative and reflective period, focusing on how he was to survive until American forces returned.

A growing guerrilla organization was forming in Misamis Occidental province, led by Captain Luis Morgan, a former Philippine Constabulary officer. He had been effective in bringing a small group of guerrillas together but had neither the inclination nor organizational ability to go beyond the provincial level. Moreover, Morgan had difficulties working with the Moros, crucial to the cause since they made up one-third of the population of Mindanao. He linked up with Captain Charles Hedges (the former superintendent of the Finlay Logging Company and a good friend of Fertig), who had worked with the Moros and knew how to deal with them. Working through Hedges, Morgan arranged a meeting with Fertig. So in September 1942, he went to Fertig's hideaway and requested that he take command of guerrilla forces throughout the island. Moreover, he recommended that Fertig assume the rank of brigadier general. Morgan would function as his chief of staff or deputy, as lieutenant colonel—he based his rationale on the fact that other emerging guerrilla groups had leaders with self-appointed ranks of major or colonel. Hedges supported Morgan's premise, and their combined arguments swayed Fertig, who agreed with Morgan's proposal, though with certain conditions. Fertig wanted the guerrilla organization to function as a U.S. Army unit, with regulations and authorities normally accorded such a unit. His first order was a proclamation that reestablished U.S. and Commonwealth authorities, reflecting the type of organizational direction Fertig had in mind for his movement.

UNITED STATES ARMY FORCES IN THE PHILIPPINES
OFFICE OF THE COMMANDING GENERAL
IN THE FIELD OF MINDANAO

September 18 1942

PROCLAMATION

On September 18, 1942, our forces under Major L. L. Morgan completed the occupation of Misamis Occidental province and northern Zamboanga from the hands of the Japanese Military Government, and raised the American and Filipino flags therein.

In behalf of the United States of America, the Philippine Commonwealth government is re-established in those regions under the military authorities. All Civil Laws and regulations will be followed except in those cases where they conflict with Military Laws. In such cases Military Laws will prevail.

This procedure shall continue to be enforced until such a time when it shall be declared suspended, or terminated.

W. W. Fertig
Brigadier General, USA
Commanding Mindanao & Sulu Force

With this proclamation, the guerrilla movement on Mindanao came into being. On October 4, 1942, Fertig assumed command of the remnants of the Mindanao Force that General Sharp had ordered to surrender in May. On November 12, guerrilla units in Misamis Occidental and Zamboanga provinces were formed into the 106th Infantry Regiment. Fertig directed Morgan to travel throughout Mindanao, encouraging unification of the other guerrilla groups forming throughout the island—this led to Morgan's meeting with my father and brothers in Tagana-an.

In the meantime, Fertig began to focus on dealing with the many administrative and organizational problems confronting the new organization. The new command made a major priority of establishing communications with MacArthur's command in Brisbane, Australia. Prior to surrender, several potential stay-behind USAFFE units on Luzon and Panay had been given equipment, codes, and communication instructions; these groups were already communicating with MacArthur's headquarters. Fertig had neither a transmitter nor communication codes. In September 1942, after he had agreed to organize the guerrillas on Mindanao, he began in earnest to advance an effort to establish communications with MacArthur's headquarters. He initially brought into the effort four Filipino radio personnel: Alfredo Bontuyan, Glicerio Lim, and Gerardo and Eleno Almendras. This group had already been collecting junk radio parts to use in constructing a radio transmitter. They also had diagrams from a correspondence course on building transmitters. Florentino Opendo, a former Bureau of Aeronautics radio operator who possessed a transmitter, joined the group. Fertig transferred these personnel to Bonifacio, where more painstaking efforts were initiated to comply with Fertig's desire to communicate with Australia. Others who had military radio experience joined them: Robert Ball, Army Air Corps; George Hall, Army Air Corps; William Konko, U.S. Navy; and William Johnson, U.S. Navy. Later on Roy Bell, a former physics professor from Silliman University in Zamboanga, worked with the group. This organization of communications personnel later became known as the Force Radio Section (FRS) of the Tenth Military District, with Lieutenant Robert Ball as its first commanding officer. When possible, the FRS station was located in close proximity to Fertig's headquarters but near a lumber camp or a mine, which usually had its own diesel generators, similar to the ones at East Mindanao.

For days on end, the FRS attempted to make contact with some Allied stations using the Army Air Corps call letters from the Del Monte airfield (KZOM). The section made initial contact outside Mindanao on February 6, 1943, when it had a communication exchange with Lieutenant Colonel Peralta's guerrilla force on Panay. On February 18, 1943, they made contact with Station KFS (a naval station) in San Francisco. This station, working with the War Department, provided the guerrilla FRS with code words to use with MacArthur's headquarters net (KAZ). FRS would use the call letters WYZB. However, it was not until later in February that MacArthur's headquarters was convinced as to Fertig's bona fides. Fortunately, Fertig had sent out a personal code with two American mining engineers, Jordan Hamner and Charles Smith. Together with another man named Smith and a small crew, they left Mindanao on a small sailboat and headed for Australia. All were successful in making it to Australia and MacArthur's headquarters.

This whole effort in establishing communications with MacArthur's headquarters raised a basic question: Were there not transmitters available somewhere on the island of Mindanao? One could speculate that there had to exist company radios, possibly used for interisland communication before the war, that could have communicated with Australia. In fact, there was one such transmitter in Anakan, Misamis Oriental. Cecil Walter of the Anakan Lumber Company had used it to communicate with the States and Manila prior to the war. Glyn Mitchell and Loyd Waters, both members of the Army Air Corps, helped make the transmitter operational, and the group made contact with KFS. (The locals affectionately nicknamed Waters *"Tubig,"* which means "water.") This effort was independent and separate of Fertig's FRS in Bonifacio—perhaps Fertig had no idea that this transmitter existed some two hundred kilometers away in Anakan. Moreover, the guerrillas were still in the process of organizing, and potential capabilities were not shared with each other.

After receiving radio contact instructions, Fertig sent his first report to MacArthur's headquarters, now designated as General Headquarters, Southwest Pacific Area (GHQ, SWPA). This report read: "HAVE STRONG FORCE WITH COMPLETE CIVILIAN SUPPORT XXX LARGE NUMBER OF ENEMY MOTOR VEHICLES AND BRIDGES HAVE BEEN DESTROYED XXX MANY TELEPHONE POLES HAVE BEEN TORN DOWN FOOD DUMPS BURNED AND CONSIDERABLE ENEMY ARMS AND AMMUNITION CAPTURED XXX THOUSANDS YOUNG FILIPINOS EAGER TO JOIN WHEN ARMS AVAILABLE XXX READY AND EAGER TO ENGAGE THE ENEMY ON YOUR ORDERS XXX."

According to Father Edward Haggerty in *Guerrilla Padre in Mindanao,* MacArthur's initial message to Fertig read: "FERTIG XXX YOU ARE NAMED GUERRILLA CHIEF XXX YOUR MEN ARE NOT DESERTERS BUT FIGHTERS XXX IN SOME WAY I WILL GET AID TO YOU XXX FOR FUTURE I REITERATE MY PLEDGE XXX I SHALL RETURN XXX MACARTHUR." MacArthur's statement that Fertig's men were "not deserters but fighters" clarified the status of those who did not surrender, thereby allaying any feelings of doubt or guilt that may have plagued some of them.

The next message was Fertig's appointment to command. "LTCOL W W FERTIG IS DESIGNATED TO COMMAND THE TENTH MILITARY DISTRICT (IS-LANDS OF MINDANAO AND SULU) XXX HE WILL PERFECT INTELLIGENCE NOT COVERING NINTH MILITARY DISTRICT (SAMAR-LEYTE) XXX NO OF-FICER OF RANK OF GENERAL WILL BE DESIGNATED AT PRESENT XXX."

MacArthur's headquarters activated the Tenth Military District, which had existed prior to the war, to provide an organizational framework upon which to build a guerrilla force and command structure on Mindanao. It should be noted that MacArthur limited Fertig's area of responsibility to the Mindanao and Sulu islands. He assigned the operational responsibility for Samar and Leyte (Ninth Military District) to other guerrilla organizations on those is-lands. Under the Tenth Military District, a number of geographic divisions were formed.

The first division established in the Tenth Military District was the 105th, under Fertig's direct control in Misamis Occidental. This was followed by the creation of the 108th Division in Lanao under Charles Hedges. The 110th Di-vision, covering the Surigao provincial area, had been established in 1942 by Lieutenant Colonel Ernest McClish. As the guerrilla organization expanded, it was incorporated into the Tenth Military District. Over the course of the war, Fertig established six divisions under the Tenth Military District organi-zational umbrella.

The division under which my father and brothers fought, and where we evaded the Japanese, was the geographic responsibility of the 110th Division. This division covered northeast Mindanao, including the provinces of Agusan and Surigao and numbered approximately 5,400 personnel. A sub-element of the division was the 114th Infantry Regiment. Going through my father's wartime records, most of which were military reports and orders, it became evident that Fertig required all levels to adhere to military regulations. He demanded that every action and request be documented at the local level and that a copy always be forwarded to the next higher level of command. On every official order, the distribution list included the infamous "File."

Initially, the guerrilla units within the 10th Military District were loosely organized and lacked many of the attributes of a viable military force. Food and money were essentials upon which the district command focused. Most important in this process had been the recognition by MacArthur's head-quarters that Fertig had a viable guerrilla organization under his command. From this recognition flowed measured support that commenced in March 1943 with the arrival of the first supplies via submarine. This was followed by authority being granted by President Quezon for the 10th Military District to print money. As the guerrilla strength grew, Fertig used the Philippine army table of organization as a template for forming divisions, regiments, and battalions. For leadership, he was fortunate to have a number of civilians with reserve commissions, like my father, and active duty U.S./Filipino military personnel who volunteered to serve in the growing guerrilla organization. This extraordinary group of people brought talents and leadership to an organization that would make a difference in the war against the Japanese presence on Mindanao. Common characteristics of this unique group of leaders included residence in the Philippines before December 1941, business background and knowledge of the Philippines, military experience, including World War I, and reserve commissions and an understanding of warfare. Several notable men were active in assisting Fertig in the formative years of the guerrilla movement. Charles Hedges was a World War I veteran and lumber executive in southern Philippines. Frank McGee, a West Point graduate (class of 1917) and a highly decorated officer in World War I, became a successful businessman in the Philippines after leaving the U.S. Army. James Grinstead, also a World War I veteran, was an officer in the Philippine Constabulary before going into business. Robert Bowler was a U.S. Army Reserve Officer who later became Fertig's second-in-command. Cecil Walter, manager of the Anakan Lumber Company and a civil engineer, brought area expertise to the guerrilla movement. Sam Wilson, a World War I veteran and naval reserve officer, had a financial background and would oversee the guerrilla money printing operation. Ernest McClish had served as a captain in the 57th Infantry Regiment of the Philippine Scouts, was seconded to the Philippine Army as a battalion commander in the 61st Regiment in 1941, and participated in combat during the Japanese invasion of Mindanao in April 1942. And Clyde Childress, a military officer with the 31st Infantry Regiment, was also seconded to the Philippine Army as a battalion commander in the 61st Regiment in 1941 and participated in combat during the Japanese invasion of Mindanao in April 1942. All of these men would have substantive responsibilities within the 10th Military District. Except for Sam Wilson, all became division commanders.

In March 1943 Commander Charles "Chick" Parsons arrived on Mindanao via the submarine USS *Tambor* from General MacArthur's Australia headquarters. Parsons had lived in Manila prior to the war and was the chief executive officer of Luzon Stevedoring. He was also the honorary Panamanian consul. This diplomatic status allowed him and his family to be repatriated to Panama after the Japanese took control of Manila. The Japanese were unaware that Parsons was a commander in the U.S. Naval Reserve and a specialist in intelligence. After his return to the U.S. from Panama, Parsons was called to active duty and dispatched to MacArthur's command in Australia. There he became the staff coordinator for guerrilla activities in the Philippines.

MacArthur's command sent Parsons to visit with Fertig's growing guerrilla organization on Mindanao; soon after his arrival he met with Fertig. Parsons was accompanied by Captain Charles Smith, who, together with Jordan Hamner, had left Mindanao for Australia on a sailboat four months earlier, carrying with him the authentication codes vital for Fertig to establish communications with Australia. Their trip was to assess the guerrilla movement, its leadership, and its resupply needs; they concluded that Fertig's group was stronger than MacArthur's headquarters had realized. During this meeting, Fertig received a set of eagles and confirmation of his promotion to full colonel. Parsons and Smith also concluded that arms, ammunition, and radio equipment were the major needs of the guerrillas. Parsons stressed that the 10th Military District was to change from an active guerrilla force, waging tactical operations against Japanese Army units, to an intelligence-gathering organization which included the development of a coast-watcher net to report on Japanese shipping passing through the vital maritime passages around the island of Mindanao. Parsons's argument further stressed that despite the valor and tenacity of the guerrillas, their Springfields and Enfields were no match for the more modern Japanese Army weapons. During Parsons's initial visit, two tons of vitally needed stores were off-loaded to a local guerrilla lighter and then moved to the beach in less than an hour. These supplies included 50,000 rounds of .30 cal ammunition, 20,000 rounds of .45 cal ammunition, radio equipment/spare parts, medicine, clothing, food, cigarettes, bandages/surgical kits, and wheat flour for making communion wafers.

No doubt Father Haggerty, the unofficial chaplain of the guerrillas, had originated the request for wheat flour. Attendance at Sunday Mass was central to the lives of Catholic Filipinos, and the reception of Holy Communion was an important part of that ritual. Those parishes that still had communion wafers when wheat flour ran out stretched their supply by dividing the hosts and distributing a tiny piece to each communicant.

While we were in our hideout in the Tagana-an area, Dad received word that an American soldier with twenty fully armed guerrillas had arrived in town. This group had heard there was an American in the area with arms, and they wanted to see him. He learned that a Lieutenant Colonel Luis Morgan led the group. Accordingly, Dad, Rudy, and Hank went into town and met Morgan and his group who had come in a big sailing banca. When Morgan asked Dad if he was involved in any guerrilla organizing, Dad replied that he wasn't but described the ill-fated meeting of the Filipino-American-Chinese group that had broken up when the Japanese arrived in town. Morgan requested that Dad not get involved in any more organizing until he received instructions from the Tenth Military District. Morgan further said Fertig was attempting to organize and consolidate all guerrilla organizations on Mindanao. Hank remembered Morgan as outgoing but demanding, almost arrogant. He had a swashbuckling air about him, with a tommy gun strapped across his chest. Even so Dad trusted him regarding the guerrilla organization he and Fertig were trying to put together. Hank recalled Morgan bragging about his American name later on in the war (Morgan's father was an American, his mother a Filipina), particularly after he had consumed several glasses of tuba. He focused on his American family's famous warriors, even ones who fought in the Civil War. After his meeting with Dad and the boys, Morgan went on to Cantilan to meet with Frank McCarthy, operator of a lumber business in the area, about throwing his lot in with the new guerrilla organization.

Several months later Dad received a message via a runner asking him to attend a meeting of the new guerrilla organization at the 110th Division headquarters in Medina, Misamis Oriental. On foot, Rudy, Hank, and Dad made the trip, carrying Dad's weapons with them—the .38 caliber revolver, shotgun, and hunting rifle. The boys hiked barefoot, but Dad was fortunate to still have his work boots, although his socks were threadbare.

On this initial trip to Medina, Dad and my brothers planned to follow the national road designated as Route 1. However, since they had no knowledge of the locations of Japanese outposts, they had to rely on the advice of the locals regarding alternative ways to skirt dangerous areas. Their route took them around Lake Mainit to Cabadbaran and Butuan in Agusan province. They continued along the coast, passing through Gingoog, and then on to Medina. It should be noted that during this trip they carried no rations. When they reached a barrio or town Dad usually met with the local *teniente del barrio* (barrio lieutenant) or the town mayor and secured a meal and lodging for the night.

Arriving in Medina after almost two weeks on the road, they were first met by Major Clyde Childress. Hank recalled that they were just rounding the bend into Medina when Childress came riding up on a big red stallion, wearing khaki pants, a white shirt, riding boots, and a garrison cap. As they met, he reached down, shook Dad's hand, and said: "Hello, I'm Major Childress. Go over to the big house and you will meet Colonel McClish."

Prior to the war, Childress and McClish had been American officers assigned to the U.S. Philippine Division in Manila. When the war started they were then assigned to the 61st Infantry Regiment, which was sent to Mindanao to reinforce General Sharp's forces. Their regiment first participated in a battle beginning at Malabang, Lanao, on April 29 and ending on May 10, 1942, near Ganassi, Lanao. With their respective units dispersed, both officers retired to the interior. They met again in November 1942 at Fertig's headquarters in Jimenez, Misamis Occidental. Their visit was prompted by the news that an American general had landed to organize a guerrilla force.

The big house Childress referred to belonged to the Pelaez family, who had large land holdings in the area and had made available the first floor of the house to the guerrilla force as headquarters of the 110th Division. McClish warmly welcomed Dad and my brothers in his office, where they also met other American officers from the newly formed group. Hank described McClish as having a quiet manner and being soft-spoken, with a low and slow Oklahoma drawl and walk to match. He approached issues and problems very methodically, a stark contrast to other guerrilla leaders, who barked out orders the minute they walked into a room. Father Haggerty described McClish as

> a handsome Oklahoman who had risen from a hospital bed rather than surrender to the Japs. For three months after the surrender he had kept a band of Americans together on the borders of Lanao in spite of constant danger from the Moros. He had become one of the most colorful guerrilla leaders in Mindanao and later became leader of all the forces in the northeast part of this big island (110th Division). When he passed through Talakag he was yellow from malaria and without shoes, but his famous slow smile was still with him.[1]

Next to the 110th Division headquarters was a school that housed a large number of Filipino guerrillas, some of whom were acquaintances of Rudy and Hank from the Surigao area. These troops, who appeared to be fairly well armed, became the mainstay of the division and grew to number over five thousand.

One might ask how the guerrillas acquired their large store of weapons. Those Filipino soldiers and Philippine Constabulary personnel who did not surrender kept theirs, and to augment this pool, they appealed to Filipino citizens. The same way Dad had been procuring for Sharp's forces in Surigao before we went into hiding, the guerrillas went into the barrios and asked the residents if they knew of anyone who had arms. They then asked that individual for the weapon, providing, of course, a proper receipt. Dad already had his revolver, shotgun, and hunting rifle and turned the last two in to the military.

Dad and McClish had a productive meeting, after which McClish dispatched a runner to Fertig's headquarters with a request for the preparation of Dad's official induction orders. Lieutenant Colonel Luis Morgan, Fertig's chief of staff, who had previously met with Dad in Tagana-an, executed the orders. About a week later, on April 11, 1943, Dad, already in the Army Reserves, was formally placed on active duty with the Tenth Military District with the rank of captain. Perhaps to maximize the value of his background and years of experience on Mindanao, he was assigned to the staff of the 110th Division as liaison officer for the Province of Surigao. In this capacity, he would work closely with provincial government officials, whose assistance was important to the success of the guerrilla operations.

On April 11, 1943, Dad received Special Order Number 8 from Tenth Military District headquarters, designating him liaison officer for the Province of Surigao. A detail of five enlisted men was assigned to his appointed office. Later in the month McClish designated him procurement officer for the 110th Division, with authority to obtain fuel oil, gasoline, kerosene, internal combustion engines, launches, et cetera, for the army.

Dad, together with the detail assigned to him, set out with Rudy and Hank toward Surigao province, Dad's primary area of operations. They traveled by banca whenever possible, thereby shortening their trip considerably. They were excited and impressed with what they had seen of the guerrilla organization. Dad could now see some light at the end of the tunnel regarding the future of the war and his role in it. Active participation in the guerrilla movement against the Japanese became something akin to a viable compensation for what they had taken from him—his self-esteem. Now he could get back at the enemy for having drastically altered his life and that of his family.

As they made their way back to Surigao, their morale was higher than it had been for many months. It soon became obvious to my father that, despite their youth, the boys were determined to serve in the guerrilla movement. They were now eager to become part of an organization that would engage the Japanese occupiers that had disrupted the lives of our family.

When Dad and his group reached the area around Lake Mainit, they met up with Captain William Knortz, who was on a recruiting mission. He was persuading various factions, largely Philippine Constabulary, to come into the Tenth Military District organization. After spending some time with

Knortz, Rudy and Hank prodded Dad about their joining the guerrilla organization. When Dad asked, Knortz turned to the boys and asked their ages. Rudy immediately replied that he was twenty-two, and Hank said he was twenty-one. (Actually, they had turned seventeen and sixteen the previous December.) With a nod and perhaps a knowing wink, Knortz simply commented, "You look old enough," and told them they could return with him and several other recruits to Medina for induction.

Bill Knortz was a colorful character and, because of his subsequent close connection to my brothers, merits a special introduction. He had a fixation on using a boat rather than walking. He had been captured by the Japanese in Lanao province in May 1942 and was interned at Keithley Barracks. In July 1942 he—along with Bill Johnson, Robert Ball, and James Smith—escaped and later joined the guerrilla movement. Their escape was almost comical, compared with the hazardous efforts of other POWs. Johnson, a crewmember on one of the torpedo boats bringing MacArthur and his staff to Cagayan, recalled their escape from the Japanese:

> My job while interned at Keithley Barracks had been in the pump house. On the morning of the breakout, for some unexplained reason, my attention had been drawn to a large crescent wrench that was on the wall of the pump house. I decided to take it with me. After meeting the others, we proceeded to an area where there were a number of disabled U.S. Army vehicles lined up in a row. Our escape route passed through these vehicles. At the end of the line of these vehicles was a Japanese guard chatting up several Filipino girls. As the guard looked at us among the vehicles, I raised the crescent wrench and pointed to the vehicles, giving the appearance to the guard that we were there to do some repair work on the vehicles. The guard, satisfied with my comical antics, returned to his discussions with the young women. He was totally oblivious to our planned intentions. We continued moving along the line of vehicles, using them to cover our route away from the barracks and the view of the guard.[2]

Within minutes they were able to leave the area and escape into the countryside and freedom.

After joining the guerrillas, Knortz was assigned initially to the Cagayan-Bugo area. His attacks against the Japanese were legendary within the guerrilla movement, but for one problem: each time he succeeded in his attacks, the next one had to be bigger than the last. He annoyed the Japanese very effectively. One day, for example, he decided he wanted some canned pineapple and went to the California Packing Corporation's cannery at Del Monte, heavily guarded by Japanese troops. He broke in and left with several cases of canned pineapple—no one could understand why he went to this trouble when he could pick fresh pineapple from the many fields around the processing facility.

Knortz was a physical fitness enthusiast, and he believed in maintaining his body at its maximum strength. He had been a football player prior to joining the U.S. Army Air Corps. He did not smoke or drink and was known for exercising several times a day. When in the field he carried a Browning automatic rifle (BAR), two belts of ammunition, and two .45 pistols. He was also a judo black belt and practiced when he could. While in prison camp, he sometimes challenged the Japanese guards and their officers.

When Dad and my brothers met Knortz, he was about twenty-two, well built, tall (over six feet), blond, and fair-skinned. He had an angular frame, like John Wayne, with a bit of a list. His long gait required the boys to take almost a step and a half for his every one. He was well schooled and had a commanding poise and voice; when he walked into a room, everyone felt his presence. Despite the age difference, he got along very well with Dad. For the teenage Rudy and Hank, Knortz was someone to emulate. Hank recalled that Knortz had a Filipino aide-de-camp, nicknamed "Dancer" (apparently because he used to dance by himself), who took care of his clothes and prepared his meals.

Rudy and Hank returned to Medina with Knortz, and on April 24, 1943, both of my brothers were officially sworn in as privates in the U.S. Forces in the Philippines (USFIP). They were issued their first weapons—Rudy a 1903 Springfield rifle and Hank an old British Enfield rifle—which, like most of the arms in the arsenal of the U.S.-Filipino military at that time, were left over from World War I. Becoming guerrillas so quickly and easily was an unexpected turn of events for my brothers. After Dad's return to active duty, they had to either go home to our hideout or ask Dad to allow them to tag along with him. There was a good possibility that Dad would have allowed his sons to stay with him as unofficial members of his detail. He had an excellent rapport with them, and they, in turn, loved being with him. I wonder what Dad's thoughts were as he watched his boys eagerly going off to join others in becoming guerrilla fighters in a nasty war.

Now, one of Dad's most difficult tasks was to explain to Mom that he had allowed their two young sons to join up and become guerrillas! We can only guess at Mom's reaction to the news. My parents had always argued or discussed problems out of earshot of their children, but in this case that would have been difficult, given our cramped quarters. Neither Peach nor I remember Mom displaying any histrionics, however, so Dad must have done an excellent job of persuading her that this was the right thing for their boys to do. Besides, at that point it was a fait accompli, and Mom, ever the pragmatist, probably realized that she should be focusing her energy on keeping us alive and out of harm's way.

Rudy and Hank were assigned to the 114th Infantry Regiment that was being formed in the Claver area. Its first commanding officer was Captain Macario Diaz, a former Philippine army officer. He had been municipal mayor of Surigao and did not surrender to the Japanese. Early in the war he had organized civilians and USAFFE personnel into FACGA. Dad had attended their meeting in Tagana-an, which had disbanded because of the unexpected arrival of a Japanese patrol. Later, Knortz became the commanding officer of the 114th with Bill Money as the executive officer.

When my brothers joined the 114th Infantry Regiment it was still somewhat disorganized. It was the charge from the 110th Division to Bill Knortz, the 114's new commanding officer, to unify the units and overcome some of the regiment's earlier separatist tendencies. Prior to establishing a headquarters in Claver, the regiment had no logistical base and was forced to live off the land in the areas in which they operated. Members of the regiment were lucky to have one full meal a day. Weapons and ammunition were in short supply; guerrillas going on patrol carried no more than ten rounds for their individual weapons. Even though the submarine resupply effort from Australia had begun in March 1943, the submarine landing sites during the early part of the mission were some five hundred kilometers west of our location, and it would take months for new weapons and ammunition to flow down to the various regiments scattered around Mindanao. This scarcity forced the guerrillas to be most prudent in their operations; moreover, the emphasis from MacArthur's headquarters that collecting intelligence and coast-watcher information was *the* priority decreased the propensity to engage the Japanese. Every round fired mattered when fighting, if only in self-defense. While Rudy and Hank had military-issue rifles, some of their fellow guerrillas had to make do with homemade weapons. A favorite was the *paleontod*—a short shotgun made out of pipe and used a 12-gauge shotgun shell. This weapon was effective at close range and could do a lot of damage with a load of buckshot. The guerrillas also employed homemade grenades—a common type consisted of three sticks of dynamite packed in cans containing metal parts. (Dynamite was still available during the early part of the war because of the mining industry.)

It is worth mentioning that within Fertig's guerrilla organization there was a generation gap. Many of the American soldiers who had refused to surrender or had escaped from Japanese prison camps were young noncommissioned officers. Nonetheless, among the Filipinos there was a respect for the American officer corps. Therefore, Fertig felt it necessary to commission these young soldiers, even though many had little leadership training or tactical military experience. This infusion of young people into the organization clashed with the old-timers like my father and many other civilians who had operated businesses in the Philippines for years. (Dad was fifty-three when he joined the guerrilla movement.) While the conflict between the two generations was contained, it was nonetheless a real part of the dynamic within the guerrilla organization. That many of the guerrillas evaded capture by the Japanese was in no small measure due to their cunning and individualism, which are not characteristics that build unit cohesion. Once MacArthur's headquarters exerted control, those who could not abide by the command policies of the district were sent to Australia on the next resupply submarine. Lieutenant Colonel Morgan, the first chief of staff of the Tenth Military District, experienced this drastic action.

Fortunately for the guerrilla movement, ten American POWs successfully escaped from the Davao Penal Colony (DAPECOL) in the southern part of Mindanao in April 1943, to the benefit of the officer corps of the Tenth Military District and the 110th Division in particular. The penal colony, originally a Philippine institution for long-term convicts, had been developed to rehabilitate prisoners by putting them to work clearing jungle and then having them apply modern farming methods to the cleared fields. By 1941, the colony had almost a thousand hectares under cultivation and was supplying food to not only the inmates but also other governmental agencies in the vicinity of Davao. While the primary crop of the prison farm was rice, it grew corn, beans, bananas, papayas and some coffee as well and did some experimental work in growing rubber trees. The Japanese, who had long had a large civilian population in Davao province, decided to move some American POWs, many of whom came from the Cabanatuan POW camp north of Manila, from the crowded prison camps on Luzon to this penal colony. DAPECOL was a positive development for the POWs after the hell of Cabanatuan. Many of them were undernourished and had come with all sorts of ailments, and the colony gave them a better diet and a chance to heal their physical problems.

After several months in the camp, a number of American prisoners methodically planned their escape; separate groups merged to maximize their supplies and individual talents. Ten finally made the breakout. After their escape, the group planned to move to the coast, steal a fishing boat, and head for Australia. Their immediate goal was a coastal barrio named Cateel, some one hundred kilometers away. Prior to departure they carefully prepositioned water and rations for the trip and recruited two Filipino inmates to guide them away from the colony. Unfortunately, after their escape from the camp they got lost; their guides really did not know the terrain as well as they had claimed. Moving north, they continued to make their way through a crocodile-infested swamp, hacking through dense thickets of sword grass and vines. Eventually a guerrilla unit interrupted them and brought them to a safe area. The guerrillas dissuaded them from going to Cateel and, instead, recommended that they travel overland into the Agusan Valley. Following this advice, and having been given guides and supplies, the escapees crossed the mountains and reached the Agusan River, where they boarded bancas and traveled toward the coast, hugging the coastline until they finally reached Medina, headquarters of the 110th Division. They traveled approximately two hundred kilometers, from the penal colony to Medina, much of it through dense jungle. The ten Americans who had escaped from DAPECOL in this group were LCDR Melvin McCoy, U.S. Navy; Major Stephen Mellnik, U.S. Army; Major William Dyess, Army Air Corps; Captain Austin Shofner, U.S. Marine Corps; Captain Samuel Grashio, Army Air Corps; First Lieutenant Jack Hawkins, U.S. Marine Corps; First Lieutenant Michael Dobervich, U.S. Marine Corps; First Lieutenant Leo Boelens, Army Air Corps; Sergeant Paul Marshall, U.S. Army; Sergeant Robert B. Spielman, U.S. Army.[3]

Hank happened to be at the 110th Division headquarters in Medina when the escapees arrived, tired, thin, and bedraggled, some suffering from malaria. Their arms and legs were covered with infected sores, and their bare feet were cut and bleeding from the long hike over rough terrain. Hank contacted a local carpenter and arranged for wooden *bakyas* (slip-on footwear with wooden soles) to be fashioned for the ex-POWs.

On April 28, 1943, shortly after assuming his responsibilities as liaison officer, my father was designated procurement officer for the 110th Division. One of his first actions in his new assignment was to retrieve the *Henry Joy* from its hiding place in the mangroves near Tagana-an and place it into service. This little launch from East Mindanao would provide him with fast and reasonably safe transportation as he traveled up and down the coast of Surigao, maintaining close contact with the various local government officials.

Dad began to receive memorandums and reports written by local Filipino officials in Surigao province concerning the activities of the Japanese occupiers and the hardships endured by innocent civilians. As mentioned before, contact with these officials was one of his major responsibilities as liaison officer. One of the first memorandums he received was of particular interest because it came from Jesus Aloyon, acting municipal treasurer of Tagana-an, our first hiding place and home of our friends Chief, Peping, and Juan Lisondra (Peping and Juan were brothers) and many others.

The memorandum described in detail the Japanese raid on Tagana-an in the early morning of May 22, 1943, which caught the townspeople by surprise and caused them to flee from their homes. It outlined the atrocities that the Japanese soldiers committed that day, notably the murder of one young girl and the wounding of another by machine-gun fire. Before leaving, they ordered Father Viola, the parish priest, to tell the residents to return to their homes within five days and stay in town.

Dad was relieved and gratified that Aloyon also sent a handwritten note reporting that soon after the departure of the Japanese he had passed by our evacuation place and found that we were safe, though it expressed his concern that the Japanese would return to the area.

Japanese soldiers repeated this brutal activity again and again in the Philippines and other Asian countries. Certainly the ultimate responsibility for this inhuman treatment resided with the Japanese military leadership, within which such violence began to appear with Japanese incursions into China during the 1930s. Most notable was the rape of Nanking, when the Japanese occupying force killed many innocent Chinese civilians. Such action showed a disregard for human life, regardless of the circumstances. Therefore, the norms of humanity could be ignored because these people did not matter— only Japanese superiority and dominance over them. The Japanese military also, particularly in the Philippines, displayed basic resentment toward the peoples of America and other nations that they felt had discriminated against them in their quest for modern technology, industrialization, and recognition as a world power. Additionally, many Japanese people believed that their culture and race were superior to all others; in their eyes, the Filipinos, who had willingly tolerated the American Commonwealth administration of their country, must now be taught a lesson. More important, if the Filipinos were to survive under a Japanese occupation, they must now demonstrate total allegiance to the new Japanese way of life in the Philippines.

The report contained another disturbing point. Combined Japanese and Bureau of Constabulary (BC) troops—Philippine troops organized by the Japanese to replace the Philippine Constabulary—conducted the raid on May 22. It must have been devastating for the townspeople of Tagana-an to be brutalized by a force consisting of both Japanese and Filipino troops, jointly commanded by a Japanese and a Filipino officer.

Anticipation of precisely these kinds of cruel acts by the Japanese that Aloyon reported had prompted the Lisondra brothers and others to prepare their bakwitans. But, as the report indicated, running to their sanctuaries would only give the Japanese cause to behave even more viciously, burning down much of the town and harshly punishing the remaining residents. Aloyon was, of course, worried about his own official duties and responsibilities relative to USFIP, as well as his personal safety. This memorandum to my father shows a growing concern and anxiety by loyal Filipinos to the dilemma faced by the local people—continued allegiance to the Commonwealth and the Americans, or accommodation to the rules of the Japanese occupation. It was a difficult decision, when one's very life might depend it. For us Americans evading the Japanese in the Tagana-an area, our immediate survival hinged on the choice made by these courageous people. At any time, we could have been reported to the Japanese, captured, and probably executed. Thank God the Filipinos chose on behalf of our safety—noble acts, given the pressure placed on them by the Japanese.

The problem of Filipinos sorting out their allegiance was one of many that my father encountered in his responsibilities as liaison and procurement officer for the Province of Surigao, particularly as Japanese units approached local towns and villages and demanded allegiance to their authority. When not obeyed, there was immediate reprisal.

FIVE

On the Move

The ever-increasing Japanese forays into Tagana-an and other towns as they traveled southward, coupled with the possibility that spies would learn of our location in nearby Red Mountain, made it imperative that the Hansen womenfolk leave the area. Mom decided to move us to Claver, further down the eastern coast of Surigao. Rudy and Hank were now involved with the operations of the 114th Infantry Regiment, which had its headquarters there, and, furthermore, it was a convenient place for Dad to obtain operational support when he was working in the area. After Dad and the boys joined the guerrillas, Mom took on sole responsibility for our safety; at the same time, not knowing the whereabouts and welfare of her husband and sons was also very stressful. The recent Japanese raid on Tagana-an prompted her to move to Claver, where she hoped she could see the boys from time to time, and Dad would have a place to hang his hat whenever he visited the 114th.

Getting to Claver was something else. Mom made arrangements for the three of us (and Princess) to travel by banca down the coast, bringing most of the belongings we had taken with us when we evacuated the mine. She had decided to leave behind, in Peping Lisondra's care, the trunk containing our jewelry, personal documents, and photos. The banca was to hug the coast to avoid being picked up by a Japanese maritime patrol, and on this particular day the weather was not good, with wind and heavy surf, making our progress doubly was slow. Conditions worsened as dusk approached so the *bancero* (boatman) put into a protected cove to wait out the storm. Because the tide was out, the last half-kilometer to the beach was only about waist-deep, but he had to navigate around large rocks. To avoid damaging his banca, low in the water because of its load, he decided to push it to shore. Mom and Peach helped by pushing the outrigger supports, and I tried to do my share, too, but it was a struggle to keep my footing on the sharp rocks and push at the same time, so I gave up and rode the rest of the way astride one of the bamboo outriggers. Concerned about the safety of his banca, the bancero decided to remain aboard but suggested we stay on shore. Already there on the beach were several fishermen taking shelter in an old nipa lean-to. They had built a fire to keep warm and invited us to join them; drenched and shivering from the cold wind, we gladly accepted their invitation. Feeling compassion for the two girls huddled together trying to get warm, two fishermen offered the warmth of their own dry backs for us to lean against. Peach and I were exhausted and fell asleep sitting back-to-back with those kind fishermen while Mom stayed awake, cradling Princess, like the rest of us, cold and hungry. The next morning, the storm abated and we continued our journey southward toward Claver. Later, as Mom recounted this adventure to Dad, she confessed that she spent the night in fear, praying for our safety— after all, she was defenseless, with two young daughters in tow, all her money now a soggy wad concealed under her clothes, and just about all our worldly possessions on the banca bobbing in rough waters off-shore. But no harm befell us, thanks to the innate goodness of those fishermen, some of whom had never even met a Westerner before. This was just one of the countless acts of kindness and generosity we received from Filipino strangers, given unselfishly and often at great personal peril as the Japanese were brutal to those caught helping Americans or other Allied nationals.

To our surprise, Claver was a fair-sized town, bustling with activity. We had no trouble adjusting to our new surroundings; compared to our previous hiding places, living conditions here were quite pleasant. Fear of a surprise Japanese raid, such as the one on Tagana-an in late May, had prompted many residents to leave town and seek refuge with relatives or friends in the surrounding farms and hills. Fortunately for us, a recently vacated house was available for rent. Our new home was much more spacious than the various nipa huts we had lived in since our departure from the mine. This house was constructed mainly of wood and, as was typical, the living area—a combination living/dining room and three small bedrooms—was about five or six feet above ground level. Best of all, it was furnished! The kitchen had fairly decent cooking facilities. A small room adjacent to it served as a washroom, with a slatted floor and a tall clay jar for water storage. Water was available from a well a short distance away, and an outhouse built on stilts stood behind a screen of bushes near the rear boundary of the property. The space under the house served as a comfortable retreat on particularly hot and humid days as well as a convenient play area for me on rainy days.

This new location afforded some of the conveniences of in-town living; for example, there were a few small shops (*sari-sari* stores) selling local goods. One of Mom's first purchases was a pair of bakyas. Accustomed to fashionable shoes custom-made for her at Pop Henderson's Independent Shoe Shop in Manila, the indignity of having to go barefoot deeply humiliated her. She soon learned, however, that bakya wearers had to be careful walking through mud, for the slap of the wooden sole against the foot often splattered drops of mud against the back of the leg.

A variety of vegetables and fruit could be purchased at the weekly farmer's market (*tabo-an*). Peach's mentors in Tagana-an had taught her well: she soon became expert at selecting the freshest greens and the most delicious fruits available, often driving a hard bargain with the vendors. Although meat, chicken and fish were in short supply, a variety of tropical fruits was almost always available. We particularly enjoyed, especially at breakfast time, the pomelo, similar to a grapefruit but larger and sweeter. My personal favorite, though, was jackfruit (*langka* or *nangka,* depending on the region), a large, rather unattractive fruit with thick, prickly skin. When ripe, it emitted a pleasantly pungent aroma and its ugly green exterior covered many delicious pulpy sections encasing large seeds that, when boiled and peeled, had a nutty flavor.

On Sundays people from the outlying areas came to Claver to join the townspeople for Mass at the old Catholic Church located in the center of town. It had been about a year and a half since our family was able to regularly attend Mass and participate in other church services. My preparation for my First Holy Communion had been cut short by the outbreak of the war, so I was not able to receive that sacrament. Still, the mere fact that we could attend Mass (something I had resisted every morning while a boarder at San Nicolas School) lent some semblance of normalcy to our lives. However, because of the war and fear of possible Japanese occupation, the local schools remained closed, and the townspeople with out-of-town connections continued to stay in areas deeper in the interior and away from the coast.

As liaison and procurement officer for the 110th Division, Dad's area of operations covered the entire Province of Surigao, and he traveled extensively, often into neighboring provinces as well. Since Claver was the headquarters for the 114th Infantry Regiment, there were always a number of guerrillas (sometimes including Rudy and Hank) either arriving or leaving. While Dad was away, the presence of these guerrillas provided a modicum of security, but a top priority for Mom and Dad was locating an evacuation point that we could run to should a Japanese patrol make a foray into Claver. They arranged for us to use as a bakwitan a small nipa hut, located halfway up a nearby hill, so we packed up a few household items not needed for day-to-day living and stored them in the hut. Thus, we could flee at a moment's notice and not be burdened by too many bundles. Mom found an old insulated beverage jug, its glass lining long since broken and discarded, that she converted into a medical kit. It had a looped handle and a tight-fitting cover that made it suitable for storing our small amount of medical supplies as well as paper money. After our experience during the banca trip from Tagana-an, when all our possessions (including money) got sopping wet, Mom decided that we needed a waterproof container in our traveling gear. Also convenient, the jug's size and handle made it ideal for a little person to grab and carry, so I was made responsible for the kit in the event of a hasty departure.

During a break in their guerrilla activities, Rudy and Hank were able to bring Old Timer down from Tagana-an and he soon found a home in a fenced area adjacent to the rice mill. The boys' departure for guerrilla service placed a heavier burden on Peach. The care and feeding of Old Timer was added to her already long list of daily chores. First she filled a small container with chaff from the rice mill at the edge of town, then stopped at the well for a pail of water. I can still remember her treks to the farm with a heavy pail of water held in one hand, her slim body leaning in the opposite direction with the other arm fully extended to balance the weight. Every few minutes she had to switch the pail from one hand to the other. I carried the chaff but only to a certain point, then I'd hand it to her. I was still afraid and distrustful of Old Timer and stayed at a safe distance. Although Peach did not have the same authority over the horse that the boys did, she tried to put up a brave front. I watched anxiously as she approached the crude fence, knowing that as soon as Old Timer spotted her he would immediately run toward her at full gallop, snorting in anticipation of his dinner. Faced with all that horsepower, Peach hastily dropped off both containers inside the fence, picked up the empties, and retreated to the safety of my position. We then nervously watched Old Timer for a few minutes until we were certain he wasn't going to jump over the fence and come after us for a second course.

Another job Peach took over from the boys—and I could not help with this either—was making coconut oil. She had not yet turned thirteen and was nowhere near the weight of either of the boys, but she gamely kept the kudkuran anchored to the stool with her right foot and grated the tough co-coconut meat without complaint. As the juicy flakes of coconut meat dropped into the container I snatched small handfuls and popped them in my mouth. Peach crankily stopped me because a lot of hard work went into grating and squeezing enough coconut meat to produce a sufficient amount of the milky gata, some of which she and Mom used to make sauces for fresh or dried sea-food and vegetables and the rest they boiled until it clarified and turned into oil suitable for cooking and for fueling our clamshell lamps. I could not help observing that Peach was always busy with grown-up work; she did as much housework as Romana and our day maids did in our home at the mine, only under more primitive conditions.

One chore I felt confident enough to take on was collecting firewood. The job did not seem difficult, and I was sure I could actually handle it. Mom was hesitant at first, but, mindful of the many household tasks already heaped on Peach's shoulders, she relented. After her many admonitions and my repeated promises to be careful, she finally entrusted me with a *sundang* (bolo or machete) to chop the thick stems of dried coconut fronds that abounded under the coconut trees in the vicinity of the town. I learned to cut the pieces into uniform sizes that fit in the space beneath the culon and still allow air to circulate. Pleased at my ability to be doing something useful, I proudly strutted off every day, with my *sundang* in its sheath tied around my waist with a piece of rope, in search of dry firewood and kindling. In the mornings, and as needed throughout the day, I made several trips to the well to haul water, half a pailful at a time, to store in the large earthen containers in the kitchen and washroom.

There was a short period after our arrival in Claver when I had to self-consciously endure the stares and giggles of the children still living in town—I must have been a novelty to them. In the year or so since we left the mine, I had grown in height and girth, and I'm sure they were puzzled that my hair was shoulder-length like a girl, yet I was dressed like a boy. Like kids everywhere, they gathered in clusters and openly remarked about my appearance—blond hair, green eyes, narrow feet with long toes—unaware that I understood most of their comments. I had never lived in a town atmosphere with neighbors and children of different ages so I did not know how to behave. I wanted to play with them but was too shy to make the first move. Eventually, however, a couple of the kids made friendly overtures that I quickly reciprocated, and in no time at all I was included in their games. One of our favorite phrases was *"Dula ta,"* meaning "Let's play." For the first time in my life I had several playmates—and our playground consisted of the town, the nearby river, the surrounding farm areas, and the seashore. I soon learned to maximize my playtime by rushing through my chores early in the day.

There was no shortage of trees for us to climb—one of our favorites was an old tree on the riverbank that leaned far enough over the water so its branches became convenient jumping-off platforms. I often thought of the tree house behind our home at the mine and felt confident that when we returned there after the war I would be able to play up in the tree house along with my older siblings. This freedom to roam around with my friends was a new and pleasant experience for me, and I did not object to Mom's rule that the church bells ringing at 6:00 in the evening (a reminder to recite the Angelus) was my signal to return home.

It was a happy event whenever Dad or the boys showed up. Their arrival was always a surprise and their stay far too short. Their wartime roles were completely different: Dad was working at a macro level with the local civilian officials to keep the more than five thousand guerrillas in the 110th Division's operational area supplied with *palay,* or unhusked rice, and other foodstuffs, such as ground corn and dried fish; Rudy and Hank were grunt soldiers in the guerrillas' frontline units, so their experiences were quite different from those of my father.

During the early months of 1943 Rudy and Hank participated in a number of small raids against Japanese units moving southward on the provincial road from Surigao. At that point in the war there were insufficient Japanese troops to cover the vastness of Mindanao, so they were forced to rely on periodic patrols to establish their occupation presence in the remote areas of Surigao province. This continued until more Japanese troops were brought in to establish permanent garrisons along the south coast from Surigao. Hank recalls that in late June 1943, the 114th Infantry Regiment launched a series of sniping/ambush raids against Japanese dispositions in the Bad-as area. Seven Japanese were killed, and guerrilla casualties were one killed and one wounded. These actions had no great significance to the guerrilla war effort, but they did build the confidence of the guerrilla troops in attacking Japanese patrols as they moved southward from Surigao.

As liaison and procurement officer, my father traveled to various parts of Surigao province, which let him get information on Japanese activities and troop movements. One of his first reports, dated July 6, 1943, described the shelling of three towns (Bacuag, Placer, and Lacandola) by a Japanese destroyer the previous day, in which nineteen five-inch shells were hurled against the three towns. Fortunately, only the church and municipal building in Bacuag were damaged and there were no casualties. The objective in shelling Placer was to destroy East Mindanao's crude-oil tank, but only the municipal building was damaged, and again there were no casualties. Apparently two shells hit Lacandola, but Dad could not assess the damage. I can imagine Dad's anger at the Japanese for aiming shells at the East Mindanao tank in Placer. After the outbreak of the war, he had considered different ways to destroy the tank and its flammable contents but did not want to risk damage to the town and possible injuries to the residents. It was fortunate that the gunners on the Japanese destroyer had, as Dad described it, "poor marksmanship"—had they hit the tank, the resulting explosion could have caused widespread destruction and loss of life. This report (and others like it) documented the wanton damage the Japanese had inflicted on various towns in Surigao province. Later, after the war, the local governments could use this documentation for reimbursement of claims against the Japanese government.

Ten days later, Dad sent another inspection report to Division headquarters, which covered a number of problems confronting the 110th Division and the Tenth Military District. The Japanese Army or its civilian agents had been offering excessive prices for livestock and other commodities, at the same time seeking information regarding the guerrillas and their activities. The Japanese were also trying to buy coins, paying one Japanese government peso for one centavo coin and two to three pesos for five centavo pieces. They needed the metal for making ammunition. A subset of this issue was the extortion of food and transportation by former USAFFE soldiers, not members of the Tenth Military District organization, falsely claiming to be on military missions. Furthermore, due to lack of military or police presence in many areas, robbers had free rein and the locals were powerless to stop them.

My father reported that the Japanese were fortifying the Mindanao Mother Lode Mine site, digging tunnels apparently for use as shelters in case of attack. Eighty to one hundred prisoners of war were working on this project. Four of them, sent out to collect firewood out of sight of the Japanese guards, appealed to some locals to contact the army and ask for diversionary action so they could all escape in the confusion.

Dad also mentioned prisoners of war being used as laborers on Japanese projects. It was not clear where these particular POWs were being interned or whether they were American, Filipino, or a combination of both. Perhaps because of the breakout of the American POWs from DAPECOL, the degree of assistance provided to the POWs being used in Japanese Army projects would have been an important matter to MacArthur's headquarters. Did the command encourage an escape by a few that may bring certain death to those who remained behind? Unfortunately, at this point the 110th Division was in no position to support a breakout by POWs.

Morale at the Tenth Military District headquarters received a boost when the submarine USS *Thresher* arrived on Mindanao (Sibuguey Bay) in early July 1943. In addition to delivering supplies from Australia, the purpose of the trip was to pick up Chick Parsons and Charles Smith, who had arrived from MacArthur's headquarters. (Also on the outbound trip were McCoy, Mellnik, and Dyess, the first of the DAPECOL escapees to be evacuated to Australia.)

Following the return of Parsons and Smith to MacArthur's headquarters in Brisbane and extensive briefings regarding the activities and needs of the guerrilla forces on Mindanao, MacArthur decided to establish an operation named SPYRON (from "spy squadron").[1] Closely held, this was a special-mission operation designed to ship, in a clandestine mode via submarine, the necessary arms, ammunition, radio equipment, and other supplies for the guerrilla forces conducting operations on the various islands of the Philippines. The goals of this effort were to deliver supplies, evacuate military and civilian personnel, and land coast watchers and special intelligence teams.

Communications equipment was a vital cargo on these SPYRON missions; radios and ciphers had arrived on Mindanao with Parsons in March 1943. The first guerrilla command radio station, FRS, was set up in the hills behind the town of Misamis in the Province of Misamis Occidental. It included a good transmitter, receiver, and a diesel generator. Once established, the Misamis FRS had a regular schedule with Australia. Lieutenant Robert Ball was the first officer in charge of this communications organization. One of the American guerrillas assigned to this fledgling radio unit was Lieutenant Beverly Perry "Ben" Farrens, who had joined Fertig's organization early on. He had been assigned to the 14th Squadron, U.S. Army Air Corps, at Clark Field when the December 8, 1941, Japanese attack destroyed most of the aircraft on the ground. With no equipment to repair, his unit was assigned to Bataan to fight as infantry troops. Shortly thereafter, Farrens was part of a group sent to Mindanao to repair, refuel, and guard Army Air Forces aircraft on that southern island. In March 1942 Farrens, along with ten others, was selected to provide protective security for the arrival and departure of Philippine president Manuel Quezon and family during a brief stopover on Mindanao prior to departing for Australia via B-17E aircraft from the Del Monte airfield. After Quezon's departure, Farrens was assigned to a unit providing support to the operation of a seaplane base on Lake Lanao. Two navy PBY aircraft had been dispatched from Australia to evacuate Army nurses from Corregidor, and the Lake Lanao facility was used as the staging and refueling base for this operation. Unfortunately, one of the PBYs was damaged, and only half of the nurses were successfully evacuated; those remaining were interned by the Japanese following the surrender of U.S. forces in May 1942.

After the surrender, Farrens and thirteen other American servicemen took to the hills rather than turn themselves in to the Japanese. For some time they lived on meager rations among the peoples of the hill country. Meeting up with other U.S. servicemen who escaped from Keithley Barracks, they made their way to the Kapai Valley, where they took up temporary residence in a Moro village ruled by Sultan Mala Mala. In early 1943, the group proceeded to Jimenez, Misamis Occidental, where they joined Fertig's guerrilla organization.

In conjunction with the command communications system, coast-watcher stations were established to monitor Japanese maritime activities in strategic passages in the southern islands. During their initial mission to survey the guerrilla organization on Mindanao, Parsons and Smith had established the first coast-watcher stations in the southernmost portion of the Philippines. Parsons had wanted to establish such a station in the Surigao area. However, because of the large number of Japanese in the vicinity, he moved to the island of Panaon, northwest of Surigao, where he established a coast-watcher station with Truman Heminway in charge. Located on the east side of the island, it afforded a panoramic view of the Surigao Strait.[2]

In the meantime, Smith traveled to the Davao area and established a station overlooking the Davao Gulf. Bill Johnson, one of the escapees from Keithley Barracks in Dansalan, spent a good deal of the war operating this station. Follow-up missions brought radio equipment to set up additional coast-watcher stations. Over the next eight months some thirty-one of them were established around the island of Mindanao, including sites in Zamboanga, Malaybalay, Cagayan, Surigao, and Iligan. Understandably, the navy was reluctant at first to commit some of its submarines to the infiltration of coast-watcher teams. However, it began close cooperation when it realized the value of the coast-watcher intelligence to submarine operations against Japanese shipping in Philippine waters.

The Tenth Military District processed the information from these stations and then communicated it by the FRS net to MacArthur's headquarters in Australia. Usually the FRS facility was collocated with the 10th Military District headquarters, where the coast-watcher messages were received, decoded, reviewed by the headquarters staff, encoded, and then sent on to MacArthur's headquarters. Additional radio equipment delivered by SPYRON missions had greatly enhanced its capability to transmit these reports, enabling it to handle between 150 and 300 messages per day. The information passed in this manner was crucial in monitoring Japanese naval activity moving through strategic passages such as the Surigao Strait. This intelligence traffic in no small measure contributed to the high casualty rates American submarines were inflicting on Japanese shipping transiting the sea lanes around Mindanao. The Japanese threatened the FRS constantly, but the FRS was off the air only once, and then only for thirty-six hours, when it was forced to evacuate from Bonifacio in July 1943. Until the end of the war it was a twenty-four-hour, seven-days-a-week operation.

With support provided by MacArthur's headquarters, the Tenth Military District under Fertig was gaining strength and becoming better organized. Although the guerrillas down the chain of command were encouraged by the news that much-needed arms, ammunition, and radio equipment were beginning to arrive by submarine from Australia, Fertig's headquarters simply did not have the logistical capability to transport these supplies in a timely manner to the divisions scattered around Mindanao for distribution to their various units.

During the start of the rainy season of 1943 skirmishes with Japanese units resulted in guerrilla casualties. A letter from Frank McCarthy underscores his heavy heart on learning about the death of his son Albert. McCarthy's July 31, 1943, letter was addressed to Major Childress, Major Shofner, or Captain Dobervich. (The latter two were among the DAPECOL escapees integrated into the 110th Division.) The first paragraph is a sad report of the death of Lieutenant Albert McCarthy, killed near Surigao in an ambush by Japanese troops. The guerrillas fought back and suffered three killed and three wounded. Casualties on the enemy side were six Japanese and thirty B.C. killed, two Japanese and ten B.C. wounded. One of the wounded guerrillas was Lieutenant Tom Baxter, with three bullets in one of his thighs and a hole through one foot. Although outnumbered and definitely outgunned, the guerrillas proved they were up to the challenge when fighting a larger, better-armed force. Robert Spielman (also a DAPECOL escapee) mentioned Albert McCarthy's death in his master's thesis on the history of the 114th Infantry Regiment. He stated that prior to the ambush McCarthy and Lieutenant Tom Baxter were literally taunting the Japanese troops between Bad-as and Surigao City. On July 4, 1943, they raised the American flag in full view of the Japanese troops in Bad-as. Moreover, the two apparently were somewhat overconfident and did not deploy flanking troops as they moved down the road. It was in this context that the Japanese set up the ambush that resulted in the death of McCarthy and the wounding of Baxter.[3]

McCarthy's letter mentioned Baxter's wounds and his evacuation for better treatment. He also reported that Captain Knortz was repairing a launch for use in transporting guerrilla supplies. This launch, later named the *Albert McCarthy,* would support resupply operations for the 114th Infantry Regiment. The rice distribution problem was also mentioned; my father had to deal with this for the next year. McCarthy made an appeal to Shofner for ammunition to equip his, McCarthy's, own army so he could avenge the death of his son. Clearly he was distraught, and his reasoning was not clear. This was the sort of undisciplined action that would have caught Fertig's ire. Most probably Shofner did not honor, or simply ignored, the request.

An August 4, 1943, communication from my father to regimental headquarters contained intelligence that would have been of value to the command. He reported that the Japanese presence in the northeastern part of Surigao province was expanding and navy vessels were constantly patrolling the outlying islands as far south as Isla General. He determined from eyewitness descriptions that one of the ships was a submarine chaser, similar to one he had run into and evaded about two weeks prior while traveling along the coast. He finished with an irreverent comment: "The Japs are fairly quiet since they got their last licking but you can never tell."

This type of information on the Japanese movements and activities was a common theme in my father's communications with the regiment and division. Since he did a lot of traveling throughout the province, Dad had many contacts among area Filipino town and barrio officials. Moreover, he was following MacArthur's dictum, delivered through Chick Parsons, that the primary mission of the guerrilla movement on Mindanao was to provide intelligence to MacArthur's headquarters—not engage the Japanese in battles they could not win.

Throughout the rainy season of 1943 the 110th Division was dealing with more immediate problems relating to the procurement, control, and distribution of dwindling food supplies. In this regard, my father received a special order designating him food control administrator for Surigao province, which meant additional responsibilities—the third hat he was expected to wear, so to speak. The order was signed by Shofner, now deputy chief of staff of the 110th Division.

On the same date, Dad received a memorandum from McClish, stating that the key element in the palay problem was transportation. The forces most often traveled by water, particularly by bancas. However, there was a shortage of them in Surigao and Agusan provinces for this task, and McClish asked Dad to go to the island of Leyte to negotiate with the Ninth Military District for its assistance in procuring more. Traveling across open waters from Mindanao to Leyte was extremely dangerous, so McClish's willingness to send Dad on this risky mission indicated the high priority on obtaining more bancas for the transportation of palay.

On this trip Dad carried with him a letter of authorization from McClish, authorizing him to sell palay, on mutually agreeable terms, to the Ninth Military District in exchange for its assistance. Of course, the Ninth Military District in Leyte, dealing with its own food shortages, welcomed the opportunity to purchase palay from the Tenth Military District. Furthermore, Dad must have successfully obtained the much-needed bancas in Leyte: a month later he received a request from the Ninth Military District's quartermaster to purchase 350 cavans of palay. (A cavan is roughly the equivalent of two U.S. bushels and weighs around sixty kilos.) The request for palay was conditional relative to a surplus in the Tenth Military District; moreover, the Ninth was willing to pay cash for the palay. The Ninth District offered to supply many different items available in the Leyte area, such as soap, cloth woven from abaca fiber, and sugar, for palay on a barter basis, to minimize the use of cash, which was in short supply. Cloth woven from fibers of the abaca plant was used to make shirts for the guerrillas.

During this sojourn to Leyte, Dad dealt with Major T. W. "Tom" Jurika, quartermaster for the Ninth Military District. Born in Zamboanga, he was the scion of an American family with business enterprises on Mindanao and received his commission as a first lieutenant in February 1942. His sister was married to Chick Parsons. Jurika also served on Fertig's staff at the Tenth Military District headquarters on Mindanao.

SIX

Life in Claver and Help from Australia

Since Claver was the location of the 114th Infantry Regiment headquarters, its population rose and fell according to the number of guerrillas visiting the area at any given time. It was a convenient and safe spot for those seeking respite from the rigors of constantly moving around without proper food and shelter while either engaging or evading Japanese forces. The occasions when Rudy and Hank came to town were causes for celebration at our house—we were as thrilled to see them as they were to be home and able to enjoy the simple comforts of shelter and family meals. In about four months of guerrilla service, my brothers had gradually changed from teenagers into more mature (and thinner) young men. For the first time, we noticed the beginnings of facial hair—Rudy's was a little darker while Hank's was lighter and hardly noticeable. Their old khaki shorts were frayed, and their shirts, already patched in some places, badly needed additional repairs. Like the majority of the guerrillas in the enlisted ranks, they were barefoot. Mom was concerned about the well-being of her boys but kept her demeanor cheerful, as she tried to make their brief visits as enjoyable as possible.

Many of the guerrillas were young and single, so it was natural that a few romances blossomed. A happy event was the marriage of Lucy McCarthy and Bob Spielman in August 1943. Paul Marshall served as best man. Bob and Paul had escaped from DAPECOL together. Our little bakwitan located up the hill served as a honeymoon cottage for the newlyweds. I only learned about this fifty-five years later, when I met Lucy and Bob at the 1998 annual reunion of the AGOM. I was touched when Lucy told me how Mom had placed in the hut a basin of water, along with soap and a towel (soap was definitely a luxury item). She had also left a note congratulating them on their marriage, adding that she wished she could have done more.

Looking back on that period in Claver, Lucy and Bob's wedding definitely stands out as a bright spot. It was a welcome diversion from the reality of life in a dangerous environment and the ever-present fear of capture by the Japanese. And yet, for our family in particular, living conditions were much better than they had been during our first months in hiding. Compared to our previous hiding places, notably the tiny one-room nipa shack perched on the roots of mangrove trees, the house in Claver was luxurious. With its limited amenities, however, the work associated with simple day-to-day living would have been disheartening to anyone with less grit and determination than my mother and my sister. Mom was fortunate to have a responsible young daughter like Peach to help her; Peach carried her share of the burden without complaint.

For me, life in Claver was almost carefree (not too dissimilar to the experiences of modern-day kids at summer camp), with limited responsibilities and only a few chores. Having the freedom to roam around the town and its environs was exciting. The families of my new friends welcomed me into their homes and often invited me to share their meals or snacks. I accepted their hospitality unhesitatingly. My fluency in Surigaonon improved, and after all these years I still remember a song that I learned during that period:

> Parong parong bukid,
> Ang buktut naligid.
> Diin dapit nalikid?
> Sa bukid na bakilid.
>
> Unsa ma'y gitambal?
> Tubig na pinabukal.
> Gracias sa Dios,
> Ang buktut natulid.

Roughly translated, it's about a mountain with lots of butterflies, where a hunchback accidentally slid down a steep slope. He was treated with water that had been boiled and, thanks be to God, he became straight. Since I had never seen a hunchback I didn't know how one could be cured by boiled water, nor did I understand the significance of the butterflies, but the tune was catchy, and it still resonates in my head from time to time.

A couple of months after we arrived in Claver, we learned that there was one disadvantage to in-town living and my close interaction with new friends—the transfer of head lice. In no time at all, those pesky creatures made themselves at home in my hair and scalp. I was constantly scratching my head, and daily washings in the river could not dislodge them. Furthermore, exposure to the sun's heat hastened the hatching of the nits that stubbornly clung to individual strands of my hair. Someone jokingly suggested that we follow one of the local customs and acquire a small pet monkey for the purpose of lice control—a monkey can expertly hunt and snatch the elusive lice and pop the little morsels in its mouth, but that process was time-consuming, with limited results. Instead, Mom used the kerosene-shampoo method. I used to cringe when she first applied the kerosene to my hair and scalp, because I could immediately feel the lice scurrying about in panic, many emerging at the hairline around my face and neck. For best results, the kerosene had to remain on the hair long enough to kill the lice. After a thorough washing in the river, Mom used a comb (usually made from carabao horn) with fine teeth set very close together to remove the remaining lice, dead or alive, as well as the larger nits attached to strands of hair. We had to repeat this procedure every month or so for me and on an "as necessary" basis for Mom and Peach.

Over a year had passed since Peach and I were given boy-style haircuts, and our hair had grown out uneven and scraggly. We learned that there was a beautician in town, and she came to our house to give us new hairstyles. To Mom's delight, she still had some cold wave solution, so Mom got a new hairdo as well. I watched in fascination as the beautician permed her hair. For the rollers, she used short pieces cut from papaya tree branches. Mom's new look boosted her morale.

Since I was a full head taller than the other eight-year-olds in Claver, I could also participate in the games and activities of the older kids. One day a couple of older boys were walking around on bamboo stilts—I had never seen this before. Each stilt was made by taking a bamboo pole, cutting a hole about two feet from the ground and a second hole about six or seven inches above it. For the foot support, a piece of split bamboo about six inches long was inserted in the upper hole so it stuck out horizontally and another (longer) piece inserted in the lower hole, protruding upward at an angle so that the two ends met to form a triangle. If the two pieces fit snugly in their respective holes, the horizontal piece (the foot support) would be fairly stable. I simply had to try it, so one of the boys lent me his pair of stilts, giving me a quick lesson on how to mount and walk on them. After a few tries, I managed to stand upright long enough to take a few faltering steps. Unfortunately, I didn't notice that the horizontal piece of bamboo under my right foot was not secure, and after a few erratic steps it became dislodged, making me hit the ground in a hurry. As I fell downward, the remaining lower support on the right stilt, still in position, scraped the right side of my abdomen. When I saw the offending piece, my heart started to pound rapidly—the tip had been cut at a slant to present a flat surface for the upper piece to rest on, so I was looking at a sharp piece of bamboo that could have impaled me. The resulting wound started to bleed immediately, and I cried from the pain. Memories of my brother Ed's death from an abdomen wound flashed through my mind, and I feared the worst. I was frantic—the wound did not stop bleeding, and I was too scared to go home, knowing my mother would be very, very upset. My playmates were equally frightened and did not know what to do. After a few minutes, we mustered the courage to look more closely at the ugly gash that ran from the groin to my waist and saw, to our relief, that it was not deep. Fearing an angry reaction from Mom for my recklessness, I decided to keep the episode secret—I sneaked into our bedroom, changed my clothes, and pretended that nothing had happened. Somehow I pulled off the deception that evening; unfortunately, Mom discovered my bloodstained clothes the following morning, and I had to tell her about the accident. To my relief, she did not show any emotion as she examined the wound. But, after she had satisfied herself that it was not as bad as she first had feared, she became angry with me for trying to hide the episode from her. Almost immediately, however, she calmed down and hugged me tightly, saying that we should thank God that the wound was not more serious.

Mom made it clear that while I waited for my wound to heal I was not to participate in activities that involved running, tree climbing, or jumping into the river. I entertained myself at home, playing with Princess and Johnny, the young pig Mom purchased from a local farmer. Although we could still find chicken and seafood, beef was almost nonexistent, and pork was becoming increasingly scarce. Mom was fortunate in procuring this piglet and planned to make adobo and tapa and preserve the rest of the cooked meat in lard, as Peach had done in Tagana-an. However, over the months we had observed free-roaming pigs in town and on nearby farms foraging for food, and some of their favorite feeding areas were beneath the elevated outhouses on stilts that were common to most households. We decided to feed Johnny ourselves and keep a watchful eye on him until he was ready to be butchered. We kept him tethered under the house, but he was so friendly and playful that Peach and I could not resist bringing him upstairs so he could move about freely. It was amusing to watch him try to interact with Princess, who did not appreciate having her domain invaded by this strange, grunting creature. Johnny loved to have his stomach stroked, and whenever Peach or I approached, he immediately lay on his back so we could rub his tummy with our toes.

During this period of curtailed activities, one or two of my girl friends often came to visit. We played games in the cool area under the house. Princess loved accompanying us, plopping herself down on the cool, hard-packed earth for a snooze. I kept the space clean by sweeping it with a stick broom, made of a large bunch of mature coconut frond spines. We particularly enjoyed a game called *sungka* (*chongka* in other parts of the world), usually played on a wooden game board with two parallel rows of seven holes each and a larger hole at each end, into which small stones (or shells) are deposited as the game progresses. Lacking a game board, we dug the appropriate holes in the hard-packed earth under the house and used small uniform-sized cowrie shells we had collected at the beach. The game involved repetitive scooping of shells from the holes with our fingers and depositing them in other holes in succession, and it could go on for hours before someone won, after which we trotted off to the river to wash our hands and remove the dirt that had accumulated under our fingernails.

We often stopped to watch the older boys shooting stones at birds with their slingshots, made from selected Y-shaped branches of the guava tree (formed when a branch split to grow two new ones of equal size). They cut the requisite elastic strips from old inner tubes. One day I borrowed one to show Mom, hoping I could have one made for me. As I demonstrated my ability to shoot stones at various objects, it became obvious I had no control over the direction or distance of my missiles, and her answer was a firm "No."

Peach turned thirteen on July 25, 1943. We celebrated the event with a special dinner and some local treats that were still available at the sari-sari stores. As a child, Peach had been considered mature for her age and now, as a young teenager, she readily assumed the role of Mom's right arm, with adult responsibilities. Although there were several young people her age in town, household chores always kept her too busy for any fun. I remember that one of her favorite pastimes while at home at the mine was reading, but there were no books or other reading materials readily available in Claver, and I do not remember seeing any paper or pencils around my friends' homes. News of the Japanese soldiers looting and burning homes had prompted those residents who remained in town to store most of their belongings at the homes of relatives or friends in the interior.

I sometimes went exploring on my own. While on an excursion into a nearby banana grove, I came upon the grandmother of one of my friends, a friendly old lady who usually had some kind of homemade stubby cigar (*tinamboy* in the local dialect) dangling from her mouth. As I approached, I could see that she was making several of these short cigars, using crushed dried banana leaves wrapped in a piece of banana leaf that was also dry but still pliable. She smiled at me and asked if I would like to try one. At first I refused, remembering Dad's rule that the boys could not smoke until they were twenty-one (although I remember them sneaking cigarettes behind our house at the mine and behind the dorm at school) and we girls were not to smoke at all. However, I could not resist the offer. Surprisingly, the cigar had a strange, sweetish flavor, not as unpleasant as I had imagined. My elderly friend and I sat smoking together as she taught me how to roll my own. Occasionally, I indulged in this pastime, but only when I was by myself; for reasons I could not understand, none of my friends smoked.

We saw little of Dad while he was wrestling with his additional duties as food control administrator. Of the various duties assigned to him by the 110th Division, the job of food control administrator was the most difficult. Surigao province was an exporter of palay to neighboring provinces. As the war went on, it was important to maintain the availability of palay to the guerrillas throughout the region. The approximate strength of the 110th Division numbered some three hundred officers and over five thousand enlisted personnel, mostly Filipino. Since rice was the staple of their diet, it was imperative that a steady supply of it be available to them.

To further complicate my father's dealing with the palay problem, several factors conspired to make the supply system uncertain. First, the Japanese Army was sending buyers deeper into the province to buy up the stores of palay. For them, this foodstuff was used as a weapon—they attempted to withhold it from Filipinos who did not cooperate or collaborate. In addition, merchants unscrupulously bought up existing stocks of palay at low prices and then sold high when shortages developed. And the guerrilla organization itself presented difficulties; some units occasionally seized supplies of palay without coordinating with my father. At one point, Dad wanted to resign this duty because of the friction developing within units of the 114th Infantry Regiment. However, McClish prevailed upon him to continue.

Despite McClish's support, Dad's preoccupation and frustration with his food control responsibilities continued to mount. Coordination became more and more difficult; in August and September, a flurry of memorandums dealt with the problems associated with procuring, storing, and transporting palay. The basic issue that confronted my father was balancing the food requirements of the whole division against the parochial needs of the 114th Infantry Regiment. Surigao province was the rice bowl of the region; however, it was also the operational area for the 114th. It is understandable that when the regiment's rations were low, its officers took matters into their own hands to ensure their soldiers were getting sufficient food. Food requirements for other units in the division and coordination with my father were not high on the 114th's list of priorities. This breakdown in coordination over the distribution of palay was a recurring problem, requiring McClish to periodically remind the regimental officers that Dad was the divisional officer responsible for its procurement, control, and distribution. Since over five thousand Filipino troops in the 110th Division required rice in their daily ration, rice imports into the Agusan Valley were vital for their daily sustenance—indeed, survival—and palay from Surigao province was an important aspect of this logistical requirement.

According to Hank, the guerrillas were both excited by news of arms, ammunition, and other supplies arriving by submarine from Australia and also discouraged by the length of time it took for these badly needed supplies to filter down to their ranks. The problem, of course, was transportation; the Tenth Military District headquarters was having difficulties moving military supplies landed from SPYRON missions to the various divisions. Whether by land or sea, transporting these supplies was fraught with danger. As an example, on September 3 a transportation convoy, commanded by Lieutenant Michael Pritz, was ambushed by a Japanese patrol en route to Medina, headquarters of the 110th Division. Pritz was killed in this attack, and the supplies fell into the hands of the Japanese. Fortunately for the guerrillas, another SPYRON mission arrived shortly thereafter with additional supplies. Included in this shipment were a 100-watt navy transmitter and navy codes. This enabled the Tenth Military District's FRS to send flash messages to Perth, Australia, and Pearl Harbor whenever local coast watchers sighted Japanese shipping moving in the waters around Mindanao. These sightings were then relayed to nearby U.S. Navy submarines.

In early September 1943, Rudy and Hank were with their commanding officer, Bill Knortz, at the 114th Regiment headquarters in Claver when word came that weapons, ammunition, and rations were available at the 110th Division headquarters at Medina. Hank clearly remembers Knortz saying: "A submarine has landed with supplies. I'm going to take the *Albert McCarthy* to division headquarters and get the 114th's share." Knortz told Rudy and Hank to stay put in Claver while he and three others took the launch to Medina. To reach Medina by sea they had to travel north from Claver, up the eastern coast and around the northern tip of Surigao province (past Japanese-occupied Surigao), then south along the western coast to Oriental Misamis. After arriving safely at Medina, Knortz learned that the Japanese had captured the entire shipment. Departing Medina, he continued on to the 10th Military District headquarters in Liangan, Lanao province, for the much-needed supplies. Successful, Knortz headed back to Claver, reversing the route he had used earlier. As the *Albert McCarthy* passed through the area near Cagayan, a Japanese patrol boat spotted it. Knortz headed out to open sea, but the water was rough and he decided to head toward Camiguin Island instead. While the launch moved by the island, a *chabasco* (sudden squall) arose. These squalls occur frequently in the waters around Mindanao and usually dissipate as quickly as they appear. Unfortunately, the launch, laden almost to the gunwale with supplies, capsized. Immediately afterward, Knortz told his men to stay with the debris while he swam to Camiguin Island to get help. He was a powerful swimmer and felt confident that he could reach shore. Sadly, that was the last time he was seen alive. The three survivors floated for hours, clinging to oil drums until the tide finally brought them to land.

Of course, members of the 114th were devastated by Knortz's death, particularly my brothers, who looked to him as a heroic figure and role model. Perhaps that is why Rudy, when more weapons were later available, went into action with a BAR—Knortz's favorite weapon. After this tragic mishap, Mc Clish sent the boys and their fellow soldiers a message by runner, asking if they wanted to stay on with the 114th until a new commanding officer could be appointed, or go back and join his command in Medina. They decided to return to Medina. When they arrived, they were assigned to the Special Troops battalion of the 110th Division, with which they would be involved in a number of special operations later in the war.

Fortunately for the guerrilla forces on Mindanao, the SPYRON missions continued. They brought in military supplies and evacuated military personnel and civilians on their return trips. On September 29, the USS *Bowfin* arrived on the north coast of Lanao province with additional supplies. This particular trip is noteworthy because Lieutenant Colonel Luis Morgan, Fertig's former chief of staff, a very important figure in the initial phases of organizing the guerrilla force on Mindanao, was one of the guerrillas sent to Australia on its outgoing trip. This was an executive decision on Fertig's part; the two leaders had major administrative differences regarding the way the guerrilla war on Mindanao was conducted, and this was how Fertig solved the problem. Sam Grashio, one of the DAPECOL escapees, was another passenger leaving on the submarine.

Among my father's records was a handwritten letter from Jack Hawkins to Paul Marshall and Bob Spielman, reporting the successful departure of three of their fellow escapees on an earlier submarine trip. While Hawkins could not directly say that Dyess, McCoy, and Mellnik had been evacuated by submarine, he indicated that their request for repatriation to the United States via Australia had been successful. (Hawkins himself was evacuated to Australia by submarine in November 1943.) Also mentioned was Tom Baxter, wounded during the skirmish that killed Albert McCarthy. Hawkins noted the importance of rice to the survival of the guerrillas and exhorted Bill Knortz to get the local farmers planting. (This note was written about a month before Knortz's death.) He stressed that the farmers in Surigao province must be reimbursed in a timely manner for the rice they were providing the guerrillas. Hawkins chronicled his World War II experiences in his book, *Never Say Die*.

Shofner and Dobervich left with Hawkins in November, two months after Grashio was evacuated. (Shofner, until his departure, was the deputy chief of staff for the 110th Division.) Unfortunately, Boelens was killed in a guerrilla action in the town of Baroy in January 1944. Marshall and Spielman remained with the guerrillas on Mindanao, serving with the 114th Infantry Regiment of the 110th Division.

The high tonnage of supplies arriving on the SPYRON missions dictated that these be absorbed quickly into the guerrilla logistical system. Each division in the Tenth Military District had weaknesses in its respective operational area with regard to supporting the growing logistical flow. The 105th (Zamboanga) was too cut off to stage supplies to the other parts of the island. The 106th (Cotabato), the 108th (Lanao), and the 109th (Bukidnon) all had a large Japanese troop presence, as did Davao province (the future operational area of the 107th).

Fertig's Tenth Military District headquarters in Liangan, Lanao province, was becoming increasingly exposed to the Japanese presence in that area. Moreover, the supplies coming in required movement over land, a dangerous and time-consuming process. In October 1943, Fertig moved his headquarters to Esperanza in the Agusan Valley, an area controlled by the 110th Division. SPYRON missions arriving at the mouth of the Agusan River could take advantage of the river's extensive tributaries. Moreover, bancas and other small craft could quickly move the precious SPYRON cargo to protected areas on the upper reaches of the river.

The FRS operation, with its expanding message traffic, was also moved and collocated with the new headquarters. Even so, Fertig decided to establish a backup headquarters in the Misamis area. Colonel Robert Bowler, commander of the 105th Division, would head this reserve headquarters and the necessary FRS backup. This reserve headquarters was designated as "A" Corps.

Fertig brought experienced personnel into the guerrilla organization who insisted that the organization abide by rules and regulations found in regular U.S. Army units, despite their being an irregular force. A communication from Lieutenant Colonel McClish underscored the theme of responsibility.

This memorandum said a lot about the command and control of the guerrilla organization that made up the Tenth Military District. It expressed the concept of responsibility, regardless of how palay ultimately flowed to the guerrillas. Money authorized by President Quezon was being paid to palay growers. Thus, it was incumbent on guerrilla officers within the 110th Division to ensure that monies expended for palay were properly accounted for. I would guess that no other guerrilla organization in the Philippines during the Japanese occupation paid as much attention to the concept of responsibility and accountability as did the Tenth Military District. This official concern for accountability underscored the quality of leadership within the command.

The control of palay was a new program in the division, and all parties had not yet implemented the working details. Beginning in October 1943, it and other food commodities played an increasingly important role in the Agusan Valley.

As food control administrator, my father implemented a plan to transport palay to the Agusan Valley by means of a flotilla of bancas. It is possible that this operation involved bancas and banceros Dad had contracted for during his trip to the Ninth Military District in Leyte. To maintain control of the shipments and discourage smuggling of this precious commodity, my father sent out a letter to mayors in Surigao province regarding the enforcement of food control regulations.

SUBJECT: Inspection of Bancas
TO: All Outposts and Military Mayors of Surigao
In order to enforce the rules and regulations of the Food Control Administration, the following should be complied with:

1. Bancas passing through your territory should be stopped and investigated as to permits having been granted them by the military authorities.
2. All bancas loaded with palay must have an export permit signed by the food control administrator or his authorized agents stating source of palay, quantity and destination.
3. Only designated persons or officers are authorized to sign export permits.

Any banca owner who does not have a permit signed by the above named persons is considered as a smuggler and his banca and palay should be confiscated and sent to headquarters under escort for investigation.

The letter also included a list of officers authorized to sign export permits. Until the Japanese exerted more control over the coastal waterways, which they did starting in late 1943, the movement of palay by banca was critical to supplying the guerrillas with their daily food requirements. Those traders not obtaining export permits for this cargo would be transporting it at their own peril. Dad's letter to the military mayors was to put them on notice as to the consequences of shipping within the guerrilla area of control without permits.

Palay from Surigao province continued to be an important part of the 110th Division's logistical requirement; a memorandum dated October 11, 1943, from Childress to Dad outlined the future resupply concept of operations.

Captain Hansen:

1. Due to the increased Japanese action in Surigao and also because of the vulnerability of the lumbering "Treasure Island" to enemy attack on the long way around the Surigao point to the east coast, that launch will no longer make the rice haul from the east coast.
2. The back door of the Agusan River is being opened up. I am personally opening up the road.
3. It is desired that you make arrangements to ship rice to Lianga. Write to me in care of Captain Khodr in Cabadbaran your estimate on this new change. I am leaving immediately for Lianga by way of the Agusan River. You could meet me in Cabadbaran about the eighteenth of this month and then go to Lianga yourself by way of the river. Good transportation will be on the river at that time. We could then arrange a system of bodegas, etc.

This communication outlined some of the resupply problems confronting the guerrillas. Clearly the Japanese were putting pressure on the maritime supply route around the northern point of Surigao province; thus, it was becoming increasingly difficult to ship rice via launch. Now it would have to be transported across the Diuata Mountains. Also, resupply of ammunition from the 110th Division quartermaster had to traverse the same route, in the opposite direction. In short, the Japanese had forced the guerrillas to resort to land resupply using mainly cargadores to actually handle the supplies through and around the mountains from Agusan province to the 114th Infantry Regiment's operational areas in Surigao province. Toward the end of 1943, the Japanese were expanding their force structure throughout Mindanao in earnest, thus prompting Fertig to move the district's headquarters and FRS from Liangan, Lanao province, to Esperanza in the Agusan Valley. Even there both Fertig's headquarters and the 110th Division elements were feeling pressure from the Japanese in two directions. Japanese Army forces were coming up the Agusan Valley from the Butuan area, and other Japanese units were pushing from Davao toward the headwaters of the Agusan River.

With food supplies dwindling, Dad's procurement responsibilities made it necessary for him to travel farther and farther away from the Claver area. On a trip to the headquarters of the 110th Division, he found Rudy and Hank in the division hospital, both suffering from malaria. The hospital had a limited supply of Atabrine tablets and Hank recalls the doctor personally ensuring that each patient swallowed his daily tablet. However, because food was woefully inadequate, the patients were too weak to combat the disease. Dad decided to move the boys to Claver so Mom could give them the personal attention they needed. It meant giving up the Atabrine, but Dad had heard that malaria could also be treated with the bark of the *cinchona* tree (origin of quinine). He loaded the boys onto a two-wheeled cart pulled by a carabao and started the long trip northward along Route 1. The trip was slow and grueling, and when they reached Bacuag the cart could not move through the terrain. Rudy and Hank were then loaded onto an abandoned baroto and pulled along the narrow trail by the carabao, sled-style, down to Gigaquit. From that point they moved by banca to Claver.

I remember the day Dad arrived in Claver with my brothers.

"Hon," he said to Mom, "I've brought the boys home—take care of them."

Mom was shocked at the boys' appearance. They were very thin and weak, and their skin had a sallow, yellowish appearance. Peach and I could not believe that these were the same boys who had eagerly gone off to join the guerrillas just a few short months before.

Several people in town had experience in treating malaria and helped us identify the cinchona trees that grew in the forested areas not far from Claver. When we found a tree, we cut some leaves and several strips of its bark to bring home to Mom, who boiled them for about an hour and then served the resulting brew to Rudy and Hank as a tea. It was bitter, but she insisted that they drink it. To build up their strength, Mom prepared hearty fare—mostly chicken, but also seafood or pork when available, with boiled rice and vegetables. She also gave them chicken broth between meals. I was glad that they were home with us but also confused by the effects of malaria on their physical condition. They were weak when they arose in the morning, but after a bit of breakfast they perked up. A short while after their morning dose of the cinchona brew, Mom coaxed them into having some chicken broth because she knew that by midday the chills and fever would start, and they would have to lie down on the mats on the floor in their room and cover themselves with their coarse olive-drab Army blankets. It was hard for me to believe that they could be shivering under several layers of blankets in the noonday tropical heat. They gradually stopped shivering, only to start sweating profusely. Mom and Peach mopped up the perspiration, helped them change into fresh clothes, and, when they felt strong enough to sit up, Mom offered them sustenance. Afterward, they again drank the bitter brew, and by evening they felt well enough to have dinner before an early bedtime. For the first couple of weeks, nothing changed, causing Mom great concern. However, in succeeding weeks the boys noticeably improved with each passing day.

As Rudy and Hank slowly recuperated, their appetites picked up, and Mom decided that the time had come for Johnny to fulfill his mission in life. With heavy hearts, we watched him being taken away by the local butcher. The boys had grown accustomed to his visits but did not feel the same attachment as Peach and I did—we could only watch as Rudy and Hank enjoyed the delicious and nourishing pork dishes Mom prepared for them. Johnny had endeared himself to us, and a feeling of sadness swept over me as I removed the fly eggs from the tapa drying in the sun, mindful of the fact that each piece was a bit of our late pet. Mom's assurances that Johnny had played a very important role in my brothers' recovery offered little consolation.

After several weeks, the boys were done with the chills and sweating episodes and, although still weak and thin, were almost their normal selves again.

This made me feel better about Johnny's sacrifice. As the boys slowly regained their strength, they grew restless. To break the monotony, Mom allowed them to take short walks around the town area so they could chat with fellow guerrillas and catch up on the latest news. It was my bad luck that on one of his walks Hank happened to meet me on the path through the banana grove as I was smoking a newly rolled tinamboy. He scolded me soundly but said he would not tell Mom if I promised not to smoke anymore. Greatly relieved, I vowed without hesitation.

On day we were surprised and pleased when Romana came to visit, accompanied by her husband, Simon, and little daughter, Rosalinda; she had learned of our whereabouts through the local grapevine and wanted us to meet her family. She gave me a hug and remarked on how much I had grown. A lot had happened to all of us since we had said our good-byes, and it took a long while to get caught up. She and Simon listened in amazement as we recounted the adventures of that first year in hiding. After they left, we were filled with nostalgia, as we remembered our carefree life at East Mindanao before the war.

As the boys recuperated under Mom's care, Dad continued his liaison and procurement activities for the 110th Division. His report to division headquarters dated October 18, 1943, outlined the military pressure the Japanese were exerting on coastal towns such as Placer and Amuslog (written as "Amoslop" in the report). He is very descriptive in his efforts and frustrations in trying to determine the exact magnitude of the Japanese effort to take control of the coastal towns such as Amuslog, located some twenty kilometers south of Surigao. When reports came to Dad in Claver on October 3 that Japanese had landed a number of troops in Placer, fifteen kilometers to the north, he set off at first light for Amuslog to assess the Japanese landing force. Arriving in the Placer-Amuslog area, his first action was to locate the 114th Infantry Regiment commander, Lieutenant Spielman. His subordinates did not know his location; however, they reported that between two hundred and three hundred Japanese troops had landed but were now in Placer. Since the reported landing three days earlier, no scouting parties had been dispatched. This lack of action disturbed Dad. He immediately led a party to scout the area. In the vicinity of Placer they ascertained that the Japanese presence was essentially a 150-man working party taking oil from the storage tank owned by East Mindanao, filling fifty gallon drums and loading them onto the "M/S Mawayan" for transport to Surigao. Other Japanese soldiers were searching for lumber.

Upon returning to regimental headquarters, Dad met with Lieutenant Spielman. The following day they received a message reporting that between three hundred and four hundred Japanese troops had landed in Placer and were moving southward along the coastal road toward Claver. During an officers' meeting at regimental headquarters it was decided to summon all available guerrillas from regional outposts and concentrate them in the Placer area. Two separate scouting parties reported that the Japanese presence was exaggerated; even so, the assembled guerrilla force of 135 men would be able to engage them. Dad led the attack from the north and Spielman from the south. Dad's party dispersed the Japanese troops around the oil storage tank and disabled a machine gun position on top of the tank. Spielman's attack from the south faltered and his group suffered four wounded.

Dad summarized the six-day action against the Japanese presence as follows:

- Japanese activity in the Placer area was very much exaggerated. Their presence there was to extract the crude oil from the storage tank.
- The guerrilla intelligence on the Japanese presence was distorted and based on hearsay information. Also, Japanese propaganda may have been a factor in the faulty intelligence.
- The behavior of guerrilla officers and soldiers under fire needed remedial action.

It must have infuriated Dad to see the Japanese helping themselves to crude oil from East Mindanao's tank in Placer. Six months earlier, Dad had been making procurement arrangements with the USFIP forces in Surigao, but the shortage of oil containers and the early May surrender order put an end to it. Thus, planning and executing the attack on enemy forces in Placer in the early morning of October 10, 1943, likely gave my father an extra measure of satisfaction.

Two days after Dad wrote the report, he met with Fertig in the town of Amparo, not far from the new location of the Tenth Military District in Esperanza. At this meeting, he briefed Fertig on developments in Surigao province and the loss of Placer to the Japanese. In Fertig's meticulously detailed personal diary from January 1942 to May 1945, two short sentences appear among his entries for 20 October 1943: "Capt. Hansen, an old American blowhard arrived from Surigao with a story of the debacle at the battle of Placer. I learn much without effort."[1] It was interesting to read Fertig's description of Dad as a "blowhard" because my father was not a boaster or braggart by nature. As a civilian, he had run a disciplined operation at the power plant at East

Mindanao where negligence could not tolerated—in the mining industry, as in military operations, a lackadaisical attitude could lead to disaster. Furthermore, as an old Army hand, he would have been a stickler for appropriate military tactics and following proper procedures, as borne out by the way he carried out his orders and responsibilities as a guerrilla leader. I can only conclude that during this meeting Dad was passionately venting his frustration with regard to the conduct of the guerrillas during the attack on Placer ten days earlier. The slight hint of sarcasm in Fertig's second sentence seemed to indicate that he was not too receptive to Dad's assessment of the "debacle" (it is not clear whether this was Fertig's or Dad's term). In hundreds of pages of Fertig's personal diary, this was the only reference to a meeting between him and my father that I could find. Fortunately, Dad worked independently, thereby avoiding a possible personality clash with Fertig that might have resulted in Dad being sent to Australia on the next submarine—Fertig's way of resolving problems or conflicts with his officers.

Although we were preoccupied with the Japanese threat in our own backyard, world news briefs, often compiled by signal corps personnel, brought us news about war in other parts of the world, making our family and friends feel we were not alone in our confrontation with the Japanese.

A November 12, 1943, news report on Armed Forces Radio, copied by the FRS, brought us an update on the war in other parts of the world. It meant a lot to us because it conveyed hope that there was progress being made against the Axis powers. While we were concerned with the Japanese forces in our backyard, others across the globe were also confronting an enemy. For example, India-based Royal Air Force planes were destroying Japanese aircraft in Burma. Closer to home, Allied aircraft were bringing destruction to Japanese airfields in New Guinea. American Marines were also having success against Japanese troops on Bougainville Island. Reports like these brought hope to us living behind Japanese lines.

News from the outside world meant very much to my family. Earlier in the war we had felt abandoned, as if we had been left to deal with the Japanese on our own. Now, news about the war on other fronts gave us a feeling of unity and hope that we would soon be liberated.

Toward the end of 1943 a report written by my father raised his concerns about a negative shift in the attitude of a portion of the local populace that was detrimental to his procurement efforts. He also noted that the sentiment of the people had decidedly changed in the past month. If not pro-Japanese, they had become at least cool toward the guerrillas, perhaps in part because of the draconian measures the Japanese were instituting against civilians who provided any aid or comfort to the guerrillas. Increasingly, people in various parts of the province were inclined not to furnish the guerrillas with food (palay) even though they were paid in cash for such transactions. Still, it was a situation of great concern to Dad as liaison and procurement officer. He recommended that the division develop a cadre of trusted guerrillas who could conduct a propaganda program to sway the local people in favor of the aims of the guerrilla movement. These rumors were especially persistent in the Tandag-Tago region, the biggest rice-producing area of Surigao province.

While Dad's sampling of public sentiment in the province was not precise, he sensed that the Japanese were making some inroads among a small portion of the population. His worry was that Japanese threats against those who supported the guerrillas were beginning to affect both the farmers and the middlemen involved in the palay trade. But of real concern to the guerrilla movement was that the Japanese agents had been effective in buying up supplies that might otherwise have gone to the guerrilla forces.

SEVEN

The Japanese Expand Their Operations against the Guerrillas

Rumors of additional Japanese troops landing on Mindanao continued to fly. Moreover, Japanese military units were now staying longer in areas they had previously only given token visits. As previously mentioned, Japanese forces were putting pressure on the guerrilla capability to move supplies by sea. Were developments all a part of the Japanese grand design to neutralize the guerrilla presence in the 110th Division's operational area of responsibility? A report my father sent to division headquarters may have had some relevance to the attack by the Japanese that we experienced a few days later in Claver.

In this report, dated November 28, 1943, Dad notes that the 114th Infantry regimental headquarters had received and passed on to the 110th Division headquarters reports of large numbers of Japanese troops landing in Surigao province as well as the island of Leyte to the north. Major Childress dispatched him to verify these reports. Upon arrival in Claver he found the information to be without foundation; however, it was confirmed that the Japanese were active in moving small numbers of troops to areas to which they had not previously deployed. The last item he reported stands out: "On the 24th of November two launches came to Claver, one a big one and the other a small one. They came right to the mouth of the river, stayed for around half an hour and took one banca which was anchored in the mouth of the river and took it to Surigao."

One item of Dad's report would have been especially disturbing to him on both military and personal bases; the increased activity of Japanese launches in particular indicated that they were on the move, confirming that their campaign to extend their control over the coastal regions south of Surigao was gaining momentum. Hank remembers being with Dad, Rudy, and many others on the banks of the river observing the two Japanese launches.

"Looks like they're up to something," Dad said to the boys.

While it was not clear whether the Japanese troops had simply paused during a routine maritime patrol for a quick look in the direction of the town or were actively reconnoitering the area in preparation for an impending raid, this brief foray into an area so close to the 114th Infantry Regiment's headquarters raised the alert level to a higher degree. According to Hank, guerrilla forces doubled the number of sentries at the various lookout points covering both maritime and land routes into Claver.

Until now our family had done reasonably well in evading the Japanese forces. However, as the end of 1943 approached, they had significantly strengthened their presence on the island and had increased the ferocity of their attacks against the guerrillas. Moreover, the Japanese commander for Mindanao issued a proclamation to the effect that any Americans found on the island would be summarily executed and anyone caught helping them would meet a similar fate. True to their word, particularly when they found a guerrilla, American or Filipino, the Japanese forces immediately executed him, usually by beheading. Afterward, they put the head of the dead person on a stake in the town plaza to demonstrate to the people the consequences of resisting Japanese occupation or aiding their enemies. Albert McCarthy, killed by the Japanese in an ambush, was treated exactly this way.

After our move to Claver, Mom and Dad believed we were relatively safe under the protective umbrella of the 114th Infantry Regiment headquartered there, especially while Dad was away on his liaison-procurement trips. However, this recent visit of the enemy launches forced them to see that it was only a matter of time before the Japanese forces extended their control into our area. Once again, we had to find another hiding place. Our designated bakwitan could serve as a temporary refuge but because of its proximity to the town was unsuitable for a long-term stay. Furthermore, a radio station had recently been established at the top of the hill, utilizing equipment delivered by the SPYRON missions. While the transmitter site was certainly logical, Dad was concerned that its location above our bakwitan would compromise the security of our little sanctuary. Still, there were no specific indications of an imminent attack, and the 114th had its warning systems in place, so my parents decided that we could stay put in Claver until Dad's return from his upcoming trip to Cantilan, where he was taking Rudy and Hank to consult with Dr. Castro, a civilian doctor serving the guerrillas, for an evaluation of their recovery from malaria and release for return to duty. Dad also planned to meet with local officials there regarding procurement matters and potential hiding places for us. The best option for us was to move southward, where numerous small towns and barrios located along the coast could provide safe havens. The mountainous areas to the west were sparsely populated, with the exception of some shy, reclusive hill tribes that kept to themselves and did not mingle with the general population.

The lifestyle I had grown to enjoy in Claver came to a sudden halt on November 30, 1943, when, very early in the morning, we were all rudely awakened by explosions so loud and powerful that our house shook. We were told that several Japanese ships had been deployed to the Claver area and were shelling the town with 5-inch guns.

The previous evening Dad had taken the *Henry Joy* to a location on the southern side of a point of land near Claver in preparation for an early departure for Cantilan the next morning. Fortunately, he, Rudy, and Hank had departed at dawn as planned, heading south and hidden from view by the jutting point; otherwise, they would have found themselves in the jaws of the attack. This totally unexpected mode of attack threw everyone into a panic. With the 114th's headquarters staff on high alert, those of us living there expected that there would be sufficient advance warning of a Japanese incursion, by land or by sea, to execute an orderly retreat to prearranged hiding places. That was not the scenario this morning. When the shells started raining down, Mom, Peach, and I went into our evacuation drill. My first responsibility was carrying the precious first-aid jug; second, I was to ensure that Princess was always with us, carrying her if necessary. Mom and Peach hastily packed their bundles, and we fled in the direction of our bakwitan up the hill. My heart was pounding, not just from the exertion of running as fast as I could but also from fright as the deafening explosions made the earth under my feet tremble. I had heard gunfire many times before, but nothing compared to the big booms followed a few seconds later by loud explosions that made us instinctively duck our heads. We learned that the shells were coming from ships offshore, but at that time we did not know whether there were also Japanese troops positioned on the outskirts of town, ready to march in and capture us all.

The arrival of Japanese forces in Claver, while sooner than expected, was not surprising, but the magnitude of the attack was astonishing. The guerrilla radio station at the top of the hill where we were heading complicated our situation. Robert Spielman, deputy of the 114th at the time, recalled the incident in his thesis on the history of the 114th Infantry Regiment.

"This action by the Japanese was more impressive than usual. A Japanese cruiser and several small craft shelled the town and the surrounding hills. They sent landing craft with assault troops ashore and moved inland to a distance of about three miles. Only two of our men were killed but the administrative personnel had to move quickly in order to get back into the hills before getting cut off.

"Our radio station on top of the hill was captured and some of the equipment destroyed. We could not understand what prompted the Japanese attack on Claver but after talking to our radio operator the cause was quite clear. Our radio operator had been in the merchant marine for several years before the war and was a radio 'ham'.

"The day by day operation was boring. To break the monotony he would get on one of the Japanese wavelengths and jam it. This was great fun, but the Japanese took a fix on the radio station and sent a force to destroy it."[1]

The prolonged shelling of the town and the surrounding hills indicated to Mom that this was not the usual Japanese raid on a coastal area but a serious attack directed specifically against the guerrillas in Claver and possibly the radio station on the hill. She also feared that Dad and the boys had been intercepted and captured by the Japanese forces as their ships headed toward Claver early that morning. For the moment, however, she had to focus on the safety of her girls. Even though our bakwitan was not readily visible from the path that led to the radio station, it was too close for comfort, so she pondered our options. Going deeper into the forested area was the only viable choice. Before abandoning the bakwitan, we threw all our belongings out the back window into the bushes that clung to the downward slope. If the Japanese did go to the radio station and stumble upon our hiding spot, Mom did not want them to find anything that indicated recent occupation, for they would surely conduct a search of the area. It started to rain when we left the hut. As the rain continued, we followed a small creek bed and took shelter under some big leaves of the gabi plant and remained hunkered down, listening intently and praying that we would not hear boots approaching. After a while we found ourselves squatting in water that was starting to flow through the creek bed, so we followed a trail leading deeper into the jungle to a small nipa hut. No one came to greet us as we approached, and when we entered the hut we discovered that the occupants had left in a hurry, their morning meal set out on long banana leaves spread on the bamboo floor. They must have fled when the shelling began. There were remnants of some dried fish and boiled ground corn. Since we had not eaten since the previous evening, we helped ourselves to the remaining corn.

I don't know how long we stayed there, drenched and shivering, but we had heard no sounds of shelling, or any other activity, for quite some time. The rain had stopped as well, so Mom decided to take Peach with her back to the rear of the bakwitan to determine whether there was any activity along the path and/or whether we could safely retrieve some of the items we had thrown out. Mom asked me to stay at the hut while they were gone, promising to return as quickly as possible. I was confused and frightened and started to protest, but Mom convinced me that they could travel faster without me (and Princess). Mom had cautioned me to keep out of sight, but after a while I could not resist the urge to sneak a peek at the trail. I had been clutching Princess and holding onto the old jug since we left our home in Claver. Setting Princess down, I knelt just to the right of the window and cautiously moved my face toward the lower corner until I could see the path with my left eye. I have no idea how long I held this position, my heart seemed to be pounding in my ears, and I recognized that same feeling of fear that I first experienced when we left the mine, only it was not a mere twinge—this time I thought I would throw up at any moment. I tried to calm myself down by repeating the prayers I had learned in catechism class.

Finally, after what seemed like an eternity, I saw Mom and Peach walking down the path toward the hut with their arms filled with some of our belongings. All was well with my world again! Mom and I both cried with relief when she came into the hut; we hugged each other, and she told me how proud she was that I had been so brave and responsible.

Peach then told me that they had ventured all the way to the path that led to the radio station, looked down toward Claver, and saw that the harbor was empty—the Japanese ships were gone! Mom and Peach did not know it at the time, but only a few hours earlier, when we were crouched under the gabi leaves, just as Mom had feared might happen, Japanese troops had hiked on that same path to the radio station and put it out of action. Possibly because it was raining hard while we were in the creek bed, we had heard nothing and were unaware that Japanese troops had been on the path just a short distance from our position—twice!

We headed for Claver late in the afternoon and soon met up with a few of our neighbors who had returned to their homes. They confirmed that all the

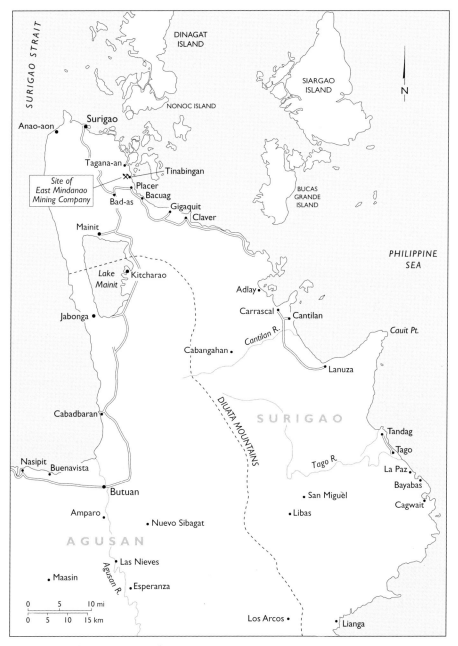

Map 1: Northern Surigao and Agusan provinces

Map 2: Southeast Asia

Above: Mom as young wife and mother, Manila, 1923.
Left: Dad holding me as baby, Manila, early 1935.

Hansen family photo, Manila, late 1935.

Dad with workers at Asiatic Philippines sawmill, Iligan, Lanao, 1938.

"The girls" (Ginger and Peach), Surigao, 1939.

East Mindanao Mining Company officials at mining site, 1940. Fred Varney, manager, is at left; Dad is third from left.

"The boys" (Ed, Hank, and Rudy), Manila, 1941.

Hank (right) and Rudy (second from left) with mineworkers at East Mindanao Mining Company, 1941.

Hank, me, Peach (holding Bucky's hands), Boots, Mom, and Rudy in front of
our home at East Mindanao mine site, November 1941. Note Princess in right
foreground.

Young Edward, Manila, 1946.

Peach and me during visit to Sydney, Australia, in 2001.

Japanese soldiers indeed had left on the ships—but not before inflicting terrific damage on the town as punishment for hosting a guerrilla operation. The troops dispatched by Japanese forces to find and destroy the radio station had also ransacked the town. We were shocked to see what had happened to the church and the homes of some of our neighbors and friends. Someone mentioned casualties but could not provide details. Mom was almost frantic as she sought information about Dad, Rudy, and Hank. It was encouraging that no one had come forward with any news of the fate of the *Henry Joy* or its passengers—if Dad and the boys had been captured, the Japanese surely would have paraded them around town, as was their custom with prisoners, alive or dead.

After the Japanese attack, it became obvious that we could not remain in Claver. The guerrillas at the 114th's headquarters were gone, and the Japanese could return at any time to establish control. Mom therefore decided to head south toward Cantilan, hoping to meet up with Dad and the boys. After a restless night in our Claver home, we retrieved our belongings from the bushes behind the bakwitan, spread the linens on some large rocks to dry, then repacked all but essential items in woven straw containers and left them with our landlord. At some point, we passed by the rice mill and Old Timer spotted us. Expecting his dinner, he eagerly approached the fence, but Peach didn't feed him that day. We took a quick glance backward as we left, and he was still looking in our direction, his head held high and cocked at a slight angle, as though puzzled. That was the last time we saw Old Timer.

We weren't the only ones moving southward; we set out on foot in the company of many Filipinos from Claver and other areas who were determined to avoid any contact with the Japanese forces gradually gaining control of the coastal areas south of Surigao. The trip to Cantilan took about a week. Normally such a trip was made entirely by banca, but now that was too dangerous, as Japanese launches were patrolling the coastal areas. Since I could not carry much more than the jug with its valuable contents and, when necessary, Princess, Peach had to take the largest, heaviest straw bundle containing our belongings. Like many of the local women, she learned that it was less tiring to carry her bulky load atop her head rather than in her arms—she alternately reached up with one or the other hand to keep her load balanced. If conditions were favorable and there were boatmen available and willing to take us down the coast, we traveled short distances by sea, hugging the coastline. Whenever we had to round a point, we braced ourselves for rough waters. There was also that little bit of apprehension regarding what might be lurking on the other side of the point. If there happened to be a Japanese patrol boat nearby, it would be almost impossible to reverse course quickly enough to avoid being spotted. On one occasion, our boatmen cut across a narrow point on foot rather than going around it. They simply put in on one side, hoisted the banca up on their shoulders, and walked to the other side, where we reboarded and continued on. After each leg of the trip Mom negotiated with locals to guide us to the next point in our journey, preferably on foot to keep the risks involved with banca travel to a minimum. Since Peach was more fluent in the Surigaonon dialect than Mom, she was a big help during these discussions. Sometimes we paid our way, other times we simply tagged along with other refugees heading in the same direction. Along the route, there were always kind Filipino families willing to share their homes and food with us. No matter how humble the abode, we received the best they had to offer.

While we were making our way southward, Dad and the boys returned to Claver after their trip to Cantilan. They were shocked to see the town virtually deserted, for they had no knowledge of the Japanese attack that had occurred on the morning of their departure. Destruction was widespread. The mature acacia trees that lined the main square were badly damaged, their tops and branches splintered and hanging limply. While the church was still standing, the Japanese soldiers had vandalized it, breaking windows and removing the front doors from their hinges. Inside, the altar had been desecrated and statues smashed. The 114th's headquarters had also been destroyed. Their main concern, however, was finding us; they had no way of knowing that we had departed and were en route to Cantilan. Fortunately, someone informed Dad of our destination, so they immediately headed back to Cantilan. During the trip the boys kept a sharp lookout for possible Japanese patrols. The *Henry Joy* was small, fast, maneuverable, and could be quickly steered toward a secluded cove, should they spy a Japanese launch

Our last major stop before reaching Cantilan was Carrascal, a lovely town larger than Claver. Mom met with local officials and, seeing that we were tired and grimy, one of them invited us to his home to rest before an early dinner. He also insisted that we spend the night before moving on. After washing up with real soap and drying off with a real towel, I was allowed to explore the surroundings of this beautiful home. It was a large house on a wide street and had a well-tended garden with flowers. Purple, white, and magenta bougainvillea blossoms cascaded from a balcony, so bright and dense that they hid the thorny vines underneath. At dinner, I was impressed by the ornately carved furniture in the dining room. The large table was beautifully appointed, and there was an enormous amount of food—bowls of steamed rice and vegetables and some kind of fried meat on a platter. It was a delicious meal, and we ate with gusto. Later on, while Mom and Peach continued talking with the town officials, I wandered off to the kitchen at the rear of the house. The woman who had served the food was eating her meal, and she was surprised and pleased when I told her in Surigaonon that I had enjoyed the food very much. She replied that she was glad to hear it because she wasn't sure that we would like the meat dish she had prepared. Then she pointed to an outside work area, and I realized what she was talking about, for there on a chopping block were the head and hands of a mature monkey. That evening, as we lay under mosquito nets on real beds with soft sheets and pillows, I asked Mom and Peach if they knew we had eaten monkey meat, and they both said "yes" matter-of-factly.

To our great relief, Dad was waiting for us in Cantilan when we finally arrived. We sought refuge at the convent, but it was filled to capacity; in fact, the nuns were also looking for accommodations for several other nuns, fellow refugees from areas to the north. They initially put us up in the local church school but then found a house that could accommodate us all. This house belonged to a woman named Buenafe "Naping" Ayado, the mother of a little boy, who was given the house by her grandmother. Located outside of the town proper and a short distance from a stream, it had a nice front yard with a few chickens roaming around. The house was spacious by local standards and was well furnished, but of course Naping had not anticipated the sudden appearance of so many "houseguests" at her home. Still, she graciously made us all feel welcome and we settled in, grateful for the home environment. Some of her relatives and friends pitched in with extra dishes, cutlery, and woven sleeping mats.

Prior to our arrival in Cantilan, Rudy and Hank, having been cleared by Dr. Castro, had departed and were en route to Rizal to rejoin their Special Troops unit under the 110th Division. Since the Japanese Army was increasingly present along the coast, the boys decided to cross the Diuata Mountains into the Agusan Valley. The terrain between Cantilan and the valley is not the tropical jungle found south of the Agusan basin, where you must cut your way through the jungle (see the map of the Northern Surigao and Agusan provinces). Instead, the boys were hiking through a forest of tall hardwood trees, uphill until the top of the range. The boys each carried a knapsack but they had no rations. At night they used them as pillows and used gathered leaves as mattresses. As they crossed the mountain range, they went without food for a couple of days. Because of hunger, it was difficult to fall asleep, so Hank developed a special technique: he closed his eyes and thought about the Chinese restaurant we used to frequent during vacations in Manila—the Panciteria Nueva, located near the Santa Cruz Plaza. The restaurant's extensive menu included pancit and bola bola—Hank's favorites. In his imagination he would relive those sumptuous dinners, and within a few minutes he felt full and sleep came easily. After they passed the summit, they descended into the valley, at which point they came upon barrios where locals always shared welcome meals with them. Days later, my brothers realized that they had spent their birthdays up in the Diuata Mountains—Rudy's eighteenth and Hank's seventeenth.

Arriving back at division headquarters, they learned that the new commanding officer of Special Troops was Fred Faust. Within days after their return, the Special Troops were on the move. McClish had decided to relocate the 110th Division headquarters from Rizal to Buenavista, northwest of Butuan. Unfortunately, the Japanese had a garrison nearby, which the Special Troops were assigned to neutralize. Faust had the unit deployed along the road between Buenavista and Rizal. Periodically they shelled the Japanese garrison with their newly acquired 81 mm mortar. Faust then decided to have the unit take a more active role and moved it down to the Buenavista area. The unit encamped along a channel that led to the sea. Early the next morning, a launch with approximately forty-five or fifty Japanese soldiers going out to sea passed in front of the unit's position. They opened fire as the launch passed, and their heavy barrage caused a fire on the launch and it sank within a few minutes. Some of the Japanese soldiers remained on board, and others jumped overboard to escape the fire. Knowing that they would retaliate, the Special Troops moved back into the hills. The next day a column of two hundred heavily armed Japanese soldiers approached the Special Troops' position. According to Hank, their unit numbered about forty. As the Japanese moved up the road, they opened fire with mortar and machine guns. The Special Troops unit melted into the jungle. Shortly after these exchanges with the Japanese troops, McClish prudently decided to move division headquarters back to Rizal. Again, as guerrillas, they kept flexible tactics and plans, open to change, particularly when the enemy had greater numbers and superior firepower.

My father's job of procuring food and other supplies for the 110th Division was becoming more and more difficult as the end of 1943 approached. To assist in his efforts, his detail had been increased and now included two young Filipino officers to help negotiate purchases. Several memoranda point to the ever-increasing importance of palay and other commodities for the guerrilla force. Moreover, it underscored the growing requirement to use inland routes, both river and trail, to move needed supplies to guerrilla units within the 110th Division.

While Mom, Peach, and I (and Princess) remained in Cantilan, its population continued to swell with the constant stream of refugees from other areas, putting a strain on local food supplies. Despite the shortage of food available for purchase, we always managed to have sufficient rice and ground corn (the nuns in the convent shared their resources with us), which we augmented with dried fish or tapa and vegetables simmered in gata. In addition to making gata, Peach provided us with a variety of wild greens and mushrooms she picked fresh daily. I often went with her on these foraging expeditions, and we enjoyed spending some personal time together. We shared food and household chores with our housemates.

I had the same responsibilities as in Claver, primarily keeping the kitchen supplied with firewood and water. Stacked against the wall of the house were several bamboo tubes for carrying water. I regularly filled a tube of hollowed-out bamboo at the stream and carried it home on my shoulder. To reduce the discomfort of carrying the rough, heavy bamboo tube, Peach taught me the trick of positioning it on the fleshy part of my shoulder closer to my neck, not on my collarbone. Sometimes these adjustments tipped the bamboo tube backward, and all the water ended up on the ground—and I would have to return to the stream for a refill. To conserve the water stored at the house, I often took the dishes, utensils, and pots to the stream to be washed. There was no soap for this, so I scrubbed them with the leaves of the *hantutungaw* plant; the surface of these leaves was rough, resembling very fine sandpaper, and worked quite well in removing grease. Rubbing a handful of sand on the dirty items also helped the cleaning process.

December 17, 1943, was my ninth birthday. Again, Mom organized a modest celebration. The entire household joined her and Peach in making the occasion extra-special for me. The nuns announced that they had offered up special prayers for me at Mass that morning. Mom and Peach prepared a delicious meal, and even though there was no big birthday cake with candles, we all had small, sweet cakes made from cassava flour and brown sugar. The close hugs and warm wishes from the group made it memorable.

A few days after my birthday the traditional star-shaped decorations were hung outside the houses, heralding the approach of the Christmas season. To our surprise and delight, Dad arrived in time to celebrate the holidays with us—I remember thinking that it would have been nice if he could have been present at my birthday celebration. He looked really handsome and snappy in his new uniform and boots. In fact, everything he wore and carried was new, including a handsome bag with shoulder strap. Since supplies brought in by the SPYRON system took time to move down to the fighting units, my dad didn't receive some of this support until early December 1943. Among his papers I found a copy of a receipt dated December 8, 1943, for several items received from the 110th Division quartermaster.

1 Carbine M1 cal. 30
100 rounds Ammo cal. 30
1 Jungle pack
1 Musette bag w/ strap
1 Field jacket
1 Shirt K
1 Pants K
1 Jungle medical kit
2 Undershorts
2 Undershirts
1 Sweater K
1 Jungle suit
2 prs. Socks
1 pr. Jungle boots
1 Molle shaving cream
1 Razor w/blades
1 Matchbox compass
1 Towel
6 bags Duke's tobacco
1 ctn Camels cigarettes
1 can Gun oil
1 Sewing kit
1 pr Leggings, canvas

These things may not be extraordinary, but to Dad, who had spent many months hiking long distances over rough terrain in all kinds of weather, such basics as a change of clothes and new socks were luxuries. The tobacco products were also welcome. (There's an old saying in the military, "Rank hath its privileges." By no means did all guerrillas receive such items: as privates, my brothers received new weapons and ammunition delivered by early SPYRON missions but did not receive boots and other uniform items until almost a year later.)

It was a welcome change to see a smile on Mom's face as she prepared for Christmas, but her face clouded over when she thought about her boys. Dad's reassurance that they had safely returned to their unit at the 110th Division's headquarters was little consolation because it also meant that they were now fighting the Japanese.

Naping, our hostess, really had a houseful at this point, but everyone pitched in to make this holiday enjoyable, even under trying circumstances. We attended Midnight Mass at the local church, which was beautifully decorated and lit with oil lamps. After Mass there were embraces and handshakes among the townspeople as they extended Christmas wishes to relatives and friends. Many strolled through the streets, enjoying the festive, colorful holiday decorations and the soft glow of light shining through open windows, as they traveled to the homes of family and friends to celebrate Christmas Day. It was a beautiful experience, and the horror of the Japanese attack in Claver less than a month before seemed like just a bad dream.

Peach and I weren't aware of it at the time, but during this visit my parents had a serious discussion about our welfare. Dad informed Mom that with the advent of the SPYRON missions, American dependents could evacuate to Australia and subsequently proceed to the United States. In fact, a number of civilians, including the group that had been hiding out at the Gomoco Goldfields, had been evacuated along with several ex-POWs from DAPECOL on the November 1943 mission. Mom was not receptive to the idea, and apparently Dad didn't push it. They had not been in touch with relatives in the States, and they both recognized that without financial support it would be very difficult for Mom to settle there with two young daughters. Besides, she constantly worried about Dad, Rudy, or Hank being killed or wounded and could not bear the thought of being thousands of miles away with no means of communicating with them or the guerrilla forces on Mindanao. It was a sad coincidence that, in fact, when Mom was emphatically justifying her resistance to the idea of evacuation to Australia, the husband of Helen Welbon, one of the women who had left by submarine in November, was killed during an encounter with the Japanese Army. Roy Welbon had been in the lumber business before the war. In fact, he, Dad, and Varney, the manager of East Mindanao, had worked together on a mission for the U.S. Army shortly after the outbreak of the war. All three had joined the guerrilla movement as soon as it was organized. Welbon's death after his wife's departure was the nightmare scenario that Mom dreaded. She was filled with sympathy for Helen.

Dad was able to stay beyond the Christmas season, extending his visit to almost a month. He was a smoker but he wanted to conserve his supply of precious Camel cigarettes as long as possible. To that end, someone had given him some dried tobacco leaves to make into little cigars. I watched him set aside several good-sized leaves before chopping the rest into tiny pieces. He then lined up these pieces along the long end of the leaf and attempted to roll it into a cylinder, but his fingers were large and he could only manage to make a loose roll, and the contents kept spilling out. I volunteered to try rolling one, and he was so pleased with the result that he asked me to make the remaining cigars for him. Little did he know that I already had some experience rolling dried leaves for smoking, although I had not done so since promising Hank to stop. So, it was exciting to be asked to help make cigars. Despite my promise, the allure of smoking was so tantalizing that I could not resist stealing one of my creations, then hiding behind a rock near the stream and smoking it from end to end. The flavor was strong and awful, unlike the dried banana leaves I had smoked in Claver. The bout of nausea and vomiting that followed was so terrible that I was convinced it was my well-deserved punishment for breaking my promise not to smoke anymore. Besides being sick, I was filled with remorse—I had not only betrayed Dad's trust, I but also wasted one of his few precious cigars. I still don't know how I managed to keep the episode a secret from Mom and Peach. Still, the unpleasant experience was a blessing in disguise: when I tried smoking cigarettes to be fashionable many years later, the taste and smell of tobacco held absolutely no appeal.

After Dad's departure in January 1944, I felt at loose ends. I missed my playmates and the carefree life I had enjoyed so much in Claver. The Ayado house was some distance from town, and there were no children my age living nearby. I was cautioned not to wander too far from home, so Naping's little toddler and Princess were my only playmates. There seemed to be a revolving door where the nuns were concerned; they spent as much time as they could at the convent in town, and when one or two were relocated, others came in their stead. Mom's attitude was subdued most of the time, and she was always anxious to learn the latest rumors circulating in town. Periodically someone on Dad's detail, usually a small, wiry man named Hilarion, arrived to check on us and bring current news and some spending money from Dad. Mom always looked distinctly relieved as she uttered the words "Thank God" when reassured that Dad and the boys were OK.

Our wardrobes needed replenishing at this point. Since there was no cotton cloth available, we had to resort to material made from the abaca fiber, similar to that used for my brothers' shirts. I once watched a lady weave this product on a loom in her home, deftly tossing the shuttle with its trailing fiber back and forth between rows of fibers stretched in front of her as her foot alternated between two pedals slightly above the floor. The finished material was a loose weave but stiff, and the shapeless shifts sewn for us by a woman who still had needles scratched our flesh. For the sake of modesty, Mom and Peach continued to wear their patched and tattered old dresses underneath. After a few washings in the stream, the abaca material softened a bit. Unfortunately, this fabric was not as durable as cotton cloth, and we broke in our new abaca frocks more often than we would have liked. The spot on my right shoulder would wear out more quickly than the rest of the garment, due to the pressure of the water-filled bamboo poles I regularly hauled from the stream. I tried switching the load to my left shoulder but the scar from Old Timer's bite was right on my collarbone, and any pressure on it was painful.

During this critical time in the war, food procurement continued to be a priority for the guerrilla units. A procurement authority document demonstrated that MacArthur's staff was providing funds to the guerrillas through the SPYRON missions. Dad was given this financial authorization for purchasing food for the 110th Division.

7 April 1944

GENERAL ORDERS
NO. 38

PROCUREMENT AUTHORITY #25

1. The Force Finance Officer, 10th MD, USFIP, is authorized to advance the amount of FIFTY THOUSAND (P50,000.00) PESOS to Captain C. HANSEN, OS, 110th Division, to be used in purchasing food supplies for the 110th Division. This amount is chargeable against the account of the 110th Division, 10th MD, USFIP.

By order of Colonel FERTIG:

S. J. WILSON
Lt. Colonel, GSC
Deputy Chief of Staff

Since it was his responsibility to disburse the funds, one might ask how the guerrillas acquired them. In the early days of the guerrilla movement money was clearly needed to pay and feed the growing organization. Initially the movement gathered funds in part by accepting voluntary contributions and issuing IOUs later honored by the American or Philippine government. However, this was not sufficient; the forces needed an emergency currency to pay the guerrillas, feed them, and procure necessary supplies for the organization. Prior to leaving the Philippines in March 1942, President Quezon created the Mindanao Emergency Currency Board (MECB). While the board did print some money, it was neither sufficient nor effective. On March 27, 1943, Fertig revived the struggling MECB. Quezon made new appointments to the board, and he authorized MECB to print up to twenty million pesos. The MECB advanced money required by the guerrillas and municipal governments with Tenth Military District approval. The early notes, however, were quite primitive, printed in "rice mills" on vintage presses with inferior paper. Later, with the arrival of the SPYRON missions, professional plates and paper arrived from Australia. The major rice mill for the island was established by the Tenth Military District in the upper reaches of the Agusan Valley in December 1943. Between then and October 1944, over fourteen million pesos were printed.

After their occupation of the Philippines, the Japanese forces had printed and circulated their own currency, which the Filipinos derisively called "Mickey Mouse money." To downgrade the effectiveness of the Japanese military notes, quantities of counterfeit notes were printed in Australia, brought in by submarine, then distributed by guerrilla units to the various provincial areas of Mindanao, causing the local Filipinos to distrust Japanese notes. The technical adviser to the MECB board was Sam Wilson, a former Manila businessman; he was responsible for monitoring and auditing the currency printing as well as maintaining a ledger on the liabilities incurred by this emergency currency. Because of his position, Wilson could authorize and sign the procurement document for my father.

Meanwhile, the Tandag-Tago area was heating up. The Japanese Army was moving more men and materiel into key towns along the east coast of Surigao province. It was no longer feasible to use the coastal waters for shipping palay or moving military supplies. And the Japanese were now landing in greater numbers with intent to remain, patrol the area, and engage the guerrillas. As the Japanese forces made their presence more permanent within the coastal areas, they began in earnest to seek out hidden caches of guerrilla palay, even enticing the local inhabitants to bring forth any hidden stores of it. For the guerrillas, it became a cat and mouse game to move caches of palay, petroleum, ammunition, and other materiel further inland, away from the growing Japanese presence.

In two reports dated May 17 and June 4, 1944, to the commanders of the Tenth Military District and the 110th Division on the situation in the Tandag-Tago area, Dad described an attack on Tandag in the early morning of April 27, 1944. Around five hundred Japanese troops on three medium-sized ships, two motor launches, and five armed landing barges landed a short distance outside Tandag. When thy entered Tandag, most of the residents fled to the nearby mountains. Dad led a small group of guerrillas that presented stiff resistance, inflicting scores of casualties, but they were no match for the superior man- and firepower of the Japanese and were forced to retreat. Dad, Lieutenant Bob Pease, and another officer were trapped in town but were fortunate enough to escape under cover of darkness.

Part of the Japanese force departed for points south while the remainder dug in and stayed in Tandag for several weeks, exhorting the Filipinos to bring in palay and other goods for purchase (on their terms), at the same time looting homes and bodegas and destroying property. A patrol was dispatched to nearby Tago in search of food and other supplies, again leaving destruction in its wake. The next contingent to Tago took supplies and equipment, signaling its intention to control and occupy that city also.

It is no wonder the frightened Filipinos fled to the interior and refused to cooperate with them. To safeguard their crop, Dad had persuaded the local farmers to harvest their palay and hide it in the mountains. He also effected the safe evacuation of all the palay and other supplies that the guerrillas had stored in various bodegas in the Tandag and Tago areas—no easy feat, considering the weight and bulk of the cavan-sized sacks used for transporting palay—with the danger of a Japanese patrol appearing at any time.

After ten days, more guerrillas arrived near Tandag under the command of Captain Marshall and Lieutenant Spielman. They attacked with trench mortars but again failed to drive out the Japanese forces. At the same time, another guerrilla unit attacked the Japanese force occupying Tago, killing eight. Angered by these attacks, the Japanese military sent out numerous patrols deeper into the interior to pursue and fight the guerrillas. Furthermore, Japanese naval forces were constantly patrolling the waters east of Surigao, sometimes anchoring in Bayabas Bay south of Tago.

Dad reported that the guerrilla organization still had over two thousand cavans of palay hidden in different locations in the Tandag-Tago area. There was certainly a chance the Japanese would find them, in which event, he issued orders for the guards to burn the bodegas rather than allow the palay to fall into Japanese hands.

He concluded his report with an appeal for twenty-five hundred tablets each of Atabrine and quinine to distribute to hundreds of local residents suffering from malaria. The nearby mountains were infested with disease-carrying mosquitoes. The quartermaster detachment guarding the bodegas also urgently needed ammunition, because they had used up their meager supply in the fight with the Japanese.

Dad's reports underscored the new strategy the Japanese were applying along the coastal areas. Rather than landing and leaving, they were now landing in force and stationing troop garrisons on a long-term basis. The Japanese were actively occupying areas previously controlled by the guerrillas, which was indeed the plan of the Japanese commander, frustrated by his inability to deal with the guerrillas and their virtual control of coastal areas. Now, that control was slowly eroding, and the very supply lines that kept them viable were being cut off.

In his diary, Fertig referred to this increased Japanese presence as a "program of envelopment."[2] During the early months of 1944, the Japanese were redeploying troops to the east coast of Surigao province. Many of these soldiers were coming from the provinces of Lanao, Zamboanga, and Misamis Occidental. Also, Japanese troops were moving up the coast from Davao. Port Lamon, south of Lianga, was occupied by the Japanese. The guerrillas had used Port Lamon for resupply operations, thus this aggressive Japanese deployment in eastern Mindanao caused many SPYRON mission landings to be shifted to western Mindanao waters. Also during this period, the Tenth Military District headquarters, located along the Agusan River, came under frequent attack from Japanese heavy bombers. This increased attention from the air may have come from the effective Japanese intelligence in triangulating FRS transmissions. This, together with the heavy radio traffic and long V-beam antennas in cleared areas, made the FRS facilities easy targets.

Perhaps the most intriguing part of Dad's report, however, was the mention of a Japanese patrol being led by twelve white men, whom the source later commented were possibly Germans. This group appeared to be a survey party; they might have been looking at expanding road or trail systems for the purpose of moving into the interior, where guerrillas had sanctuary.

The Japanese Navy continued its constant patrol of waters off the coast of Surigao, sometimes anchoring in Bayabas Bay south of Tago. The larger naval vessels cruised the sea lanes further off the coast. Eyewitnesses described a submarine attack on a convoy of fourteen Japanese ships in which three of the vessels were sunk. Of course, U.S. Navy submarines were very active in Philippine waters at this point.

In May 1944, the 110th Division sent my father a communication that reflected the pressures building against the guerrillas during that period. This memorandum, dated May 19 and signed by McClish, announced the formation of the 107th Division under the command of Major Childress. The new division would be responsible for the region south of an east-west line running between Lianga and Esperanza, including the Province of Davao. Fred Feigel, the designated quartermaster officer, sent Dad a note suggesting a meeting in Lianga as soon as possible to coordinate procurement and shipment of palay and other commodities, stressing that this be accomplished "before we are closed up by the Japs."

Creation of the 107th Division suggested an organizational change to bring more focus on the Japanese threat—the program of envelopment—that was moving from the Davao area toward the Agusan Valley, where Fertig's Tenth Military District and the 110th Division were headquartered.

In his May 19 memo, McClish outlined the problems the guerrillas were now facing with their resupply network. He pointed out that because of the increased Japanese presence in northern Surigao province, the sea route for the transport of palay and other military supplies brought in by the SPYRON program was becoming more dangerous. Moreover, he was also concerned that use of the sea route made it more likely that these critical supplies would fall into Japanese hands and be denied to the guerrilla forces. The guerrillas had also utilized an overland route, but McClish wrote, "Our route, via Lianga–Los Arcos, is entirely cut off. Our only means of obtaining foodstuffs from the Pacific coast is by trails through the interior to division headquarters. This will require human caravans, and in order to transport the supplies, we will have to use considerable personnel employed at a reasonable wage."

McClish was direct in his assessment that a new food-supply route was needed if the division and its units were to survive—the grim alternative was disbanding the guerrilla force. He asked Dad's opinion about a proposed new inland supply route from Tago over the Diuata Mountains to Sibagat in Agusan province.

Dad pointed out in his reply, dated June 4, 1944, that it took the messenger ten days to reach him in the upper Tago area using well-traveled trails. The proposed new route included approximately fifty kilometers through rugged mountainous territory known only to the Manobos. Carabaos could not be used, so all palay needed to be transported by bearers. Shortage of labor would be a major problem. The onset of the rainy season was also a major consideration. Dad laid it on the line: it would not be easy moving palay on men's backs across rugged and hostile country. The last sentence of Dad's report, underlined, reads: "*However, if there is any feasibility of getting the palay across it will be done.*"

In the meantime, the pressure on the guerrillas from the Japanese incursions continued to mount. A communication from Paul Marshall, commander of the 114th Infantry Regiment, outlined the pressure his unit had felt from the increased operational tempo of the Japanese forces. Marshall's memo presents a realistic picture of guerrilla activities on Mindanao:

> We're catching hell here. There are approximately six to ten thousand Japs now in upper Surigao and they are expecting eight thousand more. We've been at it since the 28th of May, the Japs landed in Cabadbaran on the 28th and pushed down from Surigao and met in Kitcharao about one thousand plus from Surigao. We have had about twelve to fifteen encounters up to this date. The Japs occupy Tubod, Timanana, Mainit and Magpayon, Ciana, Placer, Bacuag and yesterday they patrolled to Gigaquit and Mahonob. We've had to Buckwheat for the time being as all of our boys average about five to six rounds of ammo, however I'm hoping to get more ammo soon. We haven't got a hell of a lot of chance against such big numbers but we'll just keep on sniping them and ambush work.

Marshall's communication was a strong narrative regarding the state of his unit and the threats they were up against with the increased Japanese presence. For the 114th Infantry Regiment and the rest of the guerrilla organization, the landings in the Philippines could not come soon enough. At the same time, the 110th Division was feeling the same pressures across the mountains in the Agusan Valley.

Marshall used "Buckwheat" to mean they had to lie low for a while due to lack of ammunition; this was likely his version of *bakwit,* which could also mean "hiding out or staying out of sight." As he reported, the 114th's troops had only five or six rounds of ammunition each, despite the tons of arms and ammunition that had been delivered by the SPYRON missions; this underscored the difficulty of transporting much-needed supplies to the fighting troops.

In late June, Dad received another memorandum from McClish concerning the urgency of transporting some two thousand cavans of palay from the warehouses in the Tandag-Tago area into the Agusan provincial area. McClish realized that the only way to transport this commodity was for men to carry it in sacks on their backs across the Diuata Mountains. What could not be moved would be entrusted to the 114th Infantry Regiment for its troops. McClish recognized that my father would have to mobilize civilian cargadores for the work. He was concerned that there would be enough food for the troops until the anticipated arrival of American forces in the Philippines.

McClish's memorandum was very strong and posed a number of problems for my father. First, the palay had to be transferred from the large storage sacks to smaller *buri* sacks (woven from fibers of the buri palm) that could be carried by each individual. Recruiting civilians to carry the sacks would be a major effort. Keeping clear of Japanese patrols would be another. Perhaps the most difficult obstacle, however, was the harsh terrain over which the palay would have to be transported. McClish ended the memo by saying that if my father was unable to accomplish the task he was to come to division headquarters for a conference.

Two months later, Dad sent a memorandum to McClish reviewing his efforts to move the palay. Upon receipt of buri sacks ordered from Bohol, and with the help of the mayor of Tago in recruiting volunteers to carry the palay, he arranged the transfer of one thousand cavans to San Miguel to await shipment over the mountains. This effort took two months. In late July, after he had assembled 250 cargadores for the first convoy across the mountains, a courier arrived with news that the Japanese had occupied Sibagat, Agusan province, and controlled all the roads to Esperanza and the Agusan River, where they were heading, so the cargadores simply fled in fear. The next morning alarming reports came of columns of Japanese soldiers from Tandag, Tago, and La Paz, over one thousand strong, marching toward his location near San Miguel. Dad immediately contacted Lieutenant Spielman, whose guerrilla unit was the closest. They agreed that Spielman, who had two hundred guerrillas with him, would transport all the palay to the 114th's regimental headquarters. Dad tried to return to the Tandag-Tago area to see what could be done with the palay stored there, but he ran into about three hundred Japanese, so he and his men had to take evasive action. They took a circuitous route through the interior to Adlay, arriving a week later. Upon arrival Dad learned that the locals had safely hidden much of the remaining palay in the Tandag-Tago area in several different places.

Clearly, this resupply operation never really accomplished what McClish had hoped. It was fraught with problems. Hiking over the rough terrain across the Diuata Mountains with a heavy sack of palay on one's back would challenge even the strongest cargador. While Dad, with the help and cooperation of local officials, recruited civilian "volunteers" for this task, no one could blame them for abandoning it when faced with possible capture by the Japanese. They knew all too well the consequences of being caught helping the guerrillas. But the biggest obstacle was the ever-expanding Japanese presence in the operational territory of the guerrillas. Marshall's memo mentioned close to twenty thousand Japanese in upper Surigao, and Dad reported over a thousand from the Tandag-Tago area penetrating the interior to the west toward San Miguel. The Japanese were hitting the resupply effort from both the Surigao side and the Agusan Valley in Agusan province. Even if my father had successfully gotten the palay across to barrio Bato, would the division's quartermaster have been able to transport and store it, given the operational activity of the Japanese forces in the Agusan Valley?

EIGHT

Awaiting the Liberation of the Philippines

While Dad and the 110th Division command were wrestling with transporting palay to feed the troops, Mom, Peach, and I remained in Cantilan. One day Mom informed us, in a rather matter-of-fact way, that she was pregnant. In retrospect, one might imagine her being upset at the prospect of having a baby under such difficult circumstances. However, if Mom had any concerns, she did not share them with us. When she determined that the baby would arrive in September, she asked us to pray for a brother, so we could call him Ed to remind us of the big brother we had lost in September 1941. Still, there were certain matters to consider. We literally had nothing but the clothes on our backs, and these were made of abaca fiber. Suddenly a baby was coming, and we were without baby blankets, clothes, or diapers. Clothing a newborn baby in stiff and scratchy abaca cloth was out of the question. However, there were still some bed linens we had left with our landlord in Claver. Mom decided that she and Peach would trek back to retrieve them, leaving me in the care of Naping and the nuns. I protested vigorously, of course, tearfully reminding Mom of how afraid I was when they left me by myself in the abandoned hut in the hills of Claver when the Japanese shelled and ransacked the town. Mom gently explained that without me along they would make better time, and the circumstances were different now because there were kind people to look after me. She asked me to be brave once again and take good care of Princess. (Many years later Mom admitted that leaving me behind was very difficult, but she rationalized that if, God forbid, she and Peach happened to fall into Japanese hands, I would be spared that horrible fate and stood a good chance of eventually being reunited with Dad and/or my brothers. Not surprisingly, she chose not to share those thoughts with Peach and me at the time.)

I knew, of course, that continuing to argue with Mom was futile and I had no choice but to stay. I felt utterly miserable and could not overcome my fear and loneliness. That was the first time that I was apart from my family for more than a few hours. While my experience as a boarder at San Nicolas School was not pleasant, Peach and the boys were in close proximity. And at the mine, when the rest of the family was away from home at social events, Romana was there to take care of me. Since leaving the mine, that short period when Mom and Peach left me alone after the Japanese attack on Claver was the only one in which I felt really afraid. I realize now that Mom and Dad had always tried to shield me from situations that might scare me. They made sure I was not within earshot when they discussed matters relating to our personal safety. Furthermore, whenever Mom informed Peach and me that we were moving to a different location, she kept her demeanor normal and never expressed the apprehension and fear that she undoubtedly felt. Peach was certainly aware of the possible dangers we faced, but she, too, put up a brave front. Despite their efforts, however, I came to understand that we kept moving to avoid being captured by the Japanese because they might kill us. The memory of Ed's death in Surigao was still fresh in my mind, and the possibility of something similar happening to us, or to Dad or the boys, was a subject I could not bring myself to discuss with Mom or Peach.

While Naping and the nuns were kind and solicitous, I rebuffed their efforts to cheer me up. I knew there was a good reason for Mom and Peach to make the trip, but I was also aware that we had left Claver only a few short months earlier because it was too dangerous to remain there. And now Mom and Peach were heading back! Although Mom had assured me that they would return as quickly as possible, I remembered that it took us many days to travel from Claver to Cantilan and resigned myself to a long wait. Every day I watched the path leading to the house, hoping Dad would suddenly appear, as he had done just before Christmas, but every evening I was disappointed. I was miserable, and without Mom to discipline me, I alternated between temper tantrums and crying jags. I remember one afternoon, as I was playing hopscotch by myself in the yard, a nun approached me with a smile and started a conversation. I didn't respond and continued playing my game. While I had learned to interact with adults during our stay in Claver, they were usually relatives of my little friends, with whom I felt comfortable. Now, even though several nuns had stayed at Naping's house at different times, I still felt uneasy in their presence because they reminded me of the teachers at San Nicolas School. On this particular occasion, undeterred by my indifference, the nun continued chatting and even offered to help me do addition and subtraction, using a stick to write numbers on the ground. I knew in my heart she was only trying to be nice, but her suggestion evoked unhappy memories of my experience as a boarding student in Surigao, and I started to cry. I'm sure I hurt her feelings, but I just couldn't control my sobbing. When I recovered from this outburst, I retreated into my own world, with only Princess as company. Even Naping's cute little toddler, who usually amused and entertained me, was not welcome in my dark hole of misery.

It took Mom and Peach more than three weeks to make the round trip on foot, following the coastal road northward, reversing the route we had traveled before. In the intervening months, however, the Japanese had increased their incursions into the towns along the coast, systematically moving in a southerly direction in search of the elusive guerrillas as well as food and other commodities. They also selected strategic areas in which to establish a long-term presence. Not only were the local residents living in constant fear of a surprise raid, or, worse still, permanent occupation by the Japanese, they also had to choose between staying and being subjected to threats and possible death, or evacuating into the interior, thereby risking the wrath of the Japanese who punished absent or uncooperative townspeople by ransacking their towns and burning their homes.

My mother was usually calm and deliberate in her actions, but hormonal changes due to pregnancy must have clouded her judgment when she decided to make this trip. Surely she was aware that the Japanese threat had worsened in the areas we had traversed after we left Claver. Further, she had miscalculated her own physical strength, for after a couple of days of fast hiking she started to complain of pain and fatigue. Peach recalled their having to make frequent stops so she could rest. This was uncharacteristic for Mom, usually so energetic. During these stops she simply lay down on the grass on the side of the road until she felt well enough to continue. Peach voiced her concern, but Mom was determined to complete the mission. Still only thirteen, she was in no position to win an argument with our mother. Dad would have been furious had he known that Mom and Peach were making the trip, for at any time along the route they could have run into a Japanese patrol. Mindful of this danger, they avoided the towns and used inland trails that ran parallel to the main road whenever possible, but this delayed their progress. Peach remembers that these detours took them over colorful terrain rich in iron and copper ore. As there were a lot of abandoned houses along the way, shelter at night was a minor problem. And if they found themselves near a settlement at the end of the day, the locals living in the area graciously gave them overnight accommodations. The rainy season had started and they had to stop more often than planned to wait for the downpour to abate. These interruptions annoyed Mom, but the forced stops actually helped build up her strength for the next leg of the journey.

Mom and Peach finally reached the outskirts of Claver. The number of Japanese troops in occupied towns ebbed and flowed, depending on the number of patrols deployed to seek and engage the guerrillas, but it was always assumed that there remained a token force plus an unknown number of informants and collaborators. Mom and Peach stayed in the area only as long as it took to retrieve as many of the linens and other useful items as they could carry, leaving the rest of our belongings with our former landlord for retrieval sometime in the future.

On the return trip Mom continued to have difficulty walking, and it became clear that she could not carry her bundle for any distance. Peach could not manage both of them, so Mom decided to run the risk of taking small bancas as much as possible, trusting in God and the ability of the boatmen to successfully evade a Japanese launch, should one come to patrol the waters nearby. My siblings and I don't know whether money changed hands during these arrangements. Presumably Mom would have offered to pay in scrip notes printed by the guerrillas, but many Filipinos preferred not to have those notes in their possession—if the Japanese discovered them, they would be subjected to harsh interrogation or torture.

The joy and relief I felt when Mom and Peach returned are beyond description. We were crying as Mom hugged me tightly and told me repeatedly that she was very proud of her big girl. It was the first time she had referred to me as a *big* girl. My heart swelled with happiness and pride, and all my feelings of anger and bitterness simply vanished. I hoped and prayed that no one would report to her my bouts of bad behavior during her absence. The matter never came up, and I was grateful for the consideration of our housemates.

Mom had lost weight during the trip, which accentuated her growing stomach. One of the personal items she had retrieved from Claver was a long, loose-fitting salmon-colored nightgown. It was soft and silky and became her favorite attire as she rested, at Naping's insistence, and tried to regain her strength. She knew that it was important that she be healthy for the baby's sake. Mom had just turned forty, but the mental and physical stresses of the past two years had aged her beyond her years. Our diet since going into hiding would be considered light and healthy by today's standards, but it wasn't balanced and probably lacked sufficient protein, calcium, and iron, especially for an expectant mother.

Sometime in June 1944, my brother Rudy was assigned to a special escort mission for Captain Larry Evans. Evans had landed by submarine from Australia in December 1943. His mission was to function as the Tenth Military District's surgeon and radio officer—he had expertise in both fields. After his arrival, Fertig directed him to visit the various divisions of the military district, establishing and maintaining medical and communications capabilities within those organizations. While Evans was working in the 110th Division area, Rudy accompanied him and his group down the Agusan River to Cabadbaran. Unfortunately, Japanese troops were moving up the river and its tributaries. After their first encounter with a Japanese patrol, Evans decided to move back up river to Esperanza, avoiding the enemy when possible. In his book, *They Fought Alone,* John Keats mentions this trip and an encounter Evans and his group had with the Japanese, including the role played by my brother Rudy (note that "Hansen" is misspelled). After several days on the trail, when they chanced across a nice stream in the jungle, Evans decided that a good bath was in order. While he and the others bathed, Rudy maintained guard. All of a sudden the rifle and machine-gun fire rang through the jungle. Evans grabbed his clothes and ran to a nipa hut in a clearing. Rudy was under the hut placing the advancing Japanese patrol in the sights of his air-cooled .30-caliber machine gun. Keats describes the encounter:

The Japanese came running, more than twenty of them, not a platoon but an armed mob, haring after naked men who jumped out of streams.

The expressionless Hanson [*sic*] opened up with the machine gun, the muzzle blasts kicking dust and Japanese falling on the trail.

Evans heard the Japanese scream and saw them stagger around to go pelting back, throwing away their rifles and helmets as they went, while Hanson calmly swung the blasting muzzle as the trail curved.

When the machine gun stopped, Evans heard the heavy burst of a Springfield in the forest.

One of the bathers, his khakis wet from not having dried himself, came carefully into the clearing, carrying a rifle before him. He studied the three bodies on the trail. He watched the bodies as he edged to the house, where Hanson had gathered the spent cartridge cases and was folding the machine gun's tripod.

"Let's get out," the rifleman said.[1]

Both Rudy and Hank had Special Troops assignments during this period. While Rudy was escorting Evans, Hank on occasion had escort duties for McClish. One day they were walking near the headquarters encampment when they saw a hawk circling a tall *lauan* tree.

McClish said, "Hank, give me your carbine."

"Sir, there is no way that you can hit that hawk. It's too far away." Hank replied.

"Give me your carbine anyway, and I'll show you." McClish insisted.

McClish loaded a round in the carbine and took careful aim. Aiming for about twenty seconds, he squeezed the trigger and fired. Down came the hawk.

"Hank, I told you I could hit that bird." He then handed the carbine back to Hank.

Mom would have been relieved to know that her sons were safe. We hadn't seen the boys since their departure early on the morning of November 30, when the Japanese shelled Claver and we had to run for our lives. While Mom's concern was focused on the three of us, she constantly worried about Dad and her two sons, young guerrillas involved in a war against a savage enemy. The lack of news or communication of any kind exacerbated her feelings of frustration and helplessness. Dad maintained periodic contact with us through Hilarion, a member of his detail—it was always a happy occasion when Hilarion showed up with a message from Dad and, hopefully, some money as well. Unfortunately, most of the time Dad had no knowledge of the location of the boys or their assignments, so could not pass on any information about them. Even though weeks passed without news from Dad, in this case "no news was good news," for if, God forbid, any one of them had been wounded, captured, or killed, the guerrilla commanders would have found a way to locate and inform us. This would not have been easy, had Mom opted for evacuation to Australia then, eventually, to the United States.

The Japanese were becoming more ambitious in their patrols and deployment, and Mom became even more concerned for our safety, as well as the safety of Naping and her family. They would have been subjected to unspeakable cruelty, torture, even death for harboring us. A few weeks after she and Peach returned from Claver, Mom decided to move farther south to Tandag. Although it was dangerous to travel in open waters by banca, sometimes it was the only way to get from one place to the next along the coast. Peach and I remember being bounced about in rough waters as we rounded Cauit Point. Where a good trail existed, we hiked. Somehow, Mom always managed to arrange for one or two men to accompany us and help carry our belongings. There were long stretches when we walked on muddy trails some distance from the coast. The deeper one went into the interior, the greater the probably of encountering Manobos or Mananuas, hill people, early settlers of Mindanao who had been pushed into the interior forested areas when waves of more aggressive immigrants arrived and settled in the coastal areas. Their lifestyle was very simple, and they interacted with the Filipinos who lived in the barrios in the flatlands. Naturally there was an air of mystery about them, but they were not hostile to outsiders who traveled through their territory. In this respect they were very different from the more aggressive Magahats in the southern part of Mindanao.

If we were lucky, at least one of our guides would have a penchant for chewing tobacco because, as we moved through the interior, we had to contend with leeches of a different variety from those found in rivers: these light brown leeches seemed to either drop from leaves above or jump on us as we brushed past the undergrowth. In any event, we had to examine ourselves and each other (and Princess, too) fairly often to remove any leeches, preferably before they started to feast. Sometimes they remained undetected between our toes, concealed under mud and dirt—a few squirts of tobacco-flavored spit aimed at both ends of the leech were usually sufficient to encourage it to let go.

Food on the trail consisted mostly of dried fish or tapa with rice or ground corn and freshly picked fruit. From our local guides, we learned that a piece of hollow bamboo, the node at one end still intact and a tight-fitting piece of bamboo at the other, could serve as a cooking implement. Filling it with the proper mixture of rice and water, sealing it up, and letting it sit in an open fire for about half an hour resulted in delicious steamed rice. We then placed slivers of tapa or dried fish on top of the steaming mound of rice, where it became warm and soft. In a few minutes, we laid out our communal meal on banana leaves. Using our fingers, we wadded a small portion of the rice mixture into a ball before eating it with our fingers.

As we made our way on the trail, we stopped at barrios to rest for the night. Of course, there was no advance notice of our arrival, so our marching in created a stir among the residents. Each time, a crowd gathered and followed along as we sought the local teniente del barrio or his equivalent. Filipino hospitality prevailed, and residents always gave us their best accommodations, however modest. Unfortunately, I had to contend with the curious stares of the children. Unaware that I could understand their dialect, they commented on my towheaded appearance, suggesting that I was probably an albino. But then someone pointed out that my eyes were green and not pink like those of an albino and, furthermore, bright sunlight did not seem to bother me. This led others to conclude that I must be a *wak-wak*—according to rural folklore, an eerie creature from the spirit world that could assume different forms. Needless to say, I did not appreciate being characterized as weird and tried to cover my hair and keep my eyes downcast as much as possible.

We bypassed Tandag, a fairly large town that had been invaded and occupied by several hundred Japanese just three months earlier. Dad's report dated May 17, 1944, described his participation in the guerrillas' attempt to repulse the Japanese invasion.

As we moved on southward, the mayor of a town near the Tago River some distance from the coast offered us a temporary safe haven. (Memories fade, but Peach believes the town was Unidos and the mayor's name was Jose Acevedo.) The Japanese would have had to come through Tago to reach our sanctuary, and he had a system in place whereby we would be warned of their approach, enabling us to execute a hasty retreat to the mountains. Only a couple of months earlier Japanese contingents from Tandag, Tago, and La Paz, over a thousand strong, had combed the area after learning from an informant that the guerrillas had caches of palay stashed in different locations. Forewarned by the locals, Dad was able to arrange for most of the precious commodity to be transferred out of the area by guerrillas of the 114th Infantry Regiment. While trying to salvage the remainder, he and his men ran into about three hundred Japanese. Badly outnumbered, they retreated to the mountains.

The ever-expanding Japanese military presence prompted us to hit the road again. Sometime in August of 1944 we moved again, this time to a place called Bayabas, further south along the coast. According to Peach, Mom chose this area on the recommendation of the parish priests we encountered.[2] To foster goodwill among the Filipinos, the Japanese allowed most of the Dutch parish priests to remain in their respective parishes, which helped the guerrillas because the priests had a good information network and pretty much knew what the Japanese were up to. Apparently, they also had standing instructions from the bishop to help those evading the Japanese when they could. Whenever the

Japanese were near, they recommended our moving on to another location. When Dad was on his liaison trips, he often stayed with the local priests. One of his frequent hosts was Father Carlos van den Ouwelant, then the young parish priest of Bacuag, who became bishop of Surigao many years later. During the early part of the war the priests provided us with small amounts of money in the form of prewar Philippine pesos, which was a big help when we had to move a lot.

The consensus was that Bayabas was close to the midpoint of the Japanese program of envelopment, designed to establish their control southward from Surigao and Agusan provinces and northward from Davao. Dad reported earlier that Japanese ships had on occasion anchored in Bayabas Bay but did not land any troops. Still, Mom felt secure in the knowledge that the priests and local officials in Bayabas would certainly send us some warning should Japanese forces arrive in town. Besides, with the impending birth of a baby, we had to settle somewhere where we could stay put for several months, if possible.

By now Mom was in her eighth month of pregnancy, but she did not allow her condition to slow her down. In fact, she was a determined woman on a mission—it was imperative that we find a place where she could safely await the arrival of her baby. Again accompanied by local guides, we hiked on trails and, whenever possible, traveled by baroto on rivers and inland waterways. When the moon was bright enough, we traveled on the river at night, with two boatmen paddling a baroto, the smaller kind, without outriggers. Seated behind the boatman in the prow I fought sleep and kept myself occupied by watching him dip his paddle into the water, then move it backward toward me—when he lifted it out of the water, dozens of phosphorescent bubbles danced in its wake. (I thought they were tiny, silvery fish.) Both boatmen were careful not to bump their paddles against the side of the craft because even the dullest thud would reverberate in the still night.

In the confusion of our travels from Cantilan to Bayabas, we forgot Peach's fourteenth birthday, July 25, 1944. Birthdays were always special occasions in our family, and Mom usually tried to commemorate them with some kind of celebration. However, under the circumstances it was understandable that this important date slipped by unnoticed.

Bayabas was a small town, and it was necessary to have a nipa hut built for us. We stayed with a local family in town while this was done. Situated some distance from the town proper, the site of our new home was a pleasant enough place with a small yard, trees, and nearby stream. For added safety, the hut was located on a site not readily visible from the surrounding area.

We feared being detected by the casual passerby who might intentionally, or unintentionally, let our whereabouts become known to a spy for the Japanese. Naturally, the locals knew exactly where we lived, but we felt confident that they would not betray us. However, ever mindful of the possibility of a surprise Japanese attack, Mom also found a bakwitan in an area called Buena Suerte (good luck), located partway up a hill. Cognizant of Mom's condition, the townspeople found us a midwife who lived in a neighboring barrio.

We lived in a small rural community, and our neighbors could not have been more helpful and hospitable. Bayabas was smaller than Cantilan or Claver, and its atmosphere was quite different. With the Japanese Army and the guerrillas in fierce competition for rice and dried fish and other foodstuffs, very little extra food trickled into our area from outside sources, and we were dependent on locally produced items. To have rice for our meals, we had to separate the local palay grain from its husk, which became my task; I would go to a neighbor's house and combine our palay with theirs and help them pound the husks off using a mortar and pestle. The mortar was a large, hollowed out piece of wood about fifteen inches high with a hole about twelve inches in diameter at the top, gradually narrowing to perhaps six inches at the bottom. The rhythmic process of pounding the palay by two, three and sometimes four people (usually women) using long pestles had always intrigued me, and now that I was finally tall enough to help, I was eager to learn. The women in the community were very patient as they taught me how to gauge the rhythm of the pestles pounding the palay in the hole, then do a few practice taps beside the hole to get the timing right before actually joining in. When coordinated correctly, three or four pestles could pound the palay in quick succession without hitting each other, with just enough pressure to break open the husk without crushing the grain.

After the husks were separated, we used a round, flat woven rattan tray with a shallow lip to winnow off the chaff. I learned to grasp this tray with both hands and make circular motions (while simultaneously tapping the edge of the tray with my right index finger), then flip its contents up in the air, making the hulled grains gradually gravitate toward the bottom half of the tray, as the chaff moved to the upper part until it reached the edge. With a deft flipping movement, I easily discarded the chaff—here, a nice breeze was a big help. The end product was not completely white like polished rice; rather, portions of the rice grains retained a reddish coating. While this rice might not be considered first class, it was actually more healthful than polished rice and helped prevent beriberi.

My contribution to the preparation of our daily meals was cooking the hulled rice in a culon. I placed rice in the pot, added water, brought it to a boil, and then removed some firewood to lower the heat and let the rice slowly absorb the water. It was important that the amount of water above the surface of the rice equal the distance from the tip of one's middle finger to the first knuckle. This method was foolproof—regardless of the shape of the pot or the length of the finger, the end result was delicious rice cooked just right. After each meal I took the pots and dishes to the stream to clean them with sand or hantutungaw leaves.

It was still my responsibility to keep the house supplied with water and firewood. I also enjoyed climbing a large guava tree to pick its delicious fruit and perch on its boughs. I favored this tree because its strong, resilient limbs bent rather than broke whenever I tested their limits. Now and then I spotted a small Y-shaped branch that would have made a great slingshot, but I had no elastic strips. Stretching out these activities helped keep me occupied throughout the day. In Claver I used to rush through my chores so I could spend more time playing with my friends. We had such a range of activities that the ringing of the Angelus bells at 6:00 in the evening always came too soon to suit me. While there were a few children of varying ages in the Bayabas community, we weren't able to have the normal day-to-day interaction that usually precedes friendship. Oh, how I longed to hear the words "Dula ta" (Let's play) again. Most households were multigenerational, with grandparents and sometimes great-grandparents living with their families. The older women were particularly attentive to me, always greeting me with a smile. Many chewed betel nut, which stained their teeth and turned the interiors of their mouths bright red, and whose red juice they were constantly spitting out. It was fortunate that I had grown older and wiser and had absolutely no inclination to try it. Still, I welcomed their advice when learning a new activity, whether it be a complicated cat's cradle or making a ball out of young, supple coconut fronds by removing the spines from two coconut fronds (the longer the better) and tightly braiding the four strips inward over and over until they formed a compact, squarish ball. I learned to tuck in the ends of the strips tightly, for if one came loose, the whole ball unraveled. I made and played with dozens of these; they were disposable—they bruised easily with handling, and they turned from a pretty light yellow to brown after only a few hours of use.

While we lived in Bayabas, we began to see and hear the large formations of American planes heading for Japanese targets that had to be eliminated before the coming U.S. invasion. One formation of fighters and bombers was estimated at at least one hundred aircraft. Historical accounts indicate heavy bombers were raiding Davao, to the south of us, targeting ships in the harbor as well as the surrounding airfields. During one raid, two U.S. B-24 bombers were shot down by Japanese antiaircraft fire, but guerrillas rescued the crewmen. These heavy raids by U.S. aircraft were coming at a very critical time for the guerrillas. During the first half of the year, the Japanese had moved more troops into key coastal cities and were occupying these areas on a more permanent basis than they had earlier in the war, hence, our moving so many times after we left Claver. Moreover, this increased Japanese military presence was hampering guerrilla resupply efforts, including the SPYRON missions, which had become so vital to the survival of the guerrilla movement. However, these heavy raids that began in September would begin to work in favor of the guerrillas. The United States was gaining air superiority, and Japanese shipping was now vulnerable. In fact, one Japanese convoy met a disastrous fate as it attempted to flee bombing raids along the east coast of Surigao province, where many uncharted coral reefs caused the fleeing ships to run aground. The major contribution of this American aerial bombardment was to force the Japanese away from areas favorable to the guerrillas, such as the Agusan Valley. Now the Japanese were concentrating their troops in areas they deemed favorable for a U.S. amphibious assault. Also, Japanese troop morale was affected by this American bombing campaign. With naval support reduced, reinforcement and resupply became less likely. The ultimate fate of the Japanese in the Philippines was looking unfavorable.

Sometime around mid-September, Mom decided it was safer to wait out the days before the birth of the baby at the bakwitan, so we moved our meager supplies and belongings to Buena Suerte. We called the hut "the little shack on the hill" because it was one of the most primitive and dilapidated of the many nipa huts we had lived in since leaving our home at East Mindanao. About ten days after moving, Mom began having labor pains, so Peach asked a neighbor to summon the midwife from the neighboring barrio. She barely arrived in time. Peach describes her as looking like a witch, with long, dirty fingernails. Nevertheless, she knew exactly what to do and set about preparing for the delivery. She looked out the window at the shoreline in the distance and announced in Surigaonon, "The tide is coming in—the baby will be a boy." In the medical kit I had zealously carried from place to place was a vial of medicine called, to the best of Peach's memory, ergometrine. Unbeknown to Peach and me, Mom had a history of excessive postpartum bleeding and for years she had kept this medicine on hand for emergency use. It was supposed to be injected with a syringe, but of course we had none. With nothing to lose, Mom did the next best thing and drank it.

Not knowing what to do, I stationed myself outside the hut, ready to respond if called. Much to my surprise, I saw Dad walking up the hill to our hut not long after the arrival of the midwife. He knew Mom's anticipated due date but his arrival at Buena Suerte on the precise date of her delivery was sheer coincidence. Peach later told us that she was immensely relieved when Dad arrived—the burden of being in charge during this important event had been lifted off her shoulders.

We never heard a sound from Mom during the delivery and I had no idea what was happening until I heard a high-pitched wail. A baby boy, immediately named Edward, was born on the afternoon of September 26, 1944, exactly three years after our big brother Ed was stabbed at San Nicolas School in Surigao. I had never seen my dad so concerned and solicitous of my mom as he was in the days following little Ed's arrival. Fear of hemorrhaging must have been uppermost in their minds, but, thank God, Mom and baby Edward survived without serious complications.

From the beginning, food preparation in the crude shack at Buena Suerte had been a real challenge for Peach. Now that Mom was a nursing mother, it was imperative that Peach somehow produce nutritious meals. Fortunately, Dad had brought with him a supply of K-rations, which contained a marvelous assortment of food. The olive-drab tins of canned meat and cheese were a godsend. As Dad opened the kits and laid everything out, my eyes fixed on the little candy bars and pieces of gum. The packets of cigarettes also caught my attention. Dad called them Chesterfields and Lucky Strikes, adding that he preferred Camels, which he was sometimes issued in carton form. With suggestions from Mom and Dad, Peach prepared nourishing meals, incorporating the protein products from the K-rations.

We moved back into our hut near Bayabas as soon as Mom felt well enough to walk down the hill. When some of the women in the area saw little Ed for the first time, they commented on his length and color and dubbed him *ubud,* the heart, or innermost part, of the trunk of the coconut tree, which is white and tubular in shape. It's also tender and delicious when cooked.

Dad left Bayabas sooner than he would have liked, but he was anxious to resolve an important procurement matter. Shortly before traveling to Bayabas he had received a copy of a proclamation that Paul Marshall, as commander of the 114th Infantry Regiment, had published in August, authorizing elements of the 114th to confiscate from the local population all palay and corn that was in excess of personal need. Essentially, Marshall's proclamation made the following points:

- The 114th Regiment, 110th Division, Tenth MD which garrisons the Province of Surigao, is in dire need of food, especially rice or corn;
- There are still food supplies (rice or corn) being hoarded by civilians and being clandestinely sold at exorbitant prices;
- All rice and corn in possession of anybody in excess of his need for subsistence (including family) until next harvest shall be commandeered by the army or any agent authorized by this headquarters; and,
- Anybody who shall be found evading, or trying to evade, the purpose of this proclamation shall be considered enemy of our cause and shall be imprisoned for the duration of the war.

Marshall added a note to his battalion commanders: "You are authorized to commandeer rice or corn for subsistence of your units from anyone within your respective jurisdictions who has more than enough for his use until the next harvest."

The proclamation undercut my father's authority as food-control administrator for Surigao. A similar incident occurred in September 1943, and Dad had written a memorandum to division headquarters on the matter. To straighten out the problem once more, Dad wrote a personal letter to Marshall, in part:

> I am writing you unofficially and I am confident that when you know how matters stand you will understand that what I am suggesting will meet your approval without the necessity to bother headquarters about it.
>
> I wish to inform you that I requested that Colonel McClish revoke my assignment as food control administrator for the Province of Surigao but he refused to do so and wishes me to continue. Now a few days ago Lieutenant Mercado sent me a copy of your proclamation dated August 19, 1944. Ever since then your soldiers have been running wild robbing small owners of the palay they want to take to their homes for family consumption only. As you know I have been controlling palay so close that even at present there are several thousand cavans available for the army and I don't see any reason why small landowners and also laborers who planted and harvested here can't remove their palay to their residences.

In fact I am so strict that to my knowledge no palay has been exported for commercial purposes since I have been in this sector.

Now this Lieutenant Mercado claims he is in charge of food control in this sector interpreting your proclamation in such way and ordering his soldiers to confiscate any palay they see on the river regardless of permits issued by me.

All this palay has been taken under the pretext that all palay belongs to the army. The owners have requested to be paid for this palay or a receipt be given them but they were refused payment or a receipt. This is robbery in its worst form committed by members of the army and I don't believe that your proclamation was intended to be interpreted that way. The worst of it all is that only small people are molested this way. It seems to me that the big fellows are strictly left alone and are not bothered for obvious reasons, but the poor fellow who has nothing has his few sacks taken away from him by the army and must starve.

Another thing must be taken into consideration: during the Jap occupation ninety percent of the pigs and chickens were stolen, also thirty percent of the carabaos were killed and therefore consideration should be given to trade in salted and dried fish. Right now there is plenty of palay but nothing else.

I am requesting that you issue orders to the effect that your officers refrain from interfering with duties of the food control administrator as I expect to receive orders to start shipping palay again.

Well, Paul, I hope that this matter will be settled between us. Now for some bad news. The other day I went to San Miguel to see Waldo Neveling and he sure is in bad shape, he is absolutely dumb and cannot utter a sound and even if he pulls through I am afraid he is finished as far as fighting is concerned as he will be a casualty for a long time to come. There are other bad rumors coming from Lianga which say that several Americans got caught when the Japs pushed into Agusan. The names of two which are mentioned mostly are Captain Feigel and Captain Haratik but of course the rumors must be taken with a grain of salt and I hope they are not true.

This letter clearly showed the depth of Dad's frustration with his food control administrator responsibilities. He had worked diligently to win the land-owners' confidence and trust and was concerned that brash young officers were ruining the relationships he had cultivated. He was especially displeased because their actions were unnecessary, since he had ample stores of palay available. This was another example of noncompliance with established procedures and guidelines that made his job more difficult.

Dad also mentioned some rumors he had heard about Captains Feigel and Haratik. Dad's responsibilities kept him in the field with little access to radio communications. Information that came via the bamboo telegraph was not always accurate; sadly, however, the tale about Captain Feigel was later confirmed—he was killed in late July while on an inspection trip in the 107th Division's area of operations. Dad was greatly saddened upon learning of the death of his friend and colleague. Mom also knew his wife, Jean, and had learned that she had been evacuated to Australia by submarine only a couple of months earlier. This tragedy dispelled any second thoughts my mother might have entertained with regard to her decision to remain on Mindanao.

The rumor regarding Captain Haratik proved false. And Hank recalled hearing that Waldo Neveling, a colorful character, had suffered a stroke. A German national who had been affiliated with the Mindanao Mother Lode Mine before the war, he joined the guerrilla movement early on and was renowned for his daring attacks against the Japanese with his motorized banca. It's not known what, if anything, resulted from Dad's letter to Marshall. Perhaps the matter was overtaken by rapidly unfolding events.

October 1944 marked a watershed in the disposition of Japanese forces on Mindanao, brought about in no small measure by the intensified U.S. bombing and, later, the invasion of Leyte. By midmonth most of the Japanese troops had left the Dansalan and Iligan sectors. Moreover, Lanao province was now free of Japanese. The 108th Division was firmly in control and had established its new headquarters at Dansalan. The Japanese had now redeployed its troops in a defensive perimeter stretching from Cotobato to Davao, which would suggest that Davao was the major defensive area to be protected from an Allied invasion. Estimates of Japanese troop strength in eastern Mindanao ranged from 34,000 (Eighth Army) to 40,000 (X Corps). The Tenth Military District's estimate was 42,600, which historians deemed the most accurate.

Prior to the U.S. invasion of Leyte in October 1944, a detachment of the Sixth Army's Alamo Scouts made a landing on the north coast of Surigao. Their mission was to verify the intelligence that the guerrillas had provided. Though they only remained two days, the local Filipinos orchestrated a barrio fiesta in their honor. One can imagine the surprised looks on the scouts' blackened faces as they made this foray into what they considered enemy territory.

At this point in the war, when it appeared that the liberation of the Philippines was imminent, an unfortunate incident occurred involving the sinking of a Japanese ship carrying American POWs from DAPECOL. In early September 1944 the Tenth Military District FRS received the message from a Davao coast watcher that some 750 American POWs were put on board a Japanese freighter and left in a convoy headed for Zamboanga city. When the convoy arrived, Don LeCouvre, coast watcher in Zamboanga, sent FRS a message confirming its arrival. Unknown to LeCouvre, however, the American POWs were then transferred at night to another ship, the *Shinyo Maru*. The original ship from Davao left the following morning without the prisoners. LeCouvre reported this departure to FRS, which in turn passed it on to MacArthur's headquarters for transmittal to U.S. Navy attack submarines monitoring Philippine waters. This original ship was allowed to go through these waters unharmed. On the morning of September 7, 1944, LeCouvre sent a priority message saying he had information that the POWs were now on the *Shinyo Maru*. FRS again informed Australia, but by the time the navy and the attack submarines received this information, it was too late. The USS *Paddle* had torpedoed the *Shinyo Maru* off of Sindangan Point. From that moment on FRS notified the navy directly rather than going through MacArthur's headquarters.

As the *Shinyo Maru* was sinking, the Japanese guards machine-gunned the POWs trying to escape. The POWs who did escape into the sea were killed, wounded, or drowned. Of the 750 POWs carried on this Japanese ship, only 83 made it to the beach and safety. Many who perished were from the 19th Bomb Group. A number of guerrillas who were also from the 19th but had refused to surrender in May 1942 were touched emotionally by this tragic incident, particularly Don LeCouvre, who had passed the initial information about the ships in Zamboanga. Because of the bureaucracy between MacArthur's headquarters and the U.S. Navy, the information about these POWs did not get through in time. The fortunate few who survived were evacuated to Australia by submarine in late September.[3]

As a footnote to this tragic incident, Major Stephen Mellnik, one of the escapees from DAPECOL in April 1943, was repatriated to Australia on a SPYRON submarine in July 1943. After reporting to MacArthur's headquarters, he was sent back to Washington for an assignment at the Pentagon, where Captain Harold Rosenquist debriefed him. After a series of discussions, they came up with a concept of an operation to rescue the POWs at DAPECOL. Undoubtedly, Mellnik had strong feelings about his fellow POWs who were left behind and was eager to put his personal weight behind such an endeavor.

The idea received support from General Sutherland, MacArthur's chief of staff. Subsequently, Mellnik and Rosenquist were ordered to SWPA headquarters in Brisbane to implement the rescue. After a stint at headquarters, Rosenquist was dispatched to Mindanao on a SPYRON mission, arriving in June 1944. His mission was on-the-ground planning for a possible breakout of prisoners. Unfortunately, GHQ, SWPA did not advise Fertig about Rosenquist's mission. Even so, Rosenquist did inform Luke Campeau, a fellow passenger on the SPYRON submarine, about his assignment regarding the POWs. Campeau, sent to Mindanao on a weather reconnaissance mission to support the forthcoming invasion, still recalls Rosenquist talking about his POW mission.

When Rosenquist arrived at Colonel Bowler's 109th Division headquarters, he refused to outline specifically the extent of his mission, saying only that he was on an intelligence mission for SWPA headquarters. Bowler contacted Fertig, and Rosenquist was ordered to report to Fertig's headquarters in the Agusan Valley. When he arrived there, he briefed Fertig, who was not impressed and asked what would be done with hundreds of POWs, most of whom were weak and sick, if a breakout were successful. Rosenquist had no answer. Fertig permitted him to make a reconnaissance of DAPECOL, but that was all. Precious time was lost. Before any practical plan of action could be implemented, the POWs were removed from DAPECOL—just ten days before Rosenquist made his reconnaissance. Mellnik and Rosenquist were shaken by the news that the prisoners had been moved. Once Rosenquist and Fertig were aware that the POWs were no longer at DAPECOL, Rosenquist elected to remain with Fertig's Tenth Military District and served as the chief of staff for intelligence.

Many American POWs were fortunate enough to escape from Keithley Barracks and DAPECOL, avoiding being sent on hell ships to work as slave laborers in Japan and other parts of Asia. With the exception of three repatriated to Australia by submarine almost immediately, the ex-POWs joined the Tenth Military District organization. Many stayed on until the end of the war.

Bruce Elliott was a POW escapee from the prison camp in Puerto Princesa on the island of Palawan. He was a young sailor whose last assignment for the navy was laying mines in Manila Bay—the SS *Corregidor* hit one of them while exiting the bay in December 1941. He was taken prisoner after the surrender of U.S. forces in May 1942 and eventually arrived at the Puerto Princesa POW camp, the one depicted in the opening scenes of the movie *The Great Raid*. After several weeks Elliott and six others escaped in a banca, spending three days in open waters with little food and water before making landfall in the southern part of Palawan. During a one-year odyssey Elliott moved south from island to island until he reached Mindanao, where he joined the guerrillas and served for several months with the 125th Infantry Regiment in the Province of Sulu.[4]

Many of the Americans who served in the Tenth Military District were U.S. servicemen who did not surrender. John Starkey was with the Army Air Corps, assigned to the 440th Ordnance Company deployed to an airstrip in Cagayan. He, Jack Samples, Gerald Chapman, Fred Faust, and other Army Air Corps personnel serving inland did not surrender in May 1942. Starkey made his decision with no hesitation. He remembered the rape of Nanking, particularly the horror the Japanese had inflicted on the Chinese, and believed surrendering would be a death sentence. The group went deeper in the interior to evade capture; however, several contracted malaria and had to stay in the care of Filipino families along the way. After some months they joined the Tenth Military District. Starkey served in the 109th Division in Bukidnon; Samples with the FRS; and Faust later commanded the 110th Division's Special Troops with which my brothers served.[5]

During his initial assignment at the 110th Division's headquarters, Gerry Chapman volunteered to replace James Schoen, a coast watcher on Leyte who was stricken with a serious illness and evacuated to Mindanao. About two months later he was moved to the northwestern tip of Samar, overlooking the San Bernardino Strait; however, ever-increasing forays by Japanese patrols into the area were endangering his site, forcing him to move again and establish a new site across the strait on the Luzon side, near Santa Magdalena.

Bob Stahl, U.S. Army Intelligence, joined the guerrillas on Mindanao in December 1943, arriving on a SPYRON mission from Australia. Prior to his assignment, he had received training in radio and cryptology. After spending some time with the guerrillas, he was sent to an observation point on the northeast coast of Samar, where he encountered the same difficulties that had been common to us in Surigao. Japanese patrols were a constant threat, food often inadequate and daily living a challenge, and the jungle harbored malaria and other illnesses. Keeping his equipment functioning was a top priority. Stahl described much of his Samar adventure in his book, *You're No Good to Me Dead*.[6] While Chapman and Stahl did not have frequent radio contact, Stahl occasionally relayed Chapman's radio traffic to Fertig's FRS station when the atmospheric conditions affected his transmissions.

In the afternoon of June 15, 1944, Stahl heard Chapman's radio trying to contact Mindanao, but Japanese military stations were jamming him. Because of Chapman's repeated attempts, Stahl sensed that he had observed something really big in Japanese ship movements. He tried to relay Chapman's message traffic but was also jammed by the Japanese. KFS in San Francisco did hear his relay and asked him to move to a higher frequency. When he did so, KFS sent the relayed information to Fertig's headquarters on Mindanao as well as the U.S. military in Australia. After the successful relay, Stahl decoded a message: "Going east, two small patrol boats, ten cruisers, three battleships, eleven destroyers and nine aircraft carriers."[7]

At this time Admiral Raymond Spruance, commander of the Fifth Fleet, was about to launch an amphibious assault against the island of Saipan. He was unaware of the Japanese battle group movement eastward from Philippine waters. With this message, he ordered the Fifth Fleet southward to engage the Japanese in the historic "Marianas Turkey Shoot." This decisive sea battle destroyed in large measure the Japanese Navy and rendered its forces ineffective for the remainder of the war. Chapman's and Stahl's quick action and superb teamwork exemplified their dedication to the coast-watcher mission.

General MacArthur's headquarters also placed a high priority on weather stations to report on weather conditions as the U.S. forces were finalizing plans for the liberation of the Philippines. Lucien "Luke" Campeau was in Australia when he learned about the need for people with his expertise. He volunteered to lead a party of six enlisted men to join the Tenth Military District. Traveling by submarine, they were allowed only five thousand pounds for all of their specialized equipment; they were expected to live off the land for the duration of their assignment. Their weather station was located on a high mountain range between Zamboanga and Misamis Occidental provinces. Living conditions were difficult, and Campeau suffered from a painfully infected molar and bouts of malaria and dysentery. In a remote area with no medical facilities close by, he recovered slowly. But he and his team persevered and provided a steady flow of weather information to the planners of the upcoming landings of U.S. forces in the Philippines.[8]

Coast-watcher reports, FRS communications support, and weather analyses provided by the Tenth Military District itself underscore the importance of the district's role in the total war effort.

NINE

Light at the End of the Tunnel

As the liberation of the Philippines was drawing near, McClish sent a memorandum, dated October 4, 1944, to the field that gave some indication that the American forces were about to return to Mindanao. In effect, it ordered all units to have all of their paperwork in order and to begin planning how to support the American forces. Furthermore, Dad was needed at the 110th Division headquarters to procure supplies for the troops along the Agusan River. McClish wrote:

> It is very important that all administration be brought up to date and kept up to date. All reports in arrears must be sent to this headquarters by return courier.
>
> A practical plan will be mailed to your headquarters in a few days. In essence, your part in the plan will be to cover prominent trails in the interior when the Americans drive the Japanese back in retreat. In the meantime your combat troops should be conveniently located to cover the trails and equally to carry on local action.
>
> It is further desired that you send Captain Hansen to this headquarters and that he shall turn over all division supply to your supply officer on proper receipt. Captain Hansen is needed for procurement of supplies for the troops stationed along the river.
>
> My headquarters is now located at Las Nieves. The 113th Infantry Regiment is organized and they are taking a position along the river in order to cover converging routes in the Esperanza area, both river and trails.

I have received very little intel information from your province. It is desired that you send by return courier a resume of your intel reports from the first of June to the last of September inclusive, and also a sketch of your troop dispositions.

Clearly McClish was anticipating the arrival of the American forces and wanted the official records of his division and the 114th Infantry Regiment to be current and in good order when that happened. The memorandum suggested that he was somewhat irritated at delinquent reports and the lack of intelligence and that, moreover, he wanted a regular courier service established between his headquarters and the 114th Infantry Regiment. In effect, he was demanding more information and a tighter control over his operational units as they prepared to work with the incoming Americans.

When Dad arrived at the 110th Division headquarters in Las Nieves for his meeting with McClish, he met up with my brothers and told them the good news of the safe arrival of their new baby brother, Edward. At that time the division was in a state of flux, awaiting news of the start of the eagerly awaited liberation of the Philippines. Everyone was wondering—when and where would it start? They believed Mindanao would be the first island liberated and they would participate in the effort.

Rudy and Hank were granted leave to visit us in Bayabas, but we had no advance notice. I was perched on a branch of the guava tree when I saw two uniformed men walking in the direction of our hut, with rifles slung over their shoulders and knapsacks on their backs. For a brief, scary moment I thought they were Japanese soldiers. But before clambering down the tree and sounding the alarm, I realized they looked more like the young American guerrillas I had seen congregating in Claver when we lived there. It wasn't until I saw the familiar smiles on their faces as they approached that I finally recognized my brothers. When I last saw them they had been thin, dressed in tattered clothes and barefoot. Now, standing in front of me were two handsome young men clad in new military uniforms and boots (courtesy of the SPYRON supply missions).

Mom's elation at having her boys home, safe and sound, was beyond measure. She peppered them with questions about their activities over the past year. Peach and I stayed close by so as not to miss any details. We marveled at the improvement in their appearance since their recovery from malaria. They had saved their allotment of K-rations to bring home so we could all share these treasures. As they spread out the contents of each kit, I noticed that they quietly stuck the small packs of cigarettes and matches in their pockets. These were not for sharing—during their stay I noticed that they often went off by themselves to smoke away from the rest of us.

Dad came home around the end of November or early December. Our family unit was complete! Best of all, Dad brought exciting details of the liberation of Leyte and General MacArthur's return to Philippine soil, fulfilling his promise, "I SHALL RETURN." We welcomed the arrival of the American forces with much elation and great relief. For us, it was the beginning of the end to our wartime ordeal. Of course, we were disappointed that Mindanao had not been chosen as the first island in the Philippines to be liberated, and we wondered when our forces would come to free *us*. When would *we* be finally rid of the ever-present fear of being captured or killed by the Japanese?

Frankly, we were running out of places to hide. Did Mom have enough energy left in her to uproot her children, including a little baby, and move to still another location? Japanese forces were firmly in control of the areas south and north of us. With the Philippine Sea to the east, the only other possible direction was west, deeper into the mountainous area, which was absolutely the last resort, for it was sparsely populated and we didn't know what kind of local support was available. For centuries various hill tribes had lived in those mountains by choice, keeping interaction with the general population along the coast to a minimum. There was no way of knowing how our presence would be received.

We set aside those concerns for the time being as we reveled in the excitement of our family reunion. We had a small celebration to observe the boys' birthdays—Rudy's nineteenth and Hank's eighteenth. Three years earlier we had enjoyed a similar celebration at our home at East Mindanao, unaware that a few short hours later, Dad would rush home with news of an event that would change our lives forever. My tenth birthday came later that month, and while there was no cake with candles, I received treats that were just as special—gum and candy from the K-rations Dad and the boys had carried in their knapsacks.

Although there were no star-shaped decorations hanging outside our windows when Christmas Eve arrived, we were happy and thankful to be alive. We celebrated Christmas 1944 in a mood of joy and hope. For the first time in a long time, Mom and Dad smiled and laughed. It seemed like an eternity had passed since that unforgettable day when we abandoned our home at East Mindanao. We had all overcome hardships and survived dangerous situations, and now we were together again, with a new baby in the family!

Our little nipa hut barely accommodated us all. It reminded me of our first hideout in Binaguiohan, when we were all crowded into Peping Lisondra's bakwitan on the hill. This time, however, we had one more Hansen in our group. We slept on the floor, and Princess wandered around, trying to decide which body to plop herself next to. My faithful little companion had been neglected since the arrival of the new baby. For many years Princess had always been there for me whenever I was afraid, unhappy, or simply bored, and now the new little family member was really interesting and entertaining, and the poor dog did not receive the attention she deserved. But with the boys home there were extra hands to pet her and she even learned to tolerate some of the tricks they played on her.

Peach had to prepare enormous amounts of food to satisfy our family, especially the two lanky teenage guerrillas. I had to work overtime with the mortar and pestle to have enough rice to cook two pots for each meal. She fried any leftover rice from the previous evening in a little coconut oil with chopped onions or vegetables and added it to our morning meal. There was little variety in our menu and no distinction between breakfast, lunch, or dinner fare. She carefully doled out food from our K-ration supply to enhance the flavor of our meals. Rudy and Hank had voracious appetites, and it was a daily challenge for Peach and me to find and pick enough greens for each meal. Fortunately, our neighbors had pointed out an area where ferns grew in abundance. The young, curly new shoots, *paco,* were a delicious addition to the main dish, especially when simmered in a gata-based sauce. The boys helped by grating coconuts and extracting the milk to make gata and oil for cooking and fueling our clamshell lamps. They scoured the nearby fields for *kamoteng kahoy* (the tuberous root of the cassava or manioc plant), delicious when roasted over the embers of an open fire. Chunks of camote also stretched a stewlike meal.

Hilarion, the member of Dad's detail who had often brought news and money from Dad to our various hideouts, had grown somewhat attached to us and stayed close by. He kept his eyes and ears open for any news of possible nearby Japanese patrols. He also shared our food and reciprocated by keeping us supplied with bananas and other fresh fruit. He always left a large bunch of ripe bananas hanging by a strip of rattan near the entrance to the hut. We'd grab a banana whenever we felt peckish—I remember seeing Hank plucking several at a time for a quick snack. On occasion, Hilarion prepared a vegetable dish with the shredded flower of the banana plant (called *kasing-kasing,* for the local word for heart, because of its t shape and blood-red color) simmered in gata flavored with tiny salted fish.

In reviewing Dad's reports and memos, I can now understand how difficult it must have been for him to procure enough food to feed over five thousand guerrillas in the 110th Division alone, especially toward the latter part of
the war, when food was so scarce. Dad had the power to strong-arm the rice
producers into selling him their crops, but his reports and memos indicate
that he used persuasion rather than force to gain their trust and cooperation.
He also earned their respect by his fair negotiating approach, always allowing
them to keep enough palay to feed their own families until the next harvest.

With her family safe at home with her, Mom could relax for the first time
in almost three years. Her appetite picked up. Thankfully, the K-rations added
nutrition and pizzazz to our meals, for Mom needed to be healthy for her
baby's sake as well as her own. Mom was ever mindful of the fact that, by the
grace of God, we had all survived up to this point. She had been deeply affected by the tragic loss of hundreds of American POWs on the other side of
Mindanao; it was a stark reminder that the war was far from over. She would
have been even more upset, had she known that those POWs represented only
a fraction of the thousands whom the Japanese had shipped to various destinations to augment their dwindling workforce in mines, munitions factories,
and other industrial sites.

Hank recalls those days before and after Christmas of 1944 as ones in which
he and Rudy spent some quality time with Dad; they had a lot of catching up to
do. The boys and Dad had always enjoyed a good relationship—they had spent
countless hours together at East Mindanao's machine shop during weekends
and school holidays before the war. After we went into hiding, they were never
far from his side, right up to the time Dad joined the guerrilla organization in
early April 1943. I wonder what was going through Dad's mind when, just a few
days later, he saw them going off with Captain Knortz to Medina for their own
induction into the guerrilla force. And I can only imagine how heartrending it
must have been for him to see his young sons a few months later in a makeshift
military hospital, weak from malnutrition and suffering from malaria. Since
then, however, their paths had crossed only occasionally. And now, as they sat
and talked about their experiences, it felt like a conversation among peers, as
Hank recalls. He sensed that he and Rudy had grown in stature in Dad's eyes.
Mom, Peach, and I listened to these discussions with great interest. Mom, especially, had been very frustrated at having been in the dark about important developments unfolding over the past year, and she did not want to miss a word.

I stayed close to the family circle during this period, going outdoors only
to perform chores. Our hut had a front porch running along its the width;

though narrow, there was enough room here to suspend a small rattan hammock at one end. I can remember rocking my baby brother in the hammock—I loved stroking his little round head with its fine, silky hair. Almost three years had gone by since I had played with dolls, and here I was holding in my arms a real live doll that wiggled and cried and wet his diapers (made of old bed sheets). However, my joy at having a little brother was somewhat tempered by the fact that after the baby's arrival Dad stopped calling me "Babe" (his special pet name for me) and started referring to me as "Gin" like the rest of the family. My position as "the babe" in the family had been usurped. Our family reunion did not last long, however, as Dad soon received word via a runner that he was to report back to the 110th Division's headquarters.

At the dawning of a new year (1945) that we felt certain would bring us liberation at last, Dad, Rudy, and Hank, together with Dad's detail, left Bayabas for the Agusan Valley. Hank remembers that shortly after they hit the trail, Dad whipped out a pack of Camels and offered each of them a cigarette. The group hiked to the coast, then sailed by banca to Lianga. The Japanese had built a road from Lianga across the mountains into the Agusan Valley, which they followed until it reached the Agusan River. They could not cross because the river was so high—it had been raining constantly for a number of days. They constructed a raft of bamboo and sailed down the river to Butuan, where the headquarters of the 110th Division had been moved.

Upon arrival at the 110th in early January, Dad received orders from McClish regarding a new assignment—division ordnance officer. McClish was anticipating that Dad's expertise in ordnance matters, coupled with his knowledge of the areas of Mindanao that he had traversed so many times, would be beneficial in supporting the operations of the U.S. forces when they arrived to liberate Mindanao. However, the orders were almost immediately superseded by Special Orders from Fertig's headquarters dated January 10, 1945, directed at him and four other officers. "The following named officers are relieved of assignment and duty in the Tenth MD USFIP effective this date and will proceed by first available transportation to GHQ, USAFFE." My father was being sent to USAFFE headquarters in Leyte!

Dad had one last meeting with McClish before leaving division headquarters. Theirs was a relationship based on mutual respect that had deepened over the years they worked together. Rudy and Hank accompanied Dad part of the way to his departure point before reporting to their Special Troops unit. Although his exact departure date and mode of transportation are uncertain, around January 23 he may have made his way to Tambis, near Lianga on the coast, for a flight to Leyte via Catalina or C-46. Fred Faust, Rudy and Hank's former commanding officer in the Special Troops, was also part of the group that left with Dad.

Following Dad's departure for Leyte, Rudy and Hank embarked on a new operation for the 110th Division's Special Troops. The objective for their unit was the Mina-ano area of Agusan province, which lies between the towns of Cabadbaran and Butuan. This was a noteworthy encounter with the Japanese because it was a valiant effort by the guerrillas to prevent the Japanese from Surigao reinforcing their garrison in the Butuan region. Since October 1944, the Japanese, sensing likelihood of a U.S. invasion, were reinforcing their garrisons in places that might be objectives of amphibious assaults. When it learned of the enemy's move, my brothers' unit deployed from Tagabaca to Mina-ano on January 17, 1945. Once there, their unit hastily developed dug-in positions on both sides of the national Route 1 highway leading toward Butuan from Cabadbaran. At 6:30 A.M. on January 17, the unit made contact with 200 to 250 Japanese soldiers marching along the highway toward Butuan. Members of the 113th Infantry Regiment, assisting in the operation, had em-placed a .50 caliber machine gun on the road along with guerrillas armed with bazookas and BARs. The Japanese column was now between the two Special Troops positions. Both guerrilla units opened fire on the enemy force. Be-tween fifty and sixty Japanese fell in this initial exchange, which lasted about three hours. Later, the engagement brought more Japanese casualties. Because of the Special Troops' prepared positions, there were no guerrilla casualties. Overwhelmed by their opponents' fire superiority, the Japanese were forced to retreat. However, by noon they reorganized with reinforcements and moved again down the road, with flanking elements on each side, which resulted in an intense combat situation. Three times the Japanese assaulted Rudy and Hank's unit's defensive line but were repulsed. With their ammunition now in short supply, my brothers' unit withdrew at about 6:30 P.M. under cover of a bazooka fusillade. Their withdrawal point was Damognay—two kilometers away. Japanese causalities for this operation were estimated between 110 and 160 killed and wounded. One guerrilla was wounded.

Later, on March 3, my brothers were involved in a similar firefight with the Japanese on Route 1, toward Rizal, near the junction of a private road off the national road that led to a hacienda that had been occupied by a Japanese en-terprise before the war. Some civilians had reported seeing a large contingent of Japanese hiking along Route 1, the main road from Butuan to Buenavista. Cap-tain Dongallo, the new commanding officer of the Special Troops, assembled

Company "A" (Rudy and Hank's unit) and planned to ambush the Japanese at a juncture midway through a horseshoe-shaped bend in the road. The guerrillas dug fifty foxholes ten feet apart around the bottom of the U of the bend about three hundred feet from the road. Hank's foxhole was closest to the middle of the U and Rudy's was next to his. Hank was designated to fire the first shot as soon as he determined that the Japanese contingent was halfway around the bend. The Special Troops maintained their positions until dark, with no sign of the advancing enemy. The guerrillas assumed that the Japanese would encamp somewhere along the way and continue their advance the following morning. There was no moon that night, and it was pitch black as they waited in their foxholes.

Members of Company "A" had no watches, but they guessed that it was about 11:00 or midnight when they saw glimmers of light coming in their direction. Soon they could make out three Filipino guides holding torches, followed by four or five uniformed Japanese soldiers. This was apparently a scouting party, sent in advance to determine whether the road was clear. The Special Forces allowed this group to proceed. When they were out of sight, the still night was suddenly filled with loud creaking noises and Japanese voices as the main force approached. It was dark, and the guerrillas continued to hold their positions until Hank fired his signal. The Special Troops fired with everything they had—machine guns, BARs, carbines, with tracer bullets illuminating the action. The Japanese immediately took cover in the ditch on the opposite side of the road and returned fire. The fierce firefight lasted about thirty minutes. Strangely, the Japanese ceased firing, and in the silence the guerrillas heard the piercing sound of a bugle. After about half an hour of silence, Rudy and Hank and three other guerrillas, each with five hand grenades, ventured out of their foxholes and crawled on their bellies toward the road. On signal, all five would throw their grenades at the opposite side of the road, repeating every ten feet until they reached the ditch on their side of the road. There was no return fire, so they climbed onto the road, where they stumbled on a mountain gun—a gun barrel about three feet long and mounted on a carriage with two wheels. It was harnessed to a horse that, unfortunately, had been caught in the crossfire and killed. The five returned to their foxholes, and it remained quiet until dawn. At first light, the guerrillas confirmed that the Japanese had, indeed, left the area, leaving behind the mountain gun and three supply carts pulled by carabaos, which were unharmed. Among the supplies on the carts were sacks of rice, canned meat, and tea—but no ammunition. The Japanese had taken their ammunition and a machine gun with them on a cart further to the rear of the column but left the machine gun's tripod lying in the ditch. The gun carriage and carts explained the loud creaking that heralded the approach of the Japanese.

Several guerrillas worked to separate the horse's body from the gun carriage, no small task considering the elaborate leather harness that was used. (This was undoubtedly the reason the Japanese were forced to leave the mountain gun behind—it was too dangerous and time-consuming to release it from the dead horse.) When they had freed the weapon, they rolled it down an embankment and dragged it through a cornfield to headquarters. When Dongallo saw their trophy, he remarked, "Boy, we got a jewel today—this is going to be shipped to Fertig."

The horse was immediately butchered, and the guerrillas and their civilian volunteers had a feast. They turned over the carabaos and carts to the civilians. Shortly thereafter, with two guerrillas as escorts, the mountain gun made its way to Fertig's headquarters, where it remained on display only, because the guerrillas could not obtain appropriate shells for it.

During after-action discussions, the Special Troops and their officers concluded that their nighttime attack had been somewhat ill-conceived. Knowing the terrain, a more effective tactic would have been to confront the Japanese head-on, which would have caused a much larger number of Japanese casualties and also prevented them from taking cover in the ditch on the other side of the road. They had conceived the plan for a daytime confrontation, but the Japanese surprised them by arriving close to midnight. Thus, there were only four dead Japanese soldiers after the encounter.

Fully expecting the Japanese to return, the Special Troops took up positions guarding the highway to Rizal from their foxholes. About three weeks later, before dawn, about two hundred Japanese soldiers attacked their positions from three sides—left, right, and center. My brothers were part of the group with heavy weapons covering the right flank. Rudy and Hank immediately sprang into action, raking machine-gun fire from right to left. Hank recalls that they fired nonstop until the muzzle of their machine gun became too hot to touch. Just before daybreak, Dongallo, realizing that his troops were badly outnumbered, ordered them to retreat to the nearby river. They waded through chest-deep water carrying their weapons above their heads and reached the opposite bank before daylight broke. Later, as they were hiking toward Rizal, a fellow soldier, with a grin on his face, suggested to Hank that he remove his knapsack and examine it. Imagine his surprise when he found bullet holes on two sides—a bullet had pierced it from the right, went right through the contents, and exited on the left side. That was too close for comfort! Fortunately, Hank's knapsack was the only guerrilla casualty during this engagement. Japanese casualties were unknown, as they didn't pursue the guerrillas across the river and instead returned to their base, bringing with them their wounded and dead.

In preparation for the U.S. forces landing on Mindanao, the 110th Division's Special Troops participated in two special operations. The first was the Japanese radar station in Surigao that was monitoring the U.S. naval forces passing through the strait. It was situated on a hill behind the cemetery where my older brother Ed was buried. The 114th Infantry Regiment was designated as the major attack force. The attack was scheduled for April 27, 1945. The 110th's Special Troops unit was to land on the west coast of the peninsula at Ipil, then push east on the road to Kilometer 4. The 114th's troops were to attack from the eastern side of the peninsula and move along the coast road to Kilometer 4. Unfortunately, the landing craft that were to provide fire support never arrived, and Rudy and Hank's unit got bogged down fighting Japanese. Soon after their arrival at Ipil, they met stiff resistance and never made it to Kilometer 4. Even so, a small patrol of the 114th Infantry Regiment did destroy the radar station.

In May 1945 Rudy and Hank participated in a beach reconnaissance and scouting operation with the Special Troops near Bugo. Later in the month, the 108th Regimental Combat Team came ashore here. A U.S. Navy landing ship tank (LST) transported them to the area and they spent the night on a beach near the Del Monte pineapple plantation. On the day of the reconnaissance operation two small navy launches assisted them. Major Rosenquist was in charge of one of the boats and Major Robert Spielman, from the 114th Infantry Regiment, had command of the other. Once on board their assigned boats the group headed for the beach in the Bugo area, where Spielman's party, including my two brothers, was offloaded to provide cover for Rosenquist's mission. Rosenquist's boat remained offshore taking depth soundings and coordinating with Rudy and Hank's party on shore. All of a sudden a shot rang out, and one of the men in Rosenquist's boat fell into the water. Then more shots followed, and Rosenquist's launch headed out into open waters. The group on the beach could not ascertain where the firing was coming from. The sniper had to be high up but even so apparently could not see the boys or their fellow guerrillas. Then firing started coming into the spot Rudy and Hank were attempting to take shelter. After changing their position, they looked up and saw a Japanese sniper on a platform built between two coconut trees. They beat a hasty retreat and hid behind a fallen tree while exchanging fire. They only had carbines with them, and the Japanese soldier on the platform had a machine gun. They decided to move out of the area, passing by the Del Monte facility and adjacent water tower. As they retreated, shots rang out again, this time from the water tower. One person was wounded, but they were able to bring him along. To reach the pick-up point, they had to ford a channel, carrying their wounded comrade as well as their weapons. When they reached the other side, they could see fires that had been set by the Japanese in anticipation of the invasion. Later, the launch arrived and picked up Spielman's group. The wounded man had been hit in the back near his kidney, so Hank grabbed the first aid pouch attached to his web belt and doused the wound with sulfanilamide powder and then applied a bandage, wrapping the ends around the man's torso. Ten members of Special Troops, including Rudy and Hank, returned in the launch with Spielman, then proceeded to the place they had spent the previous night.

The next morning my brothers looked out into the bay and saw hundreds of ships. The liberation force had arrived! This was the beginning of the invasion on the north coast of Mindanao. The 108th Regimental Combat Team made this landing. During the previous month, the 24th and the 31st Divisions had landed at Illana Bay on the west coast. Within two weeks, the 108th and elements of the 31st Division linked up on the Sayre highway. The landing of the 108th Regimental Combat Team in the Cagayan area now prompted the Japanese Army to move north, eventually going inland along the Agusan River valley. Approximately thirty thousand Japanese troops were now retreating into this area—where the guerrillas had successfully evaded them previously. In the meantime, the 114th Infantry Regiment was continuing to clean up the Japanese presence in Surigao province. They later joined regular U.S. Army units in pursuing the Japanese remnants in the Agusan River valley.

At our hideout in Bayabas, the roar of airplanes flying overhead made me run outdoors and watch in awe. The many different shapes and sizes of aircraft flying at different altitudes fascinated me. Even the smallest Allied planes seemed far grander than the little Japanese zeros from Surigao I had seen flying over Tagana-an during the early part of our evacuation. I often wondered if the American pilots could see me waving my arms in excitement.

We remained in our secluded haven in Bayabas after Dad and the boys left in January 1945. Peach and I helped Mom with baby Ed while continuing with our usual activities. As we settled into our routine, I noticed that Mom was thin, there was more gray in her hair, and she just generally looked older; the constant stress of the previous three years had taken its toll on her. However, she always had a faint smile on her face as she nursed and cared for little Ed, who was growing more active by the day. Fearing that her milk was not providing enough sustenance, Mom slowly started introducing solid food into his diet, mashing a small portion of table food or banana with a wooden spoon and pushing it between his lips with a finger tip. I spent a lot of time holding Ed in my arms and hated to set his soft little body on the rough woven mat on the hard bamboo floor. Peach continued to perform all household tasks, and I helped her as much as I could. Before baby Ed's arrival, doing laundry in the stream was fairly simple—we had no soap, so we simply kneaded our clothes on a smooth rock and gave them a whack or two with a thick paddle, then rinsed and spread them on other rocks or draped them over bushes to dry. With a baby, however, there were soiled diapers to contend with. To my relief, Peach took charge of them, spreading them on flat rocks to let the sun thoroughly dry them and bleach out the stains.

Without the men with healthy appetites to cook for, Peach had more time and proceeded with a project she and Dad had discussed during his visit. Among the items Dad carried in his Musette bag and left with us was a small canister containing sulfanilamide, a new medicine that had come with supplies delivered by submarine. He explained that this was a new sulfa drug that had proven effective in the treatment of gunshot wounds. One of our neighbors was a kind old man with an ugly sore on his leg that apparently had been festering for a long time. He was constantly chasing off the flies with a branch from a small tree. Before Dad left, Peach asked him if she could try treating the sore with sulfanilamide, and he agreed. Dad also advised her that fresh air and sunlight would speed up the healing process, but the flies had to be kept away. I watched as Peach poured water over the ugly wound to try to clean it before sprinkling the powder on it. Then Peach took a piece of one of our old abaca frocks, folded it over several times, and put it on the wound, securing it around the man's leg with string. It formed a barrier for the flies, yet allowed air to circulate.

In time the man's sore improved and, of course, word got around that Peach had some powerful medicines. Soon other people came with various ailments, and she had to explain that the medicine that Dad had brought was suitable only for the treatment of open sores. By using the sulfanilamide powder sparingly she was able to successfully treat several "patients" while we lived in Bayabas. The whole community appreciated the efforts of my fourteen-year-old sister who, in addition to carrying the full responsibility of running our household while Mom tended to the baby, willingly took the time to treat their sores.

As the months went by, little Ed developed into a cute, active baby boy, with hazel eyes and silky, blond hair. I learned from one of the women in the neighborhood that certain people in the community considered baby Ed an *engkanto* (enchanted one) and, according to folklore, the hair of such a creature had curative powers; when it was combined with pieces of coconut husk then set on fire, the resulting smoke, when inhaled, was supposed to cure illnesses or promote good health. I related this to Mom and she smiled and dismissed it as superstitious folklore, adding that she hoped no one would come asking for a tuft of Ed's hair, for she certainly would not want to offend anyone by refusing such a request. I couldn't help feeling jealous because these people thought little Ed was enchanted while others (especially the children) in the remote barrios we had passed through considered me a kind of weird wak-wak creature!

Large formations of U.S. planes continued to fly overhead, and rumors abounded about American forces having landed on Mindanao and fierce battles being waged on Mindanao as well as other islands. However, there was no way any of these stories could be confirmed. We had heard no news about Dad or the boys for several months. Hilarion, Dad's emissary, had not made an appearance since leaving with Dad and the boys in January. We had no inkling that Dad had been ordered to USAFFE headquarters in Leyte. Mom was beside herself with worry about the whereabouts and welfare of her husband and sons. We seemed to be living in a time warp while so much was happening in the outside world. The conclusion to World War II was fast approaching, and we had no knowledge of events, their import, or how they would affect our lives in the months and years ahead. Of course, we had no way of knowing that by February 1945 Operation Victor had commenced, with its overall objective the liberation of the remaining Philippine Islands, including Mindanao. Such news would have boosted our morale considerably. Also unbeknown to us, my brothers and their fellow guerrillas were working with elements of the U.S. liberation forces in these efforts. This knowledge, too, would have helped allay Mom's worries. By late February 1945, the liberation of Manila was complete. As we were ignorant of that momentous occasion, we could not celebrate its return to rule by Filipinos and an interim American government.

Father Luis soon sent word that American forces had landed on Mindanao at last. However, it was anticipated that, because of its size and rough terrain, the liberation of our island would take some time. The most encouraging development was that the Japanese were retreating into the interior and relinquishing control of the coastal towns. Shortly thereafter Father Luis told us that he had decided to carefully make his way north, toward Surigao.

For the first time in years, Mom felt optimistic enough to acknowledge the possibility that our long ordeal might be coming to an end. However, there remained the challenge of somehow reconnecting with Dad and my brothers. For weeks Mom was consumed with uncertainty. Unable to endure it any longer, she decided to move us one step closer to normality, which involved our eventual return to Surigao. We would go first to Tago, where she would seek the assistance of local officials. She thought that if conditions in Tago proved too dangerous for us, we could always return to Bayabas.

Gathering up our worldly goods, we said goodbye to our friends and neighbors in Bayabas and commenced our homeward journey. Fortunately, by then it was safe to travel by banca—traveling on foot with a wiggly nine-month-old baby would have been difficult. When we arrived in Tago, Mom immediately sought news from the mayor and the priests, but, unfortunately, nobody had any information about Dad or the boys. In fact, they noted that Dad had not been in the area for many months. However, the good news was that the Japanese no longer occupied the east coast of Surigao province—they had been ordered to the interior of Butuan province to the west, in the vicinity of the Agusan River. But the best news was that U.S. forces were now in control of most of Mindanao.

Many of the homes in Tago had been burned or otherwise destroyed. Accommodations for our family were set up in the local Puericulture Center (these centers had been established in major cities throughout the Philippines to provide assistance to new mothers and their babies). Meals were prepared for us in the kitchens of the priests or the mayor, both of which were in close proximity. Thankfully, conditions in the Tago area had improved considerably since our trip the year before. Only then did we realize that a year had passed since we left Cantilan to seek a safer location in which to await Ed's birth. For the second consecutive year we were on the move on Peach's birthday on July 25 (her fifteenth), though in the opposite direction this time and under less frightening circumstances.

As we paused in Tago we were joined by Sarah and Annie, two of Frank McCarthy's granddaughters, who, along with their sister, Agnes, were schoolmates of my brothers at San Nicolas School. Sarah was now married to Bob Pease, one of the young American guerrillas, and they, too, had lost contact. The sisters were headed south to Lianga to look for him. Hoping that there might also be information about Dad and the boys there, Mom decided to send Peach and me with Sarah and Annie while she stayed in Tago with baby Ed and Princess. We were able to travel on a banca carrying a load of goods to Lianga the following morning.

The trip was going well until a chabasco materialized out of nowhere, catching our banceros by surprise. A big wave swamped the banca, immediately filling it with water. In the blink of an eye, we found ourselves in water up to our shoulders, still holding onto the sides of the boat. The waterlogged cargo kept the banca partially submerged—even the stout bamboo outriggers could not rise above the surface of the water. Perhaps because I was afraid and anxious, I have only vague memories of the details of this voyage, but Annie recalls that the banca's progress was so slow that it took three days for us to reach Lianga.

The wife of the mayor of Lianga immediately took us into her care, giving us food and a change of clothing. It soon became evident that I was running a fever. The mayor's wife had a remedy—she prepared a mixture of vinegar and chopped local onions (similar to shallots), warmed this concoction and applied it to my chest and back, and then wrapped me tightly in a crisp, fresh bed sheet. I distinctly remember the feel of that soft cotton sheet against my skin and its aromatic camphor scent.

There was no news about Bob Pease or of the Hansen menfolk, so our adventurous trip did not produce the results we had hoped. And we could do nothing else until I was well enough to make the return trip. One evening there was a dance party and the young ladies were invited. Sarah would not think of it, but Annie and Peach, like typical teenagers, were not averse to having a little fun. Knowing that I was in good hands, Peach went with Annie to the dance. Looking back, I can only imagine that my sister must have felt like Cinderella that evening. At fifteen, she was going to her first dance, wearing a dress lent to her by our kind hostess.

I made a quick recovery, thanks to the warm-vinegar–and–onion treatment, and we headed back up the coast to Tago. This return trip was uneventful, thank God. Mom was full of concern when she learned that I had fallen ill, but was soon reassured that I was well. Amazingly, that was the first time that I had gotten sick since my school days before the war. (At school I was known as the sickly one because of my frequent absences.)

The news coming into Tago from the north was encouraging. The Japanese troops that had been occupying the coastal towns up the east coast of Surigao were gone. This made travel by banca safe. The refugees that had fled south over the preceding eighteen months or so were now returning to their homes. So Mom decided that we should continue on to Tandag. Once again we were welcomed, but still no news about Dad or the boys. Tandag had also suffered much damage. A gracious lady named Adela Serra Ty insisted that we stay in her home. She was a member of an influential political family and was so hospitable and solicitous of our needs that it was easy to simply relax and let her pamper us. For the first time in years, Peach did not have to perform any of the multiple household tasks that had fallen on her young shoulders, as Mrs. Ty had a full complement of household help. I was relieved to see that the staff included an elderly man who made sure the kitchen was well supplied with water and firewood for the stove. Although Mom also enjoyed the respite, she was anxious to continue our quest for Dad and the boys.

This trip was much different from our hasty departure from Claver in November 1943 after its early-morning shelling, when we were fleeing for our lives. On this trip we had a baby with us. There was also a noticeable difference in Mom's physical condition. She had lost weight and it seemed to me (possibly because I had grown taller) that she had actually shrunk in size. Little Ed had developed into an active ten-month-old, and I remember having to shift his weight from one hip to the other when it was my turn to carry him. After making arrangements for a banca that could take us all the way to Surigao, we pushed on northward. Once or twice a day, we put into a seaside town to inquire about not only news of guerrilla presence in the area but also the safety of our next destination. We sought the advice of the local officials, who had fairly reliable and current information about conditions within a certain radius of their towns. Although the Japanese troops had been ordered to proceed to Butuan, there was still a possibility that small contingents of stragglers could unexpectedly appear on the scene. At this point in the war, it was a foregone conclusion that it was only a matter of time before the Japanese surrendered or were annihilated. However, the cultural belief that death was preferable to the disgrace associated with surrender caused many of them to be even more dangerous and unpredictable. There are numerous instances in which Japanese soldiers killed mercilessly as their final acts before their own demise. Thank God we did not encounter any of this as we proceeded north, but we were sad to see the destruction the retreating Japanese forces had left in their wake. The towns along our route to Surigao were within the operational area of the 114th Infantry Regiment; the locals supported the guerrillas and had suffered the consequences of their loyalty and cooperation.

We made a brief stop in Cantilan, which had been badly damaged during the occupation, but only to confer with town officials. Mom also asked them to extend her greetings and best wishes to our friend and hostess, Naping Ayado. Since Mom was anxious to proceed to Surigao without further delay, we kept stopovers to a minimum for the rest of the trip. Strangely, Mom deliberately bypassed Claver, possibly because of bittersweet memories associated with it. I was disappointed because I would have enjoyed seeing my old playmates and showing off my little brother.

We eventually reached Surigao, where we were shocked at the destruction the war years had wrought. Many houses stood empty, and others were mere skeletons. Walls were pockmarked with bullet holes. There were piles of rubble everywhere. The tree-lined streets that used to be so pretty were now full of potholes, and only a few trees were left undamaged.

A few inquiries yielded information about temporary living quarters for us at the home of the Meehlieb family. We actually had the entire lower level of their large house; they provided us with basic furnishings, and we soon settled in fairly comfortably. It was certainly luxurious compared to the places we had lived in since leaving East Mindanao. As I explored the house and the surrounding neighborhood, I was surprised at the feelings of happiness and relief that slowly swept over my whole being. It felt wonderful to be back in familiar surroundings! I knew that this was a temporary living arrangement, a place where Dad and the boys could easily find us when they returned to Surigao. Then we would go to our own home at the mine.

One of the first things we did was visit the cemetery where our big brother Ed was buried. Like the rest of Surigao, it was in sad shape—Ed's gravesite was overgrown with weeds, and Mom did not say a word as she gazed at it, little Ed wiggling impatiently in her arms. There was a look of incredible sadness on her face but she did not shed a tear, nor did she share her thoughts with us. I believe it was Peach who broke the silence and suggested that we say some prayers, so we knelt on the grass and recited the Our Father, Hail Mary, and Glory Be, followed by another prayer, "Eternal rest grant unto him, O Lord, and let perpetual light shine upon him. May his soul, and the souls of all the faithful departed, through thy mercy, rest in peace. Amen." I didn't know the last one, so I just knelt silently, keeping an eye on little Ed, who had freed himself from Mom's grasp when she knelt and was on his hands and knees crawling on the grass. I have a clear recollection of the sad expression on Mom's face as she gazed at Ed's grave almost four years after his death, but as usual, she kept her thoughts to herself. Writing about our wartime experiences has helped me to understand and appreciate my mother's strength of character, and I feel safe in speculating that even as she gazed at Ed's grave and mourned her dead son, she was also focused on reuniting her family and moving us forward to some semblance of normalcy.

COMMENTARY ON THE RETURN OF U.S. FORCES

The return of the American forces to the Philippines began with the amphibious landings on Leyte in October 1944. It had been generally assumed all along that Mindanao would be one of the first Philippine islands liberated, particularly given the advance of the American forces through New Guinea during the summer of 1944. The likelihood of the American invasion of Mindanao was further supported by the liberation of Biak Island that positioned the Americans some 1,450 kilometers from Mindanao. However, the liberation of that island was to be postponed; the Sixth Army landed instead on the east coast of Leyte on the morning of October 20, about 300 kilometers north of the Hansen hideout in Bayabas. In fact, there had even been discussions in Washington and Pearl Harbor about bypassing the Philippines entirely, moving either to Formosa or the home islands of Japan. General MacArthur strongly petitioned the Joint Chiefs of Staff (formerly the Joint Board) on keeping the Philippines as the next invasion target. At a July 26, 1944, Pearl Harbor meeting of senior commanders, including General MacArthur and President Roosevelt, they decided to continue planning for the invasion of the Philippines. "Leyte and then Luzon," said General MacArthur at the meeting. President Roosevelt and Admiral Nimitz agreed.[1] Even so, planners persisted in advocating an invasion of Formosa after Leyte was under control, bypassing Luzon. MacArthur objected, strongly pushing for the liberation of the Philippines before moving against Formosa and the Japanese homeland. In early October the joint chiefs decided to go ahead with the Luzon invasion in early 1945.

The initial planning in June 1944 called for the invasion of Mindanao in November 1944, followed by Leyte the following month. The operation was to be launched in the Sarangani Bay area, near Buayan in southern Mindanao. The purpose was to establish airbases that could be used to augment aircraft flying from carriers. However, this timeline and objective area was changed at Admiral Halsey's insistence. He was convinced that the Japanese defensive capability in the Philippines was a hollow shell, particularly regarding control of the air. Instead, he proposed that the liberation timetable be accelerated, with Leyte the site for the first landing. Mindanao had been relegated to a backseat on the schedule. American troops would not land in Mindanao until April 1945, long after Manila's liberation. Sarangani Bay became the site of the last amphibious assault in the Philippines on July 12.

Concurrent with the invasion of Leyte, an epic sea battle was developing between U.S. and Japanese naval units. The objective of the Japanese thrust was to destroy two U.S. fleets and the massive force that had invaded Leyte. Parts of this battle were fought in the Surigao Strait. The extensive sea battle raged for three days. Some of the individual skirmishes were as far as five hundred miles apart. In the end, the Japanese Navy lost twenty-six of its warships and much of its strength as a major naval force. More important, the U.S. invasion force on Leyte was kept from harm's way. However, because of the lack of air support (diverted to oppose the Japanese naval forces), the Sixth Army was commencing to meet stiffer resistance on Leyte. The Japanese Army had moved some forty-five thousand troops from Luzon and Manchuria to reinforce their positions on Leyte. Despite this increased Japanese presence, the campaign slowly shifted in favor of the American forces, and by Christmas 1944 the Sixth Army had secured the island.

Though the Japanese troop strength on Mindanao was being gradually diminished by combat actions, the remaining troops continued to pose a significant land threat in the southern Philippines. Surprisingly, after the landings on Leyte and Luzon, MacArthur's command had no mandate to use U.S. forces in liberating the islands to the south. Washington planners had counted on the joint American and Filipino guerrilla forces and the Philippine Army to accomplish this task. Fertig and his Tenth Military District would have been hard pressed, had this been the case. The redeployment and expansion of the Japanese military presence along the coastal areas of Mindanao in the early part of 1944 had reduced the guerrilla capability for resupplying food and ammunition. Many guerrilla units were on the margin relative to any sustained engagement with the estimated forty-three thousand Japanese troops remaining in eastern Mindanao. However, the landing of American forces on Leyte in October 1944 began to ease the pressure the Japanese had been putting on the guerrilla organization. Now the Japanese were feeling the effects of Allied bombing and submarine warfare. Realizing that an American invasion was coming soon, the

Japanese began in October 1944 to redeploy their troops in strongholds that were likely sites for amphibious assaults. This resulted in guerrilla units gaining supremacy in several provinces, particularly Lanao. In late February 1945, materiel arrived from Leyte to ease the logistical base of the 110th Division. Several U.S. Navy landing craft unloaded much-needed supplies in the Claver area, by now free of Japanese. Included in this over-the-beach offload were ammunition, arms, food, and other military items. Even with this logistical flow to the guerrilla forces, the Tenth Military District would have had a difficult task in dislodging the 30th and 100th Divisions of the Japanese Army on Mindanao. Though the remaining Japanese forces were not first-rate and had lost much of their logistical capability because of Allied bombing, their troops were a fair match for any American invasion force. With just the Tenth Military District troops to contend with, the Japanese could have resisted for several years. On the other hand, the 114th Infantry Regiment did secure Surigao province in the summer of 1945 without the assistance of U.S. Army ground forces. Even so, a U.S. military invasion of Mindanao was necessary to remove much of the Japanese presence.

It had always been General MacArthur's position that he had a moral imperative to liberate all the islands of the Philippines, including those bypassed by the drive to retake Leyte and Luzon. To leave the central and southern islands still under Japanese occupation would be a breach of his oft-repeated promise, "I SHALL RETURN." Moreover, the Filipino population in the central and southern islands would remain at the mercy of a frustrated and losing Japanese Army. Many casualties and concurrent atrocities could have occurred. Also, there remained pockets of American civilians and military personnel still in hiding on the other islands, members of the Hansen family on Mindanao among them.

TEN

The War Ends

Initially, Mom's attempts to gain information about the whereabouts of Dad and the boys were fruitless. Some guerrillas passing through told her of rumors that Dad and several others had been sent to USAFFE headquarters in Leyte before the American landings on Mindanao and that Rudy and Hank were in Butuan or Surigao. After a while, however, bits and pieces from different sources led Mom to believe that the rumor about Dad's having gone to Leyte might be true. After learning that the Japanese no longer patrolled the ocean and interisland banca traffic had resumed, Mom began making plans to go to Leyte and inquire at the U.S. Army headquarters there. To this end, she arranged for a large two-masted sailing banca equipped with a thatch canopy—very important to protect the tender skin of our now almost one-year-old brother Ed—to take us to Tacloban, site of the USAFFE headquarters. During this important trip, Princess remained in Surigao with the Meehlieb family. Our purpose in going was twofold: first, to locate Dad and the boys through the military and the American Red Cross, and second, to seek the medical treatment, food, and clothing assistance that Mom hoped would be available to people like us who had been in hiding for almost four years. (In fact, American civilian internees from Santo Thomas and other internment camps were brought to Tacloban for medical attention, rest, and some decent clothes before repatriation to the States.)

About midway between Mindanao and Leyte, we ran into some rough weather. A large swell hit the banca, and it tipped precariously, the outrigger on one side rising toward the sky while its counterpart disappeared beneath the surface of the water. As was customary on these large bancas, long poles extended from the hull to the large hollow bamboo floats and narrow slats of bamboo were lashed to these poles to form makeshift platforms. A crewmember was squatting in front of a simple cooking stove preparing a meal and would have been washed overboard had he not grabbed a bamboo slat and hung on, although he couldn't prevent the food and cooking paraphernalia from sliding into the water—hot boiled rice was not part of the menu for the remainder of the trip. The outriggers enabled the boat to right itself, but not before those of us who were in the cabin got drenched as water poured in.

Thankfully, warm breezes filled our sails (also helping us dry off) for the rest of the voyage, and we soon arrived at our destination. It was thrilling to pull into the harbor in Tacloban, with so many U.S. Navy ships of various sizes moored there. As we went up the channel, past the ships, the sailors leaned over the railings to get a closer look at us, probably wondering where we had come from. They seemed genuinely delighted to see Mom with her scrawny kids, including a baby. Many waved and shouted greetings at us, while others threw pieces of candy, chewing gum, and even an apple or two in our direction, but unfortunately most of the treats bounced off the canopy of our banca and fell into the water. Our boatmen did catch several of the goodies, though, and gave them to Peach and me, politely declining our offer to share with them. Once ashore, we went to a convent where, as always, we felt confident that the nuns would put us up or help us find alternate accommodations. True to form and without hesitation, they gave us rooms at the convent, near the cathedral in Tacloban. This proximity to a church allowed us to attend Mass again and offer many prayers of thanksgiving for the survival of our family and the gift of a healthy baby boy. We also prayed that we would soon be reunited with Dad and the boys.

The first order of business, however, was a visit to the Red Cross, where Mom initiated the process of tracking down Dad's whereabouts. While awaiting results of their search, we took advantage of the care and assistance offered by the military authorities. Our next stop after the Red Cross was the relief-clothing center, where we must have looked a sight with our abaca fiber shifts and bare feet. There was not a great selection of clothing, for a multitude of internees from Santo Tomas and other internment camps had already outfitted themselves prior to repatriation. Still, we managed to find several dresses suitable in style and size for each of us. We were not too picky about size, since alterations could always be made back in Surigao—we mainly wanted to have the luxury of a few changes of clothing. Shoes for me were a problem, as my narrow feet swam in the ones that were the right length. So we selected a pair that was smaller in size and cut out the toe area so my toes could extend fully. We also found several cute little boys' outfits for Ed. And, of course, Rudy and Hank would need civilian clothes as well. The end of the war would bring a drastic change to the lifestyle forced on them by the war—they would have to readapt to their previous lives as high school students!

Not to be overlooked was the variety of bed linens available, precious material that we could cut up and make into dresses or shirts if necessary. Trusting that the sewing machine she had left in Claver had survived and was still operable, Mom also helped herself to needles and thread in different colors. As I watched her making her selections from the piles of soft blankets, pressed sheets and pillow cases, I was reminded of the time we were preparing to leave our home at East Mindanao, when she methodically went through a similar pile to choose what we would take with us to Tagana-an.

Then we went to the medical clinic, where we were given cursory physical exams. Peach, little Ed, and I were pronounced in fairly good shape, but Mom was underweight, anemic, and in general poor health. This was not unexpected, considering the physical hardship and emotional stress she had endured for almost four years. The visit to the dental clinic was not a pleasant one for me—after years of negligible dental hygiene, I needed one of my molars extracted. I can remember the army dentist saying, "Little girl, this is going to hurt me more than it will you." (From my perspective, that definitely was not a true statement.) This was the first proper medical or dental attention I had received in four years.

We were absolutely overwhelmed by the amount and selection of available food. We picked up as many cases as we thought could be safely transported on our banca—American delicacies we had not seen in many years, such as canned meats and sardines, powdered milk, sugar, coffee, tea. We were also given cases of C-rations—we'd already sampled these military-issue meals when Dad and the boys brought home boxes of K-rations on their last visit. I, of course, was most interested in the candy and chewing gum that came with each meal.

One day I looked out of the front window of the convent and saw an empty military jeep parked on the street. I went out to examine this strange-looking vehicle at close range, then sat behind the wheel and pretended to drive, just like the soldiers I had seen speeding around the city, leaving a trail of dust behind them. As I was sitting in the jeep, I saw a uniformed soldier walking toward me. To me, he represented the wonderful American forces responsible for ending years of hiding and living in fear of capture by the Japanese. He seemed surprised to see me sitting there but said nothing as he continued walking. As he passed me, I saw that he happened to be an African American. I felt compelled to say something nice to him. Finally mustering enough courage to address him, I called out, "Hello, nigger." He whirled around and said, "What did you say, little girl?" There was no anger in his voice, but I sensed that I had done or said something wrong. Seeing the stricken look on my face, he must have realized that I had intended no offense, and with a slight smile and a wave he turned and went on his way. I have not forgotten that incident and what it must have meant to that poor soldier. We had grown up in a multiracial society, and I had no basis for any prejudice. I can only guess that the movies I had seen before the war had left me with the impression that such a word was acceptable. Since I had never lived in the States, my notions of American social norms had all come from movies and magazines.

Multiple visits to the Red Cross provided information on Dad. To Mom's relief, she was informed that he had been sent to Luzon. I believe the Red Cross also said that they would try to locate him and tell him we were all well and would wait for him in Surigao. We shared some of our bountiful supply of canned goods with the nuns in appreciation for their hospitality and assistance, and they were almost speechless with gratitude. On the day before our departure for Surigao, there was a huge celebration in Tacloban in honor of the ceremonial signing of the Japanese surrender on the deck of the USS *Missouri* in Tokyo Bay. It was a fitting end to our trip to Leyte. Although we didn't get a definitive answer about where Dad was on Luzon, we knew that the Red Cross had begun a search that would eventually reunite Dad with us in Surigao. Laden with our huge bounty, we sailed back to Surigao. Mom was nervous about the weather because of our precious cargo, but we completed the return trip without incident and were soon back home in Surigao, reunited with Princess, who had been well cared for by the Meehlieb family. She was beside herself with delight when we arrived, nuzzling and licking each of us in turn. During all her years as a member of our family, this was the only period that our faithful little dog had been separated from us.

The school year at San Nicolas had begun prior to our arrival. Father Luis had already settled in. The nuns from the Little Flower Dormitory were all there and were pleased to see us back safe and sound. Mother Adela and her community had been among the first to return to Surigao after the Japanese surrendered to the U.S. Army. When the Japanese forces occupied Surigao, they took over the school buildings as well as all government facilities, and the nuns, like most of the other residents, had to retreat to the interior to stay out of harm's way. Now Mother Adela was faced with the daunting task of restoring San Nicolas School to the famous respected institute of learning it had been before the outbreak of the war. She was determined that all her students not be deprived of a single day of school beyond the four years already missed. The nuns cleared classrooms; collected and repaired desks, tables, and chairs; retrieved, sorted, and catalogued textbooks and library books; assigned teachers—and school was back in session!

I started school almost immediately. My teachers gave me an accelerated course in the three Rs, and this time there was no resistance on my part—in fact, as I neared my eleventh birthday, I was probably their most eager pupil! Peach, however, had to take time off to retrieve the belongings we had left in Claver. Her ability to take on grown-up tasks, and Mom's confidence in her, never ceased to amaze me. When she soon returned with all our belongings, including the sewing machine, she reported that Claver looked much improved from its post-shelling state—the church had been repaired, and she saw little evidence of the terrible damage the town had suffered. She didn't tarry in Claver and didn't inquire about Old Timer, so his fate remained unknown to us. Because she had missed those crucial first weeks of school, she had to be tutored in several subjects to catch up with the class, which upset her very much.

As soon as I learned how to read, I discovered the magical world of books. Fortunately, a limited number of library books had survived the war and the nuns instituted a good system of sharing what was available among the students. To Mom's delight, she didn't need to prompt me to get ready for school every morning. Uniforms were not yet required, so I carefully selected from my new wardrobe of secondhand dresses that had come all the way from the States, courtesy of the relief center in Tacloban. To complete my school outfit, I wore the shoes with the cut out toes, but they were ill-fitting and gave me blisters, so I couldn't wait to get home after school and kick them off.

One afternoon, when my shoes felt particularly uncomfortable, I decided to hitch a ride on a *tartanilla,* a horse-drawn carriage that carried customers from one end of town to the other. It had two-person seats facing each other lengthwise in the cab, and there was a metal step hanging from the rear that one climbed to board it. I had seen teenage boys hopping onto the step and holding on for a block or two, much to the chagrin of the *cochero* (driver). The added weight at the rear made the carriage tip backward, which annoyed the passengers as well. I found that getting up on the step and holding on with one hand was easy, but I did not realize that there was an art to getting off a moving tartanilla, even a slow-moving one. On dismounting, I tried to simply stand still but was pulled forward by inertia and fell flat on my face, my schoolbooks scattered about. The cochero was very concerned and I quickly assured him that I was all right. I gathered up my books and made my way home, fighting back tears of embarrassment and pain—my knees and the palms of my hands, badly scraped by the rough pavement, were bleeding. Needless to say, I received a sound scolding from Mom when I reached home.

After school I usually wandered around the waterfront. It looked totally different than it did when the SS *Corregidor* used to sail into port every Thursday before the war. The neighborhood had suffered much damage, and the old bodegas had been destroyed, leaving piles of mangled and rusted metal scattered about. Quite frequently there was a small U.S. Navy ship alongside the wharf, and I enjoyed watching the crewmembers as they went about their duties. To my secret delight, I learned that if I walked around the pier area the sailors noticed me. They were half a world away from the States, and I probably reminded them of a young daughter or kid sister back home. Sometimes they called out and admonished me about walking barefoot among rusting debris, perhaps not realizing that the soles of my feet had been toughened by years of walking over rough roads, sharp stones, and broken seashells. Most often, though, they asked me over and invited me on board to show me around the ship. The first couple of times I was too shy to go aboard and simply accepted the gum, candy, or fruit they offered me. Whenever I returned home with my goodies, Mom cautioned me about pestering the crew. After a while I felt more comfortable and readily went up the gangplank whenever I was asked, anticipating the delicious treats I might come away with. On one unforgettable occasion, the skipper invited me into his cabin and gave me a colorful box containing a brand new ocarina. He told me that he had bought it for his son but that he wanted me to have it instead, adding that he could probably get another present to bring home. I had never seen an ocarina before and was dumbfounded that a complete stranger would give me such a gift. I was too shy and tongue-tied to thank him properly, but I will never forget that skipper's kindness. Although I never actually learned to play the ocarina, I could make it produce some pleasant sounds, and it was one of my most treasured possessions for many years.

At this juncture, we knew very little about the participation of my brothers in the liberation of Mindanao. After the Bugo operation, which paved the way for the American invasion, Rudy and Hank's unit returned to its base at Gingoog via Route 1. Arriving at Gingoog, they were equipped with heavier weapons (for the Bugo reconnaissance operation they had been only lightly armed). They then boarded an LST, which ferried them to Butuan in Agusan province. From there another transported them up the Agusan River to Las Nieves. Their unit was later deployed farther up the river to Esperanza and Guadalupe. They were now working in conjunction with U.S. Army troops. Across the river from their position was the 114th Infantry Regiment from Claver. The retreating Japanese elements that had come into the area from Surigao and Davao were further up the river. U.S. Army forces had now moved up the valley in pursuit of the fleeing Japanese. However, bands of Japanese soldiers, short of food, were infiltrating back down into the valley at night. While they were encamped, the Special Troops slept in foxholes and set up their own alarm system. They strung tin cans from their rations around their perimeter and shot when the cans rattled. The guerrilla units were receiving food drops from Army Air Corps cargo planes, and the Japanese managed to retrieve some of the bundles from these drops. The footprints made by their hobnail boots—standard issue in the Japanese Army—were telltale signs of their intrusion. Often while on patrol, the Special Troops ran into Japanese soldiers bathing in the river, and a firefight ensued as the Japanese escaped into the jungle. As part of its overall strategy, the U.S. Army had launched several psychological warfare operations using leaflets and loudspeaker broadcasts. These efforts, combined with the lack of food, took their toll on the Japanese.

During many long conversations with Hank about his wartime experiences, he told me of an incident that had occurred sometime during this period. He was squadron leader for "B" Company of the Special Troops. He and ten other guerrillas were on patrol in an area where there was evidence of a large contingent of Japanese soldiers. Truck tires had left deep impressions in soil softened by a recent rainstorm—the water in the tracks was still muddy. For some reason Hank did not send his scout on ahead, opting to be the scout himself. With his men some distance behind him, he followed a trail that veered left. As he rounded the curve, he suddenly came face to face with a lone Japanese soldier. They both reached for their weapons, but Hank was a split second faster and shot first. As it turned out, the Japanese soldier was the scout for a patrol numbering around forty or fifty that hurried to the scene after Hank's shot rang out. Hank's platoon, badly outnumbered, retreated quickly. That was the first time Hank had seen a Japanese soldier up close, and this was obviously a young man. Perhaps toward the end of the war the Japanese, like the Germans, were sending young conscripts into battle. Hank was only eighteen at the time, and almost sixty years later, his memory of that encounter has not faded.

Finally, in early September 1945, the Japanese commander on Mindanao came down to Butuan and surrendered. My brothers' Special Troops unit assisted in organizing concentration camps for the surrendering soldiers. Hank clearly recalls the formal surrender of Japanese commander General Tomochika. Attired in full dress uniform with white gloves, he bowed and presented his samurai sword to the senior American commander. Mindanao, our home for seven years, was returned to American control. The war was over for my brothers and their fellow guerrillas. While they had received generous logistical support from the U.S. military beginning in February 1945, the 114th Infantry Regiment of the 110th Division had liberated Surigao province without help from regular American forces.

Rudy and Hank's Special Troops unit was deactivated in Butuan. My brothers both received about three hundred pesos in back pay and were discharged on September 30, 1945. Hank recalls that they had to sign forms indicating that they were not making any further claims against the U.S. or Philippine governments. One last hurdle they had to tackle was finding a way to return home—but where would home be? When they had last seen Mom and the rest of us, we were at the hut in Bayabas. They assumed, however, we were no longer there and that Surigao was the logical place for the family to converge. At the end of the war there was no existing bus service; however, a truck operator with a flatbed truck offered to take them to Surigao for twenty pesos each. Joe McCarthy and other former guerrillas who lived in or near Surigao joined them.

The boys returned home to a tearful but happy welcome from their mother and siblings. We had had no news about them for nine months! With our family almost complete we needed more space; Mom was able to find us a two-story home, with running water for its real kitchen and washroom, conveniently located near the pier. One of our favorite spots was the second-story veranda on one side of the house, where we sometimes had our meals and where we could see the large avocado tree, which produced luscious fruit, growing in the yard. The veranda continued around the rear corner of the house and eventually ended at the toilet facilities (nice and private, with an enclosed chute to a cesspool). Though large, the house was not as well laid out and definitely not as nicely furnished as our home at the mine, but it was comfortable, and we settled in gratefully. Electric power had not yet been restored, so we used locally made lanterns (similar to present-day Coleman camping lanterns).

Reluctantly, but at Mom's insistence, Rudy and Hank resumed high school—Rudy had one more year to go and Hank, two. Sitting in classrooms learning about theories and abstracts must have seemed tame in comparison with their adventures as young guerrillas in a long and nasty war. Periodically, they visited Waldo Neveling at his boatyard in Surigao. His postwar business was refurbishing surplus U.S. Navy landing craft for use in trade between the various islands. He enjoyed sitting with my brothers and revisiting their shared guerrilla experiences.

During a school break, Hank went to Tagana-an to retrieve the carved trunk containing our precious photographs and important documents that we had left at Peping Lisondra's little storage shed not far from our hideout at Red Mountain. It had remained undisturbed for more than three years. Peping and Mano Juan and their families were very happy to learn we had survived and promised to come and visit us in Surigao and see the rest of the family, including the new little addition. It was a happy day when Hank came home with the trunk and we all gathered around examining its contents, all in perfect condition. Many of the photos and documents are now in my possession.

To add to the amenities of our new home, Mom acquired a small generator and light bulbs from an entrepreneur who made trips back and forth to Leyte and Samar on a large sailing banca to purchase a variety of military goods. The boys ran the generator for three or four hours in the evening, affording us the luxury of electric lights. My siblings and I cannot help wondering where Mom got the money to pay our mounting expenses. Hank believes that she had saved a good amount of Dad's guerrilla pay and converted it to "real" pesos when the war ended. We also suspect that many of her purchases from local merchants were on credit, which was a common practice before the war.

Dad arrived home in Surigao sometime in late October—he was able to hitch rides on several U.S. Navy vessels and eventually reached us. It was a wonderful surprise to see him again after almost ten months! He told us that after arriving in Leyte he had been sent to Luzon and put in charge of a contingent of military police that directed and assisted the liberating of American forces on their way to Baguio and other points in the northern part of Luzon. His area knowledge proved invaluable during this operation. After he completed this assignment, he had participated in various mopping-up operations and was now waiting to be discharged. Before coming to Surigao, he had sought our old friends and learned, to his sadness, that Pop Henderson had died while interned at Santo Tomas; however, Boots and Belle were fine. The entire Holmes family had survived and were repatriated to the States at war's end.

Dad tried to reassure us that in short order our lives would return to normal. There was every indication that mines, lumber companies, and other businesses would resume operations as soon as personnel could be put in place, including East Mindanao. He urged us kids to continue doing well in school. When Peach complained that she was having trouble with algebra, he encouraged her to try harder, telling her "You can do it, Peach!" over and over.

Again hitching rides on navy vessels, he made his way back to Manila, first stopping off in Cebu to meet with Henry Gasser, majority owner of the East Mindanao Mining Company, and inquire about plans for the mine. Unfortunately, the news was not good: Gasser informed Dad that it was doubtful the mine would reopen, claiming that the one man—Fred Varney, the manager—who could have helped him assess the situation and formulate a plan, had already been repatriated to the States and was believed to be living in the San Francisco area. Gasser further asserted that he did not know the status of East Mindanao's finances and that he, personally, was without funds, having incurred considerable debts while hiding out in the hills of Cebu during the Japanese occupation. (In this respect, at least, our family had fared better than Gasser. Because of the kindness of the people of Mindanao, money was never a factor in our survival.) For the record, however, Dad reminded Gasser that he had not received his salary from November 1941 through February 13, 1942, when the mine was officially declared closed.

Dad was bitterly disappointed when it was confirmed that the East Mindanao Mining Company would not be resuming operations. He immediately sought other employment and obtained an engineering position with the U.S. Army Air Forces, primarily in rebuilding the facilities at Clark Field in Pampanga, north of Manila. Dad's next priority was bringing his family back to Manila. By a stroke of good luck the Holmes family home in the Manila suburb of San Juan was vacant and available. Dad immediately asked Mom to make the necessary arrangements for our move from Surigao to Manila.

We moved back to Manila at the end of the school year. Once the rebuilding of Clark Field was complete, Dad decided to continue on with the air force, moving to Okinawa for the rebuilding of an airbase there. At that time, unfortunately, family housing on Okinawa was very scarce. Since we were comfortably settled in a suburb of Manila, and back in school, Mom and Dad decided that Mom and the rest of us would remain in Manila and Dad would come home twice a year for a holiday.

Peach and I attended a Catholic convent school run by Spanish nuns of the Order of Preachers, the Dominicans. Rudy and Hank studied engineering and in their spare time rebuilt and repaired surplus army jeeps left behind by the American forces. I loved riding along when they road-tested these jeeps, hanging on for dear life as we bounced along on bumpy roads. Ducks and chickens scampered to get out of our way, and barking dogs chased us. I could catch only snatches of my brothers' conversations and often heard them talk about shocked observers, which I assumed referred to the people who watched us whiz by. Many years later, I learned that they were, in fact, discussing the performance of the jeep's shock absorbers.

Our family life continued in a state of flux for the next few years. Dad, having achieved civil service status, decided to continue working for the air force until he reached retirement age, even though it meant separation from the family. In the 1930s and early 1940s Mom and Dad had planned to build up their economic resources in preparation for a comfortable life in the States; this was back on track after suffering a five-year setback.

We survived the war as a family and came through it with one additional member—little Edward. I cannot forget the shock we experienced on the morning of December 8, 1941, when our world—the one Mom and Dad had so tirelessly worked for—drastically changed. In short order, we lost our home and many associated conveniences. We left the mine with little more than the clothes on our backs and a few personal possessions. With help from our Filipino friends we met the challenges that faced us. Certainly that first year of evasion from the Japanese was the most difficult; at every turn we had to improvise, whether relative to food, shelter, or personal health. But survive we did, under some very difficult circumstances.

As I trace our journeys through the war years on the map, many memories surface. I first remember the trip from our home at the mine to Tagana-an. There we encountered our first primitive living conditions. As we moved southward along the Surigao coast we spent time in Claver, Carrascal, Cantilan, Tandag, Tago and, finally, Bayabas. But it was in Tagana-an that Dad met Lieutenant Colonel Morgan, one of the early leaders of the guerrilla resistance movement. For Dad and my brothers it was the chance to participate in an organized movement to fight Japanese domination and oppression. Involvement with the guerrillas was a major challenge for my father, as his main responsibility was to keep the guerrilla forces of the 110th Division of the Tenth Military District fed and sustained while they engaged the Japanese. My brothers, as first-line troops in the field, experienced the action and fury of fighting Japanese soldiers in close quarters.

When the war broke out in December 1941, Dad had lived and worked in the Philippines for twenty years. In most cases, his work experience involved the management of Filipino colleagues in engineering-related responsibilities.

This experience proved vital in carrying out his duties as liaison officer for Surigao province. With this office, he represented the division and its district to the many local government officials functioning throughout the province. At the time, the province was roughly sixty-five hundred square kilometers, with an estimated population near two hundred thousand (sometime in the 1960s, it was divided into two provinces, Surigao del Norte and Surigao del Sur). Thus, Dad's mission was most important as a communication channel between the guerrilla leadership and the civilian Filipino leadership that re-sided in the province's many municipalities, towns, and barrios. Later, when he was appointed procurement officer as well as food control administrator for the 110th Division, his Filipino governmental contacts became crucial in allowing palay in the rice-growing areas to be purchased and moved into guerrilla logistics channels for the feeding of over five thousand men in the division. Since the division's operational responsibilities went beyond Surigao province, guerrillas in adjacent provinces were also affected by the availability of palay. In some cases, other military districts could purchase it from 110th Division stocks. Thus, Dad's contributions to the guerrilla cause had an im-pact that went beyond the boundaries of Surigao province.

I believe one can see the qualities of maturity and experience that my fa-ther, like his other older business-oriented colleagues, brought to the guerrilla organization. What he accomplished could not have been done by younger military personnel that had only resided in the Philippines for a short time. These younger men did the fighting and had the heroics; Dad combined mili-tary actions against the Japanese with the unexciting task of getting food to the frontline guerrilla units through his successful liaison efforts with the civilian leadership in the province.

My father received his final discharge from the U.S. Army on November 10, 1945. His awards for service in two wars included the World War I Victory Medal with service clasp for Siberia, Philippine Defense Medal, Philippine Liberation Ribbon with two Bronze Service Stars, World War II Victory Medal, and Asiatic-Pacific Campaign Medal. Dad was not a grandstander in the guerrilla movement. Others received more prestigious awards because of specific actions recognized by the 110th Division headquarters. Dad's respon-sibilities were large and arduous—his efforts kept over five thousand guerrillas fed and active during the war years. As they did in many wars, individual acts of sacrifice in World War II often went unrewarded. At war's end he was fifty-five years old with a wife and five children to support. The war had destroyed his savings and livelihood, and he was forced, at an age when many contemplate retirement, to seek new employment.

In 1998, my husband and I attended the annual reunion of the American Guerrillas of Mindanao for the first time. It was a pleasure and an honor to meet the members of a relatively small U.S. military force whose contributions toward the planning and execution of the liberation of the Philippines were unique and valuable. At the reunion, I sought out AGOMers who might have worked with my father. One of them, Tom Baxter, said to me: "Sure, I remember your Dad very well. He was a maverick, all right. It's a good thing he didn't work at the 10th Military District's headquarters with Fertig. He probably would have been sent out to Australia on one of the early submarine trips." Although I wasn't sure what he meant at that time, I believe Baxter felt that my father's personality would have clashed with Fertig's. I found only one reference to a brief meeting between Fertig and my father in his personal diary, when Fertig described Dad as a "blowhard" after my father had described the debacle at Placer. It's not hard to imagine that, had Dad worked more closely with Fertig, he might have suffered the same fate as other officers reassigned to MacArthur's headquarters in Australia. If that had been the case, Mom, Peach, and I would have been evacuated to join him there, and this would have been an altogether different story.

Rudy and Hank went into the guerrilla organization as young teenagers, missing high school and all that goes with it. Sure, to the outsider, it may have seemed macho to be a guerrilla, carry a weapon, and engage the enemy. The two boys went through a lot in their three years serving with the guerrilla movement. They saw men killed, and they fired at a savage, brutal enemy. It was kill or be killed. Many of their comrades were killed or wounded. They grew from boys to men at breakneck speed. When they were boys at the Ateneo de Cagayan, the Jesuit school in Cagayan where Father Haggerty was rector, no one could have anticipated that within a few years they would be involved in a guerrilla war against the Japanese. Although their paths did not cross during the war, I am sure that Father Haggerty, the unofficial chaplain of the guerrillas on Mindanao, would have been proud of my brothers' service with the movement.

I recently read a copy of a letter Captain William Knortz wrote to his "Mother and Pop," in the United States, in October 1942. Knortz was one of the younger guerrillas my brothers served with, a leader and role model. After surrendering as ordered and subsequently escaping from Keithley Barracks, he and his companion Bob Ball eventually wound up near the Del Monte plantation, where the Antiporta family took them in.

Knortz joined the guerrilla movement and in April 1943 was instrumental in Rudy and Hank becoming guerrillas. My brothers served under him and were devastated when he perished at sea.

The first part of Knortz's letter to his parents detailed his experiences from December 8, 1941, to mid-October 1942.[1] The last part of his letter is very touching:

> If I do not ever get home please believe that I did what I thought right. I have no obligations to the U.S. Army right now—that all stopped when I surrendered. I do, however, have a duty to myself and to my country, which I shall always endeavor to fulfill to the best of my ability.
>
> I have instructed Mr. Antiporta to send this to you, after the war is over.
>
> Please send 50 pesos ($25.00) to the address on the envelope. I owe him and his wife many times that amount for all the kindnesses they have shown me. Please send the money from my army salary, which the army will send you.
>
> I took out a ten thousand dollar insurance policy in March, which I pray reached you. This will not near repay you for all you have done for me, but I hope you will use the money to make your future life happier.
>
> Please believe I've thought of you all, many, many times since I've left home. I pray God will spare me to arrive home safe and sound, so that I may bring into your lives a little of the happiness you have given me, since I was a baby.
>
> By the time you receive this I will either be well and safe, or will not be returning home. If I die, it will be as I want to die, as a soldier. There could never be a finer or better death. No matter what may come I will always pray to God for courage, that I may be a fearless American, whom you will always be proud.
>
> I seem to have a special "pull" with the Blessed Virgin. When I pray for help, she always helps me, but I'm sure that I could never have lived this long, were it not for the many prayers you all have offered for me.
>
> Please—if you learn that I'm dead—try to get the information to Miss Frances Young (530 Bailey St., Camden). Also show her this letter. I have no more paper to write her, as I had to search for weeks for this.
>
> Please tell her I thank her for the many candles she has lit for me, and for her memory and her love.
>
> Please write to Mr. Antiporta a nice letter and thank him.

He doesn't expect any pay for all he has done, but you will remember the twenty-five dollars.

>With all my love,
>Your Soldier and son

Bill

P.S. If I do not return please light a candle and have a Mass said for me.

>B.

The Antiportas sent Knortz's letter to his parents on April 13, 1946, together with a note:

Dear Mr. & Mrs. William Knortz:

I am sending this letter to you left by your son Bill Knortz. This is delayed because our communication is difficult. Please inform me about him. I'll be very glad that he was able to go home and live with his father and mother again.

I hope you will inform me about him. Best regards to you all.

>Your friend,
>Ramon Antiporta

I can only imagine the sorrow Mr. and Mrs. Antiporta felt when they learned that Bill had died off Camiguin Island.

Mom, Peach, and I had a different experience, but one that also included the constant threat of Japanese troops intruding on our lives. The Japanese landing on Claver in November 1943 was probably the closest we came to being captured or killed. Periodically, the men of the family visited our makeshift homes—I will never forget when Rudy and Hank returned, suffering seriously from malaria, nor how Mom, with determination and tenacity, nursed them back to health.

When we commenced our odyssey of hiding from the Japanese, Peach was just a slip of a girl, only eleven years old. After we left the mine for Tagana-an, her day-to-day responsibilities increased, as did her maturity. I did not realize this at the time, because I was called upon to do little in the early stages of our evacuation. I lived in a fantasy world of playtime and no school, but my obligations and duties picked up as the war progressed. During our first few weeks in Tagana-an Peach learned how to carve up a freshly butchered pig and make adobo and tapa, pick fresh local vegetables, and grate coconuts to make gata for sauces and oil for cooking and for our lamps. Later on she also learned to shop at the local tabo-an, selecting the freshest food for the family table, which required learning the local dialect, Surigaonon, and dealing with money and bargaining with the local shopkeepers. Eventually she took over most of the household chores and the preparation of food for our meals, which she prepared in the most rudimentary of conditions, including using clay pots over an open fire. During the first year of our flight, Dad and my brothers were with us most of the time. Thus, every meal posed a major logistical problem for my mother. Gone were Romana and the maids who had borne much of this burden when we were at the mine. Peach and my brothers became vital helpers to Mom, ever ready to provide assistance and take part in food planning and preparation. Whenever Mom was away, the responsibility of running the household fell on Peach.

Peach's learning curve for life excelled in areas outside of the kitchen, too. Before Dad's departure for service with the guerrillas, she was his assistant for administrative matters, for example, preparing a simple newsletter on our portable typewriter after my dad had made notes from shortwave news broadcasts. Dad passed this newsletter around to Filipino friends. The departure of the Hansen men put Peach in an even more indispensable role, particularly in dealing with our evacuation problems. Probably her most noble contribution was accompanying Mom back to Claver to retrieve items for the coming baby. Mom, several months pregnant, was in no condition to be traveling by foot through Japanese-controlled areas. But travel they did, with Peach bearing a major responsibility throughout the trip.

Later in the war Peach was instrumental in helping Filipinos afflicted with skin diseases treatable with the new sulfa drug brought in by the SPYRON missions. We had a small quantity of this drug, and Peach made the most of it by helping our local Filipino friends. Perhaps there was a touch of Clara Barton in her nature; if she had had the calling and the inclination, she might have had a career in medicine.

Looking back at this turbulent period in our lives, I marvel at the changes in Peach from age eleven to fifteen. Her personal growth into adulthood was remarkable, as she increasingly took on grown-up responsibilities. Only with the passing of years have I been able to understand and appreciate the sacrifices Peach made for her family and others with whom she came in contact. Certainly her ability to tackle difficult tasks not only lightened Mom's load enormously but also made my own wartime experience seem like an exciting adventure instead of the dangerous situation that it was.

Certainly the star at the end of our wartime odyssey was my mother. The

1940s had dealt her many setbacks that would have caused most mortals to despair. In September 1941, the death of her eldest son Edward, upon whom her maternal hopes and dreams rested, was killed in a senseless act of rage. When she was still recovering from that ordeal, the Japanese invasion came, and it would destroy the physical aspects of a comfortable life—a family together, a home, and modest prosperity. These were all smashed with the Japanese attack on Pearl Harbor on December 7, 1941. The next four years were for my mother a journey of danger, anxiety, and a drive for self-preservation. To meet these threats required the strength of a saint. Leaving the mine in May of 1942 and going to Tagana-an was a turning point in her life. Now, survival for herself and her family was her central concern. Next to the death of our big brother Ed, leaving the mine was probably her most painful life experience to that point. The house and garden with a view of Surigao Strait were very dear to her; I can recall vividly the tears she shed when we departed for a new life in the unknown. Those first days of living on the run must have been terrifying for her, although she never let on to her children. But then the reality of having to keep her family housed and fed displaced her anxiety and uncertainty. She had the grace to come to terms with what God had decided for her family and herself. She commenced to concentrate on those things in her surroundings that would help her address the problems ahead. Once she was convinced of the loyalty of the Filipinos of Surigao province with whom we came in contact, she did not hesitate to place her trust in them—and they never betrayed it. This mutual respect became the mainstay of our survival during the war years. When Dad and my brothers left to serve with the guerrillas, Mom's ability to bring us under the mantle of the local Filipino society guaranteed our survival against the forays of the Japanese occupation forces.

One of our first flirtations with danger was the boat trip from Tagana-an to Claver. Imagine if you will a mother and two young daughters going out to sea on a banca under weather conditions that quickly turned stormy and then having to spend the night on the beach with unknown fishermen in a Japanese-patrolled coastal area. Then, in late November 1943 she confronted the reality of a Japanese incursion into the town of Claver while Dad and the boys were down the coast in Cantilan. Implementing her escape plan, the three of us melted into the jungle until the Japanese troops departed. After this event she sensed that moving south to Cantilan was the appropriate option given the Japanese strategy of systematically raiding coastal towns in a southerly direction. With a few of our worldly possession on our backs we moved southward from the growing Japanese threat.

Perhaps her greatest act of bravery was the trek of many kilometers she made with Peach to retrieve items stored in Claver. These were to be used in the forthcoming birth of her son. Several months pregnant, she and Peach set out on the coastal road to the north in order to reach Claver. Traveling through areas that had already experienced Japanese assaults, they were in constant danger of possible capture. This three-week journey was one of extreme self-sacrifice. Each day brought the unknowns of finding food and shelter. Thanks to the gracious hospitality of Filipinos along the way, Mom prevailed in bringing back the items she needed to properly receive her new son.

While Mom's decision to make the trip through areas where Japanese maritime patrols had already made forays was ill-advised, she never doubted that she and Peach would receive help and protection from Filipinos along the way. Mom's total trust in the loyalty of the Filipino people was the basis for her decision to remain in hiding rather than be evacuated to Australia. She lived in constant fear for the safety of her husband and her sons and could not bear the thought of being on another continent, out of touch with the situation on Mindanao. The tragic deaths of Roy Welbon and Fred Feigel after their wives had left for Australia strengthened her resolve to remain on Mindanao. Besides, a baby was on the way and she wanted to ensure that Dad and my brothers could welcome the new member of the family. She was unshakeable in her faith in God that she and the baby would survive the ordeal of a delivery in the mountains without benefit of proper medical attention. And she was right!

Mom's crowning achievement of the war years was reuniting the family. Chartering an ocean-going banca, with three children in tow, she set out on an epic voyage from Surigao to Tacloban, Leyte. She had two objectives. First, she hoped to locate Dad through the Red Cross. Second, she wanted the family to have the medical care, clothing, and food available to Americans who had been either imprisoned or evading the Japanese; having been on the run for almost four years, we were certainly in need of all of these.

Yes, Mom was a courageous individual who brought us safely through the war. Without her diligence and sacrifice, we might not have survived. I only hope that my children and grandchildren can appreciate the great qualities that my mother exhibited during this trying period. She demonstrated the utmost of grace under fire. God gave her a role to play during the turbulent years of the war, and she played it with fortitude and self-sacrifice; she must have known and acknowledged that this was the path that God had destined for her. How else could she have done the things that she accomplished—all with grace and dignity?

Despite our hardships, we were grateful to be alive at war's end. Thousands of Americans who were in the Philippines at the outbreak of the war were not so fortunate. We have several friends whose fathers became POWs after the surrender of U.S. forces in early 1942. Shortly thereafter the Japanese started systematically sending large numbers of those POWs to Japan, Formosa, or China to work as slave laborers in mines, munitions factories, and other industrial sites. Weak and malnourished, many died en route due to the horrific conditions aboard the hell ships, and, later in the war, others were killed when the ships came under attack by U.S. aircraft or submarines. Of course, the ships had no markings nor did the Japanese make any notification to the International Red Cross that POWs were on board. (Those of us on Mindanao cannot forget the loss of the POWs off Sindangan Point near Zamboanga when their ship was torpedoed by a U.S. submarine.) For the survivors who reached their destinations, life became a living hell, and a good number later perished as a result of malnutrition, disease, absence of medical care, and a grueling work schedule.

Among my father's papers is a copy of a communication from General MacArthur to the commander in chief, Japanese military forces in the Philippines, Field Marshal Count Terauchi, addressing the brutal and degrading treatment of American POWs. MacArthur writes:

> The surrender of American and Filipino forces in previous campaigns in the Philippines was made in full reliance that prisoners of war would be accorded the dignity, honor and protection provided by the rules and customs of war.
>
> Since then unimpeachable evidence has been furnished me of degradation and even of brutality to which these gallant soldiers have been subjected, in violation of the most sacred code of martial honor. For such violations the Imperial Japanese Government will of course be fully responsible to my Government.
>
> As Commander in Chief of the Allied forces in the field, I shall in addition, during the course of the present campaign, hold the Japanese military authorities in the Philippines immediately liable for any harm which may result from failure to accord prisoners of war, civilian internees or civilian non-combatants the proper treatment and due protection to which they, of right, are entitled.[2]

As a grim testament to the Japanese treatment of their prisoners, over ten thousand American POWs in the Pacific area were killed or died after capture.

Most of these deaths occurred in the Philippines or while the prisoners were being transported on Japanese hell ships to various destinations for slave labor. One can only wonder whether the American public ever knew of or paid attention to this major atrocity. Many members of my generation are familiar with the Bataan Death March, but does the current generation understand the magnitude of the Japanese Army's treatment of U.S. servicemen during World War II—over ten thousand dead? Kent and I have attended the annual conventions of the American Defenders of Bataan and Corregidor since 2002. These veterans, a closely knit group who still display the courage and patriotism that sustained them through those terrible years of imprisonment, have been meeting continuously since 1946. Japanese academic researchers also attend these conventions to observe and listen to the veterans' stories and gather material for their reports.

We have several friends who never really knew their fathers because of World War II and their imprisonment by the Japanese after May 1942. Since the war's end, descendants of the "greatest generation" have painstakingly sought information, however fragmentary, that would satisfy their need to understand what happened to their respective fathers as POWs—more importantly, how and where they may have perished. This brings them some closure regarding the ultimate fate of loved ones alive in their memory but with whom contact ceased when they were very young. Duane Heisinger wrote a moving and poignant account of his ten-year search for details of the last years of and ultimate resting place of his father, Major Lawrence Heisinger, a JAG officer who surrendered on Corregidor and was interned at several POW camps. Anyone who reads his book, *Father Found,* will be deeply touched by his yearning to connect with the father he last saw when he was ten. Descendants of other POWs in the Philippines who never came home have embarked on similar quests for information. Paul Arnold learned that his father, Captain Paul Pearson, surrendered following the fall of Bataan, survived the Bataan Death March, and was interned at the POW camp at Cabanatuan. The father of John Lewis, Lieutenant Colonel John "Buck" Lewis, was wounded and taken prisoner on Mindanao and interned at DAPECOL and Cabanatuan.

In December 1944 Heisinger, Pearson, and Lewis were among 1,619 POWs crammed into the cargo holds of the *Oryuku Maru* bound for Japan to become slave laborers. The hatches were kept closed and the prisoners were packed so tightly that they could not sit or lie down. Many fainted from lack of air and eventually suffocated. This hell ship, unmarked like the others, was hit by U.S.

aircraft and later sank off Subic Bay. The three men survived but were boarded on another hell ship, the *Enoura Maru,* which was sunk by U.S. aircraft after reaching the Formosan port of Takao. Heisinger and Pearson died in this attack. Lewis survived and was reboarded with the other survivors on yet another hell ship, the *Brazil Maru,* bound for Japan. Unfortunately, Lewis did not survive this latest voyage—he and hundreds of his fellow POWs perished en route, probably from suffocation, lack of food and water, cold weather, inadequate clothing, and complications from malnutrition and other health problems. A Hellships Memorial has been erected near Subic Bay to honor the thousands of POWs who perished on Japanese hell ships during World War II.

We were the fortunate ones, and I cannot emphasize enough our gratitude to the Filipinos on Mindanao who contributed to the survival of not only our family but also countless others. In his book, *Guerrilla Padre in Mindanao,* Father Haggerty expressed the sentiments we all felt much better than I ever could.

Much has been written in praise of Filipino hospitality; too much cannot be written of it. Every American alive and free in the Philippines today owes his life and liberty to the hospitality of Filipinos, rich and poor.

Our young Americans who were in the mountains know what this hospitality was like—pagan *datus* bringing them a share of the harvest, Christian Filipinos traveling half a day up into the hills to bring them sugar, salt, and some prewar canned food they had bought at outrageous prices to give to these men in hiding. You may eat at any house as a matter of course, and the owners are ashamed if they cannot borrow plates and a tablecloth, rice and sugar for you. People will give you their only bed or, having none, their best mat and pillows; they will serve you their last chicken, eggs, and rice and silently go hungry themselves.

Our family had certainly experienced the same generosity and hospitality that Father Haggerty described with respect to the young servicemen who had escaped and were hiding out during the initial stages of the war. What impressed me even more was that each time the Filipino civilians helped us, they were laying their own lives on the line, as the Japanese brutally punished those giving aid to anyone they considered an enemy. I speak for my entire family in expressing gratitude for the bravery and loyalty of the numerous Filipinos on Mindanao who came to our rescue during those difficult years of World War II.

General MacArthur and Philippine President Quezon recognized and sanctioned Colonel Wendell Fertig's command, the Tenth Military District, as the official American-Philippine resistance on Mindanao. This organization became a rallying point for the Filipino population resisting the Japanese occupation. The arrival of the SPYRON missions to support Fertig's military efforts was an added visible sign for hope and proof that the Americans had not forgotten them and would return, as promised by General MacArthur. Moreover, where civil authority was free from Japanese domination, local governments continued to administer laws and facilitate order as supported by the guerrillas. Quezon officially sanctioned this and authorized the printing of money under the supervision of Fertig's command. This visible resistance to the Japanese occupation in no small measure helped the Hansens successfully evade the Japanese. The individual acts of kindness by the Filipino people, fostered by the hope that the Americans would return to free them from Japanese occupation, allowed the Hansen family and countless others to survive.

In a macro sense, the operations of the guerrillas and the efforts of the sixty-five coast-watcher stations provided the American forces with actionable intelligence upon which to attack the Japanese. This was particularly true for U.S. submarines operating in Philippine waters. Also, anticipating an eventual invasion by American forces, emergency airfields were repaired or built on strategic locations for use by U.S. forces against the Japanese. Some also provided emergency sites for damaged American aircraft.

The Tenth Military District was like a phoenix, rising from the ashes of the American defeat by the Japanese in May 1942. Starting out as disparate bands resisting the Japanese occupation in the summer of 1942, the movement became a well-organized force of seven divisions consisting of about thirty-five thousand Filipino troops, former members of the Philippine Army and the Philippine Constabulary. While their officers were vital elements in the organization's leadership, over one hundred American military and civilians provided the spark to make the organization effective. Certainly Fertig's insistence that the movement function as a U.S. military command, with accompanying paperwork and discipline, helped make it successful. When supplies were short the ingenuity and resourcefulness of the Filipinos prevailed. American penchant for organization and results were also important. The meeting of these qualities created a synergy that would endure until the American forces returned in 1945.

With the onset of the American invasion, the U.S. forces had a working guerrilla counterpart that could perform a variety of missions to ensure the success of the military mission. The guerrillas provided intelligence, functioned as blocking forces, and rescued downed American fliers. The bottom line, however, was that the guerrillas saved countless American lives and accelerated the liberation of Mindanao. The liberation was vital to the survival of the Hansen family in the late days of the war; by August 1944 their backs were against the wall as the Japanese pressed ever closer. Thank God for the American invasion of Leyte in October 1944, marking the beginning of the liberation of the Philippines. Yes, the Tenth Military District was a success story that may never be duplicated, as, like the stars and planets, the elements for making a successful guerrilla movement may not again align at such a strategic moment. A number of factors conspired to make the district successful. Loyalty of most Filipinos to the commonwealth government and their hatred of the Japanese occupation aided their support for the guerrilla movement. American organizational skills, as well as sensitivity to the religious and cultural dynamics of the various provinces, were vital in making the guerrilla movement a success. The American businessmen who joined Fertig's command served him well in this delicate arena; Charles Hansen was typical of these American civilians who provided adult supervision to the brash young American servicemen new to the Filipino culture. Finally, the supply triage by the SPYRON missions was crucial to the success of the Tenth Military District. While the missions brought in substantive supplies of arms, ammunition, and communications equipment, as well as mission critical personnel (coast watchers, radio operators, and weather observers), their mere existence provided a significant boost in morale for both guerrillas and civilians on Mindanao. These missions signified that the U.S. liberation of the Philippines would soon follow. Moreover, the American support brought in on these missions gave the guerrilla units the capability to contribute to the greater war effort by providing intelligence and laying the operational groundwork for eventual return of the American forces.

Epilogue

In the early 1950s, my brothers moved to the San Francisco Bay area. Rudy took a job as an airplane mechanic at the Pan American World Airways maintenance base, and Hank opted for the same position at United Airlines. Upon reaching the States, they registered for the draft and were immediately called up for service in the Korean War. Rudy served in the Army Corps of Engineers and Hank in the air component of the Marine Corps. Rudy decided to make the Army his career and slogged through a lot of red tape to receive credit for his service as an American guerrilla in the Tenth Military District on Mindanao. He achieved the rank of commissioned warrant officer in the Army Corps of Engineers. He served two tours in Germany and two in South Vietnam. He was an adviser at Pleiku when the North Vietnamese attacked, and he escaped injury by jumping out the back window of his quarters. Afterward he commented that the episode reminded him of Dad's escape from the Japanese in early 1942 when he was attending the meeting of the Filipino-American-Chinese Guerrilla Association in Tagana-an.

Hank became a Marine quite by chance. Upon reporting to the Army induction center in San Francisco on the appointed date, he and his fellow draftees were instructed to line up. Then, every other man was ordered to step forward; Hank was among these. This group was inducted in the Marine Corps to help fill a manpower shortage. After his Korean War service, Hank resumed his employment with United Airlines and remained there until his retirement.

After graduation from high school and completion of a secretarial course, Peach became secretary to the chief brewmaster at San Miguel Brewery. He was a talented German who had developed the formula that made San Miguel

Beer famous worldwide. Peach's office career ended when she met and married a young San Miguel Brewery executive named Jaime "Jimmy" Cabarrus, member of a family of Spanish lineage that had remained in the Philippines after the Spanish-American War. One of his older brothers had survived the Bataan Death March; another was involved in the resistance movement. Other members of his family also participated in underground activities, including the husband of his older sister, who was arrested by the Japanese at their home late one night, never to be heard from again. Toward the end of the war Jimmy served in the U.S. Merchant Marine, for which service he was granted U.S. citizenship.

After high school I, too, completed a secretarial course and succeeded Peach as secretary to the succeeding chief brewmaster at San Miguel Brewery, but my secretarial career was short-lived. I developed itchy feet and joined Philippine Airlines (PAL) as a flight attendant, where I cultivated a love for travel. I was also involved in PAL's Air Education Program as part of a team sent to various places to encourage airline travel, which required my traveling throughout many of the islands in the Philippines, including my old stomping grounds on Mindanao. As soon as Hank completed his military service, I joined him in San Francisco and took a position with Pan American World Airways as a flight attendant, or stewardess, as we were called in those days. My work schedule and vacation benefits gave me many opportunities for worldwide travel, including return visits to Manila.

Upon Dad's retirement, my parents and young Ed also moved to northern California, settling in Burlingame. Mom and Dad enjoyed life in retirement. The favorable climate enabled Mom to indulge her passion for gardening with Dad as her able assistant. Ed attended parochial and public schools in the Bay Area and served a tour of duty in the Air Force after high school. Later he graduated from San Francisco State University and went on to a long career with Hewlett-Packard. When the Army assigned Rudy to Fort Ord in California, he invited Mom and Dad to live with him and Clarissa and their daughters Kristina and Annette. However, Dad died there of heart of failure in 1963 and was buried at Golden Gate National Cemetery in San Bruno, California. Mom decided to move back to the area south of San Francisco that had become home to her; it was also close to Dad's resting place. Ed lived close by and was of great assistance to her; Hank, Bobbie, and their children Mark and Judy were only a few miles further down the peninsula, and Peach's second daughter Charlotte also lived nearby while earning her B.S. in nursing at the University of California in San Francisco. Mom lived independently and loved to travel.

Rudy's subsequent assignment to Germany afforded opportunities for visits with him and his family and travel to other parts of Europe. Her favorite destination, though, was the Philippines, where she enjoyed long visits with Peach and her family. Sadly, Mom suffered a massive bilateral stroke in 1976 that paralyzed her on both sides and radically affected her throat muscles, requiring round-the-clock nursing care. Rudy, now retired from the Army and living in San Francisco with his family, found that options for the level of care she required were limited and costly. Peach made a very gracious offer to take Mom to the Philippines where she could receive excellent care; Rudy, Hank, Ed, and I gratefully accepted. Peach and Jimmy had an addition built to their home in suburban Metro Manila to accommodate Mom and her nurses. Under Peach's watchful eye she received the required medical care and physical and speech therapies. With her usual grit and determination Mom fought hard to regain her ability to walk and talk, but it was a losing battle. One small triumph was stringing words together to form simple sentences, although she could make her wishes known in other ways as well. Even though the nurses and household staff were caring and attentive she preferred to communicate directly with Peach and, later on, her eldest daughter Annie, who was earning her Master's in Clinical Psychology at Ateneo de Manila. Mom enjoyed being a part of the hustle and bustle of a busy household that also included Annie and Charlotte's siblings—Chuck, John, Dodie, Tony, and Jerry. One activity that always pleased her was a car ride that extended to the residential areas of Manila where our family had lived before moving to Mindanao. During my visits I would often accompany her on these outings and wondered what memories those familiar sights evoked, wishing that she would share them with me. Mom spent the last fifteen years of her life among loving family members, only a short distance from where she and Dad had started their married life in 1922. She is buried with Dad at Golden Gate National Cemetery.

In 1956 I met Kent Holmes, a Navy officer stationed in Hawaii, and we were married in June 1958. Incredibly, a month before our wedding he received orders for an assignment to U.S. Naval Station Sangley Point near Manila. Unlike Douglas MacArthur, I had not made a promise to return to the Philippines. And yet, less than four years after leaving it to see the world, I was back again! Like my mother and father, Kent and I started our married life in Manila, and we welcomed our first child, Catherine, there as well. Peach, Jimmy, and their family also lived nearby. At some point Peping Lisondra, our friend and host from Tagana-an, had reestablished contact with Peach. His daughter, Doret, came to Manila and joined our household as Catherine's nanny.

A few years later, Kent changed careers and joined the Central Intelligence Agency. In time, Catherine was joined by three siblings—Christine, Diana, and Edward. Our family spent fifteen years living in various overseas posts on three continents—Asia, Australia, and Europe. Perhaps some day one of my children will take the time to chronicle our own family's experiences— including a two-year tour in Laos under wartime conditions not too different from my own World War II experiences in the Philippines.

SURIGAO REVISITED—1975

In 1975 Peach and I, together with members of our respective families, made a pilgrimage back to Surigao and the mine where we had lived before the war. Kent and I and our children were living in Manila at the time, because of Kent's assignment with the U.S. government. The group included my family and Peach's children (at the time her husband, Jimmy, was vice president of Marinduque Mining Company). We traveled from Manila to Cebu via inter-island steamer, similar to the SS *Corregidor* that used to take us to and from Manila during school vacations before World War II. In Cebu, we caught a Marinduque Mining corporate aircraft to Nonoc Island, site of that company's large open-cut nickel mine. On Nonoc we stayed at the company's guest quarters. Romana, our maid from our pre–World War II life at East Mindanao Mining Company, met us there. Romana had kept in touch with Peach through the years. With her assistance, we planned an all-day excursion to the mine site and Surigao City, located across the strait from Nonoc. We used the company boat, and Romana was our guide for the day. After packing a picnic lunch, we traveled from Nonoc directly to the location of the old pier used by East Mindanao Mining Company before the war. Landing at the deteriorating pier, we followed Romana up to the administrative part of the mine. This included the machine shop (where Dad's office was located), various office buildings, warehouse, and other facilities. It was sad to see the place in ruins. In most cases, all that was left were the cement footings used to support the buildings. Romana and Peach, having the best memory, pointed out what buildings had existed and where—administration, movie theater, machine shop, store, and so forth. Continuing up the path toward the site of our old house, we came upon a cement bunker that had been used to store dynamite for mining operations. Attached to it was a nipa hut. We knocked at the front door and out came this old man. Romana conversed with him in

Surigaonon, asking him if he knew where the old Hansen house was. Peach and I added that we were Charlie Hansen's daughters. "Oh yes," he said in English. "I used to work for Mr. Hansen." He left us for a couple of minutes then came back sporting a miner's helmet with lamp. He said he knew where the house had been and would take us to the site. So, up the trail we trudged, following the old miner. We passed the location of the dispensary and the spot where the Studebaker used to be parked. We then found the remains of the steps that led up to the house. Peach and Romana remembered in great detail where everything had stood. We arrived at the site of the house. How it brought back memories of those days before the war! In the area where Mom had her garden, we espied the spider variety of the hibiscus plant growing wild—after thirty-three years. This was one of the many plants and flowers she and the gardeners had so carefully tended. The cement footers that had supported the house now outlined its former location within the invading jungle. I remember those footers so well, their concave tops that contained pools of oil to keep insects from the wooden supports under the floor of the house. As we walked among the debris, Kent found the nameplate from the Hotpoint refrigerator Mom had brought back with her on the SS *Corregidor* just before the outbreak of the war. After we evacuated the mine in May 1942, looters made off with all of our household effects. Since there was no electricity to run the refrigerator, however, they took it apart for the scrap metal.

While we were at the site of our house, the old miner who had led us there climbed a coconut tree and brought down some young fruits. The fresh coconut juice tasted wonderful on that hot, humid morning. As we rested and enjoyed this refreshment, the miner mentioned that a firm from Manila had resumed working the former East Mindanao mine shafts. He offered to guide us there—a short distance over another hill. The new company could not run its operations from the old East Mindanao site with the pier because of a dispute regarding ownership of that property. However, since the government owned the mine shafts, it granted the new company permission to mine for gold.

Arriving at the mine site, we met the manager and some of his engineers. They offered to give us a tour of the operation and a ride to Surigao City afterward. Since the company boat from Nonoc had to leave because of the low tide, we retrieved our lunch coolers and agreed to meet the boat in Surigao City in the afternoon. It was quite an experience seeing the old East Mindanao mining shafts in operation. Later we all shared lunch in their dining facility. Over lunch the mine manager told the story of a former American mining official (whose name they did not know) who had returned to the mine with another Caucasian sometime in the early 1960s. The two came by yacht and anchored in the bay. They said that they were exploring the possibility of re-opening the mine. Their immediate objective was clearing the main shaft and some locals were hired to do the job. (This was the same shaft where my father and Fred Varney had deposited a box containing East Mindanao's gold bars, and then dynamited, prior to the Japanese taking over Surigao.) After several days of clearing debris, using the bucket and winch method, they located a wooden box. They brought the box up and dismissed the workers, saying that they would resume work on the following day. The next day the yacht was gone along with the two visitors and the box. Was the box the same one Dad and Varney had placed in the mine shaft prior to abandoning the mine? Who were the two men? It was an intriguing story—or was it simply a rumor that took on a life of its own? We never found the answer.

Later in the afternoon, a Jeep picked us up for the trip back to Surigao. Our first stop was San Nicolas School, which was still there and had become an even more active academic institution. Walking through its courtyard and corridors brought back many memories of our boarding school days. Some of the older nuns on the school staff remembered us.

After visiting the school, we went up to the cemetery where the remains of my older brother Edward are in a crypt that is part of a long wall. Because space is tight in the cemetery, after so many years the remains are dug up, taken out of their coffin and placed in a crypt with an identifying inscription. Sometime after our move to Manila, Mom had visited Surigao and the cemetery and had talked to the caretaker who had moved Ed's remains. He told her that he remembered seeing tufts of Ed's light brown hair, and he commented that his bones were so much larger than those of the average Filipino. Visiting Ed's final resting place after so many years moved all of us.

Appendix

A copy of Charles Hansen's communication from General MacArthur to Field Marshal Count Terauchi, addressing the brutal and degrading treatment of American POWs.

GENERAL HEADQUARTERS
SOUTHWEST PACIFIC AREA
OFFICE OF THE COMMANDER-IN-CHIEF

To: The Commander in Chief, Japanese Military Forces
      in the Philippines, Field Marshal, Count Terauchi:

The surrender of American and Filipino forces in previous campaigns in the Philippines was made in full reliance that prisoners of war would be accorded the dignity, honor and protection provided by the rules and customs of war.

Since then unimpeachable evidence has been furnished me of degradation and even of brutality to which these gallant soldiers have been subjected, in violation of the most sacred code of martial honor. For such violations the Imperial Japanese Government will of course be fully responsible to my Government.

As Commander in Chief of the Allied forces in the field, I shall in addition, during the course of the present campaign, hold the Japanese military authorities in the Philippines immediately liable for any harm which may result from failure to accord prisoners of war, civilian internees or civilian non-combatants the proper treatment and due protection to which they, of right, are entitled.

DOUGLAS MacARTHUR,
General, U.S. Army,
Commander in Chief.

Notes

1. THE GATHERING CLOUDS OF WAR

1. Ronald Dolan, ed., *Philippines: A Country Study* (Washington, D.C.: Library of Congress, Federal Research Division, 1993), 32.

2. Stanley Karnow, *In Our Image: America's Empire in the Philippines* (New York: Ballantine, 1989), 255.

3. Surigao was the capital of the Province of Surigao, which was divided into two provinces in 1960. Surigao became the capital of Surigao del Norte and was designated a charter city in 1970.

4. Catholic missionaries were active in many areas of Mindanao. American Jesuits were generally located in the northwestern part of the island. Dutch Missionaries of the Sacred Heart had schools and parishes on the east coast while Irish Columbans were to the west. American and Canadian Oblates of Mary Immaculate were active in the Cotabato and Jolo regions with the Canadians of Quebec Foreign Missions in the area of southwest Davao.

5. Louis Morton, *The War in the Pacific: The Fall of the Philippines* (Washington, D.C.: U.S. Army Center of Military History, 1989), 18.

6. Ibid., 39–43.

7. Ibid., 45–47.

8. Dolan, *Philippines*, 35.

2. MOVING TO WAR AND AWAITING THE INVASION OF MINDANAO

1. An open city is officially declared demilitarized and it is by official agreement not subject to attack. Note: By late December 1941 most U.S.-Filipino forces had been withdrawn to Bataan and Corregidor.

2. Thomas Mitsos, "American Guerrillas of Mindanao," unpublished collection of articles and letters between members, chaps. 10–12.

3. Edward Haggerty, *Guerrilla Padre in Mindanao* (New York: Longmans and Green, 1946), 38.

4. Morton, *The War in the Pacific,* 146.

5. Pacific Wreck Database, "Extract on the Royce Mission." http.7/www.pacificwrecks.com/people/veterans/heiss.html (accessed Apr. 10, 2005).

3. EVACUATING THE MINE AND EVADING THE JAPANESE

1. Mitsos, "American Guerrillas," chaps. 3, 9–10.

4. A GUERRILLA MOVEMENT IS FORMED, AND FAMILY FIGHTERS JOIN

1. Haggerty, *Guerrilla Padre in Mindanao,* 37.

2. Bill Johnson, interview by Kent Holmes at American Guerrillas of Mindanao reunion, San Diego, Calif., June 13–17, 2001.

3. Mellnik, *Philippine War Diary,* 223–58.

5. ON THE MOVE

1. William Wise, *Secret Mission to the Philippines: The Story of "Spyron" and the American-Filipino Guerrillas of World War II* (New York: Dutton, 1968).

2. Travis Ingham, *Rendezvous by Submarine: The Story of Charles Parsons and the Guerilla Soldiers* (New York: Doubleday, 1945), 66.

3. Robert B. Spielman, "The History of the 114th Infantry Regiment, 110th Division, 10th Military District, U.S. Forces in the Philippines" (Master's thesis, University of Texas, 1953), 39.

6. LIFE IN CLAVER AND HELP FROM AUSTRALIA

1. Wendell Fertig Diary (Personal Diary), MacArthur Memorial Archives and Library, Norfolk, Va., 129.

7. THE JAPANESE EXPAND THEIR OPERATIONS AGAINST THE GUERRILLAS

1. Spielman, "The History of the 114th Infantry Regiment," 43–44.

2. Fertig Diary (Draft Narrative), 372.

8. AWAITING THE LIBERATION OF THE PHILIPPINES

1. John Keats, *They Fought Alone* (New York: J.B. Lippincott, 1963), 377–78.

2. The Catholic priests in the northern and eastern parts of Mindanao were from Holland and belonged to the Order of Missionaries of the Sacred Heart of Jesus. They often simplified their difficult-sounding first names. Serving in the Philippines was a lifelong commitment for most of them, and they returned to Holland only for rare visits. The Dutch bishop of Surigao, Giovanni (John) Vrakking, was interned at Santo Tomas, as was Bishop Hayes, the American Jesuit bishop in Cagayan. Father Luis, rector of San Nicolas School in Surigao, hid out in Bayabas with two other priests.

3. Mitsos, *American Guerrillas of Mindanao,* chapters 10, 11–12.

4. Bruce Elliott, interview by Kent Holmes at American Guerrillas of Mindanao reunion, San Diego, Calif., June 2001.

5. John Starkey, interview by Kent Holmes at American Guerrillas of Mindanao reunion, San Diego, Calif., June 2001.

6. Bob Stahl, *You're No Good to Me Dead: Behind Japanese Lines in the Philippines* (Annapolis: Naval Institute Press, 1995), 100–102.

7. Stahl, *You're No Good to Me Dead,* 100–102.

8. Lucien Campeau, interview by Kent Holmes at American Guerrillas of Mindanao reunion, San Diego, Calif., June 2001.

9. LIGHT AT THE END OF THE TUNNEL

1. Samuel Eliot Morison, *The Liberation of the Philippines—Luzon, Mindanao, the Visayas 1944–1945* (Edison, N.J.: Castle Books, 1959), 3.

10. THE WAR ENDS

1. Letter is included here by permission of Leo Conniff and the Chestnut/Frey family.

2. See Appendix for entire letter.

Bibliography

BOOKS AND THESES

Dolan, Ronald, ed. *Philippines: A Country Study.* Washington, D.C.: Library of Congress, Federal Research Division, 1993.

Haggerty, Edward. *Guerrilla Padre in Mindanao.* New York: Longmans, Green, 1985.

Ingham, Travis. *Rendezvous by Submarine: The Story of Charles Parsons and the Guerilla Soldiers.* New York: Doubleday, 1945.

Karnow, Stanley. *In Our Image: America's Empire in the Philippines.* New York: Ballantine, 1989.

Keats, John. *They Fought Alone.* New York: J. B. Lippincott, 1963.

Kerr, E. Bartlett. *Surrender and Survival.* New York: William Morrow, 1985.

Manchester, William. *American Caesar—Douglas MacArthur, 1880–1964.* Boston: Little, Brown, 1978.

Maynard, Mary McKay. *My Faraway Home.* Guilford, Conn.: Lyons, 2001.

Mellnik, Stephen M. *Philippine War Diary, 1939–1945.* New York: Van Nostrand Reinhold, 1969.

Morison, Samuel E. *The Liberation of the Philippines: Luzon, Mindanao, the Visayas, 1944–45.* Boston: Little, Brown, 1959.

———. *The Rising Sun in the Pacific—1931–April 1942.* Edison, N.J.: Castle Books, 2001.

Perret, Geoffrey. *Old Soldiers Never Die—Life of Douglas MacArthur.* New York: Random House, 1996.

Quirino, Carlos. *Chick Parsons—Master Spy.* Quezon City, R.P.: New Day, 1984.

Schmidt, Larry S., "American Involvement in the Filipino Resistance Movement on Mindanao during the Japanese Occupation, 1942–1945." MA thesis, U.S. Army Command and General Staff College, Fort Leavenworth, Kans., 1982.

Schultz, Duane. *Hero of Bataan—Story of General Jonathan M. Wainwright.* New York: St. Martin's, 1989.

Spielman, Robert B., "The History of the 114th Infantry Regiment, 110th Division, 10th Military District, United States Forces in the Philippines, 1953." MA thesis, University of Texas, Austin.

Stahl, Bob. *You're No Good to Me Dead—Behind the Lines in the Philippines.* Annapolis, Md.: Naval Institute Press, 1995.

Steinberg, Rafael. *Return to the Philippines.* Alexandria, Va.: Time-Life Books, 1979.

Wise, William. *Secret Mission to the Philippines: The Story of "Spyron" and the American-Filipino Guerillas of World War II.* New York: Dutton, 1968.

U.S. GOVERNMENT PAPERS AND RECORDS

Cannon, Hamlin M. *Leyte: The Return to the Philippines: U.S. Army in World War II: The War in the Pacific.* Washington, D.C.: U.S. Army Center of Military History, 1954.

Morton, Louis. *The Fall of the Philippines: The U.S. Army in World War II, the War in the Pacific.* Washington, D.C.: U.S. Army Center of Military History, 1989.

Smith, Robert R. *Triumph in the Philippines: The U.S. Army in World War II.* Washington, D.C.: U.S. Army Center of Military History, 1993.

ARCHIVAL SOURCES

Fertig, Wendell. U.S. Army 1941–45. Personal diary, 1942–45. MacArthur Memorial Archives and Library, Norfolk, Va.

———. U.S. Army 1941–45. Draft narrative of diary 1942–45. MacArthur Memorial Archives and Library, Norfolk, Va.

Hansen, Charles. 1943–45, papers. Author's collection.

Mitsos, Thomas. Guerrilla Radio—AGOM, American Guerrillas of Mindanao, Philippine Islands, 1941–1945. A history of AGOM members during World War II.

Pacific Wreck Database. "Extract on the Royce Mission." Available at http://www.pacific.wrecks.com/people/veterans/hass.html.

Index